Mattie Sue Athan

GUIDE TO
COMPANION
PARROT
BEHAVIOR

With full-color photos and
instructive line drawings

BARRON'S

Dedication

For Sam, my constant friend.

All inquiries should be addressed to:
Barron's Educational Series, Inc.
250 Wireless Boulevard
Hauppauge, New York 11788
http://www.barronseduc.com

Library of Congress Catalog Card No. 98-52812

ISBN-13: 978-0-7641-0688-0
ISBN-10: 0-7641-0688-0

Library of Congress Cataloging-in-Publication Data
Athan, Mattie Sue.
   Guide to companion parrot behavior / Mattie Sue Athan:
Illustrations by Michele Earl-Bridges.
     p. cm.
   Includes bibliographical references (p.) and index.
   ISBN 0-7641-0688-0
   1. Parrots—Behavior. 2. Parrots. I. Title.
SF473.P3A845   1999
636.6'865—dc21   98-52812
                                 CIP

636.6
ATH   H   9/11/09

Printed in China

19 18 17 16

Photo Credits

Susan Green: pages iv, 2, 3, 4, 6, 10, 11, 13, 21, 25, 31, 33, 36, 37, 41, 42, 51, 54, 71, 72, 75, 76, 96, 97, 110, 111, 116, 118, 124, 127, 128, 133, 134, 138, 154, 155, 156, 173, 177, 181, 182, 203, 205, 219; Joan Balzarini: pages 7, 19, 26, 30, 32, 40, 48, 50, 58, 59, 63 lower right, 65, 66, 68, 73, 77, 84, 87, 88, 89, 90, 91, 92, 93, 94, 106, 108, 149, 184, 186; Mattie Sue Athan: pages 15, 23, 57, 80, 100, 125, 161, 167, 196, 197, 213, 215, 216; B. Everett Webb: pages 16, 47, 60, 63 upper right, 81, 125 lower right, 195; Kelly Dolezal: pages 43, 69, 70, 95, 109.

Cover Photos

Front cover: Joan Balzarini; inside front cover: Joan Balzarini; inside back cover: Susan Green; back cover: Joan Balzarini.

About the Author

Mattie Sue Athan is one of a handful of bird behavior consultants in private practice in the United States. Since the mid 1970s, she has studied the development and modification of behavior in parrots living as companions with humans. While much of her early work dealt with wild-caught birds, since the 1980s the bulk of her practice has been with domestically raised parrots. She is particularly interested in the development of behavior problems such as aggression, screaming, and self-mutilation in hand-fed birds. Her work has appeared in *Bird Talk Magazine, American Cage Bird Magazine, The Pet Bird Report, Positively Pets,* and numerous other specialty publications.

Important Note
While every effort has been made to ensure that all information in this text is accurate, up-to-date, and easily understandable, we cannot be responsible for unforeseen consequences of the use or misuse of this information. Poorly socialized or unhealthy parrots may be a danger to humans in the household. Escaped non-native species represent an environmental threat in some places. Outdoor release or unrestricted outdoor flight is absolutely condemned by the ethical parrot keeper. This book recommends that a parrot's wing feathers be carefully trimmed at least three times each year.

Contents

Foreword

Who would have predicted in 1993 that *Guide to a Well-Behaved Parrot* would still be the best selling book with the word *parrot* in the title half a decade later? We should have known. There was, at that time, a great clamoring for the information provided by that book.

Just as I was aware of the widespread need for *Guide to a Well-Behaved Parrot,* I've become increasingly aware that there's a tremendous need for a book describing differences between the birds. Where can a would-be parrot owner go, at any given moment, to look up the needs and specific requirements of the many different types of parrots?

I hope to fill that need here. Drawing on my 20-plus years of companion parrot observation and the counsel of quite a few other talented and experienced parrot folk, I've tried to describe how each type of common companion parrot can be expected to differ from other types. This is not an easy task. Every parrot is an individual, and anyone who tries to predict a particular individual's behavior is wading into deep water.

In researching the chapters on expected needs and characteristics of common companion parrots, I tried to find many people with experience with the same type of bird so that I could compare the information each person provided. If several individuals with multiple experiences with the same type of bird reported similar experiences, then I felt that these experiences might be consistently observed by others.

Some of the anticipated characteristics described here are undeniable physical manifestations of the species, such as powder on the feathers, the extra power provided by a larger beak, or the presence of a mobile crest. On the other hand, behavioral characteristics described here are anecdotal reports of the interactions with humans who live with a particular bird. Some of these observations may seem arbitrary. They are. However, the observations related here are assembled from the direct personal experience of very experienced individuals. I will endeavor always to make a distinction between elements contributed by multiple individuals and elements contributed by only one source. Full details of each source's expertise are given at the back of the book, listed under Contributors (p. 223).

Publishing anticipated behavioral characteristics of the different types of parrots is risky. Among other things, anyone writing about such subjects might be accused of prejudice or bias. However, since I have no birds of a particular type to promote, I have no conscious bias based on anything but anticipated behavioral characteristics. I have been influenced by my experience, and my observations will certainly reveal my responses to my experience. Because I do not breed birds or sell birds, I suspect that my opinions are probably less prejudiced, more unbiased than anyone with a particular kind of bird to sell. My primary agenda is the successful long-term adjustment and adaptation necessary to allow companion parrots to survive physically and emotionally in their indoor homes.

This book is intended to be primarily about companion parrot behavior. I have tried not to replicate elements that are dealt with better and at greater depth in other places. If you're looking for information about diet, go to *Feeding Your Pet Bird* by Burgmann. If you're looking for breeding information, try Barron's *Handfeeding and Raising Baby Birds* by Vriends. For recapture and home safety information, go to Barron's *Guide to a Well-Behaved Parrot.*

A parrot is a big responsibility. I've tried to be totally candid about what each type of bird needs. A companion animal is completely at its owners' whims. Humans must know what each bird needs in order to provide for it appropriately. If a companion parrot needs something that isn't there, its health, demeanor, and behavior will certainly suffer. Indeed, many behavioral responses are directly influenced by missing or inappropriate elements of the indoor environment.

In writing *Guide to a Well-Behaved Parrot* and the subsequent books in this behavioral series, I have been keenly aware of a need to present the information in a special, nonjudgmental way. Over the years, it's become obvious to me that this blame-free method of providing behavioral information is more likely to be well received by the humans who own birds, by the breeders who raise them, by the dealers who sell them, and by the veterinarians and other professionals who help to care for them. Any advice that inspired guilt in any of the chain of providers for the bird could ultimately cause a backlash and could result in further damage to that bird or in damage to subsequent birds under the care or influence of an offended person. All information provided here is phrased in a manner intended not to ascribe blame, but rather to provide guidelines for improvement for all parties involved. I must thank Jill Owen for guiding me down this path to improved language usage.

I gratefully acknowledge my consulting editor, Dianalee Deter. I'd like to thank Kelly Doelzel, who has helped with photos on two books now; Barb and Gary Steffens for their ongoing emotional support; Vera Herst for her always on-target grammatical advice; Jean Pattison for her professional guidance; and my editor, Mark Miele, for his continued patience.

Mattie Sue Athan
December 1998

Preface

When *Guide to a Well-Behaved Parrot* came out, I was already involved in the retail sale of parrots. Many customers wanted a book to help them raise their birds. There were many articles around, many techniques; but when someone had a problem, it was a challenge to dig up the answer. Mattie Sue Athan's first book received criticism for not being anything new. These techniques had been used by many people for many years. When I asked my veterinarian what he thought of the book, he said it wasn't earth-shaking stuff, but it sure was nice that someone finally put it in a book.

It was a place to start. While many of those techniques have been revised and expanded, the book was one of the focal points for revolutionizing parrot training and letting everyday parrot owners access the wisdom of professionals.

Now this book is in the same category. Many of my customers ask for a book to help them choose a parrot, a book that will help them know what is involved in taking care of the birds before they make the commitment that will often be for a lifetime. The author has again taken a leap. She has worked very hard to gather information, sometimes about species she knew little about. This placed her at the disadvantage of having to trust the opinions of others, and possibly being criticized for doing so. But active critique is the good part. This is the part that helps get more people talking and writing and presenting the information to the people who will use it.

This book might be considered "incomplete," for no one book can completely cover the complex field of companion parrot behavior. However, this book covers many of the questions that prospective parrot owners have. This book needed to be written. Thank you, Mattie Sue.

Dianalee Deter, Consulting Editor

Chapter One

What Is a Companion Parrot?

Somewhere between a wild animal and a pet is the brave new world of the companion parrot—a creature that lives in human homes, developing both verbal communication and cooperation skills while pursuing its own agenda. The behaviors with which a companion parrot pursues that personal agenda are genetically programmed and make the addition of a parrot to the household more like adding a child or a spouse than adding a pet.

Companion parrots talk with understanding (sometimes even before they can eat independently), dazzle us with their brilliant colors, amaze us with acrobatics, and amuse us with unpredictable antics. Companion parrots often prefer people to other parrots.

A companion parrot is not a pet. It's an exotic, undomesticated animal that exhibits instinctual wild characteristics, especially sexual ones, that do not usually appear in pets. It is precisely this fiery independence that makes parrots such irresistible companions. (How fascinating is the story that Andrew Jackson's Amazon parrot was ejected from the former president's funeral for foul language!) Although much of a companion parrot's behavior will be motivated by a desire to please humans, there will be many times when those desires to please will be totally self-directed.

Our treasured companion parrots' behavior more likely resembles human behavior than that of any other companion animal. The field of companion parrot behavior modification is relatively new, being first described and practiced by Chris Davis, starting in 1974. The basic principles of modern parrot behavioral training—patterning for cooperation, rewards for appropriate behavior, and a behaviorally correct in-home environment—can maintain human-acceptable social behaviors for a companion parrot's lifetime. As with dogs and horses, early and enduring behavior training can minimize the manifestation of unwelcome instinctual behaviors in companion parrots. Without ongoing behavioral support, many, possibly most, companion parrots will gradually or quickly revert to instinctual wild

skills: They must know how to find and separate good food from toxic plants; how to defend territory; how to recognize and avoid predators; how to find safe water; and how to rejoin their families when separated. They must be able to do all this, sometimes in blinding rain or oppressive drought. They must face the challenges of finding and keeping a mate alive; of developing role-appropriate behaviors; of competing for and defending nesting sites; and of creating, nurturing, and teaching their extremely helpless offspring to do the same. They must have some mechanism by which to evaluate the food supply in order to determine whether a nesting process should be completed.

A very different set of behaviors is necessary for survival in the living room.

A Parrot Needs More than a Cracker

Dreaming of a perfect feathered companion, aspiring parrot owners envision themselves enjoying idyllic evenings with a calm bird snuggled on the shoulder, sharing simple conversations as they read or watch TV. Some picture a dazzling creature in an immaculate ornamental cage on a perch surrounded by lush vegetation, objects d'art, and colorful baskets.

And the premium handfed baby parrots offered for sale do seem to

behaviors. Some wild behaviors fit in well to the living room environment and some do not. Because many of the larger parrots live such a very long time, the acquisition of only one difficult-to-live-with behavior every year or two can produce a pretty obnoxious bird by the time the bird's a teenager.

Most of today's companion parrots are only a few generations out of the wild, and the behaviors they improvise are generated by instincts that enabled their ancestors to survive in the wild. The wild parrot lived, loved, learned, and evolved through thousands of generations in order to have the skills necessary to meet nature's challenges. Wild parrots must learn a diverse assortment of transportation and communication

be perfect in every way: beautifully feathered, interactive, and talkative. Even their price demonstrates that they are the finest product of the aviculturists' art. However, there's a very real temptation to believe that because that expensive baby parrot is perfect when it comes home, it will stay that way. Certainly some will; a percentage of untrained parrots grow up to be perfectly noninvasive companions. Most parrots, however, will more likely want to "practice" plastic surgery by removing little moles, go ballistic when we leave the room, try to outscream the telephone, chew through computer cords, unweave baskets, harvest household plants, and decorate the walls with brightly colored, cement-like food or droppings. With little planning and no behavior training, some parrots develop traits that can make them about as welcome as a telephone solicitor.

Learning Indoor Survival Skills

A premium handfed baby parrot is preferably weaned but under six months old when it goes to its new home. This is the ideal time to begin behavior training; it's a window of opportunity for teaching the baby parrot both human-interactive behaviors and independence. In the wild, the baby parrot would be learning what to eat and where to find it, how to find friends and avoid ene-

mies, and how to get "home" at night. This is probably the most important developmental period in the bird's life, for if appropriate skills are not learned at this time, the wild bird will not survive.

Human behavioral development isn't much different. If behavioral training is neglected during these important baby days, then either aggression, shyness, overbonding, excessive screaming, or other acquired misbehaviors can develop. If the new owner of a medium or larger hookbill has not planned the bird's environment and begun behavioral training by the time the bird is 18 months old, possibilities for the bird's future can begin to look pretty scary. That is, if a misbehaving parrot is not judiciously socialized either before misbehaviors appear or immediately after, the bird might be moved to the back room or sold through the newspaper (emotionally or physically abandoned).

These baby Timneh African greys are still too young to go to their new homes.

But what kind of problems can parrot owners expect? How could a relatively small creature like a bird—a very expensive creature—drive normally reasonable humans to such extravagant and reprehensible behavior?

The most common reasons humans give up companion parrots are the behavior problems: screaming and biting and the natural behaviors—chewing and messiness. These issues must be addressed separately, for only the former are true behavior problems. Chewing and messiness are innate behaviors that must be planned for and accommodated.

Mutual trust and enjoyment of each other's company are the most important elements in maintaining good human/ parrot relationships. (Greenwing macaw and hyacinth macaw.)

Patterning for Cooperation, Confidence, and Trust

A successful companion parrot must learn both cooperation and independence. A handfed bird first learns cooperation by being fed by humans. The weaned juvenile should be able to presume that food and water will always be available. How, then, are cooperation skills generated and reinforced after weaning?

An effective relationship with a parrot must begin with and maintain both mutual trust and respect. Step-ups and all behavioral practice must be administered regularly and sensitively. If bird and humans achieve no mutual respect and compassion, the relationship is lost. If, for example, the baby parrot begins to treat a human like a piece of property rather than a respected flockmate, everybody could be in trouble. Although most parrots go through at least a nippy stage (this is part of the normal development of independence and personality in many juvenile hookbills), the appearance of biting behaviors around a particular person or location can signal the development of territorial or bonding-related aggression.

Step-up practice inspires, facilitates, and habituates cooperation in a baby parrot. The predictability of the human's and the bird's responses to one another provides a comfortable standard for all other interactions.

Step-up Practice

From its first days in the home, the baby parrot should practice the step-up command at least twice most days. The routine need be no more than a few minutes' duration and may initially have to take place outside the bird's established territory in the home. A laundry room or hallway is usually perfect, as the bird will probably never spend much time in these types of areas, and therefore should not develop territorial behavior in them. The pattern works best when it includes:

1. practice stepping the bird from the hand to and from an unfamiliar perch;

2. practice stepping the bird from hand to hand;

3. practice stepping the bird from a hand-held perch to and from an unfamiliar perch;

4. practice stepping the bird from a hand-held perch to a hand-held perch; and

5. practice stepping the bird from a familiar perch to and from both hands and to and from hand-held perches.

Although you may be able to begin step-up practice with a cooperative baby bird in familiar territory, unless a bird is cooperative enough and well patterned enough to step up from an unfamiliar perch in unfamiliar territory, it may refuse to step up from the cage or other familiar perch. A cooperative bird can be successfully patterned to this exercise anywhere.

Be sure to offer affection and praise after each completed step-up. Always discontinue step-up practice only after a successful completion of the command. This is crucial to good patterning. If the command is not successful, you must alter technique, approach, or prompting mannerisms rather than continue with unsuccessful methods. Be careful not to reinforce unsuccessful patterns. Even if the bird must be placed on the floor to achieve a successful step-up command, unless the bird is having a panic reaction, don't return it to its territory until just after a successful cooperative interaction.

There is no substitute for warm, genuine human enthusiasm as a reward for the bird's success in stepping up. Especially with shy or cautious birds, the most important part of this exercise is probably the bird's enjoyment of the process. If the bird is not eagerly, or at least willingly, cooperating with step-ups and step-up practice, something is going wrong, and the owner should consider finding professional help immediately.

Each human expecting to interact with the bird should practice step-ups most days for a minute or so and in a routine variety of ways.

Never forget that the bird's enjoyment of the cooperative interaction is always the most important part. Frequent, exciting, or soothing verbal reinforcements are necessary components of successful step-up practice. Reinforcing the bird to enjoy step-up practice not only acts to prevent the development of normal parrot aggression, but also prevents the occasional development of shyness. While an aggressive juvenile parrot gains cooperation skills from step-ups, the shy or fearful bird can learn confidence from the joy and predictability of the interaction.

Early patterning is also necessary to prevent the development of stress reactions to toweling. A companion parrot requires annual veterinary examinations and grooming at least twice yearly. Cuddling, snuggling, and playing "peek-a-bird" in a towel will improve trust and condition the baby to enjoy or at least tolerate being restrained during these potentially stressful interactions.

We must be empathetic and predictable in the handling of all baby parrots, but the maintenance of trust is especially important to the African greys, lovebirds, the small cockatoos, and the small African parrots *(Poicephalus)*. This group has an occasional tendency to acquire sudden-onset phobic behaviors, sometimes exhibits heightened reactions, and appears to have a tendency to what might be called exceptional bonding-related behaviors. We use extra care and consistency with these species to compensate for these traits.

Bonding and Effective Socialization

In order to maintain an outgoing and social disposition, it's important to avoid allowing a parrot to become overly possessive of a particular human or territory. The bird should have relationships with as many humans and other safe animals as possible and should spend as much time as possible in diverse locations inside and out of the home. Access to appropriate choices, outings where the bird will meet sensitive, interactive humans, and regular changes in the cage and home environment will pattern the bird to toler-

Trust is especially important to potentially cautious birds like this Jardine's parrot.

A cavity-breeding parrot that is blissfully destroying wood may be saying "Look how sexy I am!" (Male Solomon Island Eclectus.)

ate the inevitable twists of fate that plague all creatures.

Vocal behaviors can develop almost any time before or after weaning. This might be babbling, talking, or screaming. The most usual source of early screaming is immediately perceived abandonment combined with failure of independence and overbonding. A companion parrot's ability to play independently greatly influences the nature of vocal behaviors. From the moment a baby parrot is aware of its surroundings, interesting tools (toys) must be provided to generate self-rewarding play behaviors. If a baby parrot does not learn to amuse itself, no amount of ignoring screaming in the other room will improve the bird's behavior.

Just as a well-planned environment stimulates activity and appropriate behavior, appropriate human behavior also stimulates appropriate behavior in companion birds. For example, any parrot learns to eat what it sees others eating. If humans in the household fail to eat diverse, nutritious foods, a human-identified companion parrot in that household will likely learn to do the same.

Accommodating Chewing and Messiness

Most hookbills are cavity breeders—they lay eggs and raise their babies in hollowed out, mostly wooden, spaces. When a cavity-breeding parrot is gleefully turning the priceless antique clock into toothpicks, it's really saying: "Look how sexy I am! I would be a fantastic mate! I could make a nice big nest cavity for you and our babies!"

If a cavity-breeding parrot is not provided with appropriate chewables, the furniture or woodwork could suffer or several troubling parrot behaviors could develop. Provision for chewing behaviors will help to prevent biting, screaming, nail biting, overpreening, feather chewing, and other innovative displacement behaviors.

Chewing and its ugly cousin, messiness, are innate behaviors, not behavior problems. That is, they must be accepted and accommodated because they are part of the parrot's nature that cannot be changed. A good quality cage is especially important here (see p. 112). The cage may be the most sig-nificant factor in whether or not the bird succeeds in its first home. A hard-to-clean cage or environment can easily inspire resentment in humans responsible for cleaning and can damage the human/bird bond.

Would You Enjoy a Parrot's Companionship?

A parrot is a wild (undomesticated) animal and not, necessarily, a perfect companion for every human. The bird must be trained to cooperate, guided to emotional independence, and accommodated for its natural behaviors. If you love a thunderstorm or busy children dismantling toys, or if you love watching a flower open (and close), you would probably love a parrot. If you think you could live with something like an occasional indoor tornado and are willing to accommodate some hot air and mess in order to share the company of sublime feathered joy, then you can probably enjoy a companion parrot.

All the potential behavior problems discussed here are usually very, very easily prevented. A new parrot owner who applies the principles set forth in *Guide to a Well-Behaved Parrot* and this book might never see habitual problem behavior.

Chapter Two

Finding the Right Bird

The Search for the Perfect Baby

A typical bird shopper in the United States probably has a choice of well over 50 different types of available parrot-type birds. So, unless a first-time bird buyer does a great deal of research or knows somebody who knows birds, there's a pretty good chance that the first bird won't be the "right" bird and that it won't last long in its first home. An example of how this might work goes something like this: a gorgeous movie star housewife with a couple of boisterous children is smitten with a lovely baby sun conure and talks her best friend, also a gorgeous movie star, into buying clutchmates. All goes well for about 48 hours until the young conures find their voices, and they are back in the store before the following weekend.

Another example: Forrest, an antiques dealer, loses his canary to old age. Browsing the bird store for a replacement, he happens upon a totally charming off-white bird just the beige/peach color of his fainting couch. Selecting a lovely domed brass cage 24 inches (62 cm) in diameter, he takes his new Goffin's cockatoo home to his lavishly furnished high-rise space. There's a clash coming between antiques and beak and between human and parrot needs. A Goffin's cockatoo will scream nonstop or absolutely self-destruct when confined to such a small cage. It will destroy all that antique wood if it is not confined. The bird will last less than three months in its first disastrous home.

As I have said previously, a parrot is not an impulse purchase. A parrot is both expensive and needy, and it's difficult to know who to believe about which kind of bird to buy, because every breeder, bird store staff person, veterinarian, and behavior consultant seems to say such different things. It's easy to see that a bird breeder or dealer who breeds or sells a particular type of bird will probably not only be partial to that type of bird, but will have a strong desire to place that particular baby in an appropriate home just after weaning, which is the most desirable age. Certain species might sometimes be produced in great numbers, flooding the market in a particular geographic area, then at least a few of those birds might languish a little longer before they are

Many different types of domestically-raised parrots are readily available in the United States. (Sulphur-crested cockatoo, African grey parrot, red-lored Amazon.)

adopted. For this reason, it is highly desirable for breeders to have waiting lists for their babies so that they can produce exactly what is needed and not have to watch their babies grow up without homes.

It's only natural that a bird dealer will be very accommodating in helping a potential client select a type of bird that is available for sale at the time. Unfortunately, that doesn't always mean that a bird shopper hears all the potential behaviors, both good and bad, for a particular type of bird. This book was written so that would-be bird buyers could have one place to look to compare expected behavioral characteristics and specialized needs of all the common companion parrots. Previously, a would-be bird owner would have to research each different type of bird, often in old books written by breeders who loved a particular type of bird so much that there was never mention

of a downside regarding the bird's expected needs and behaviors.

It's extremely important for a potential new bird owner to have some notion of what he or she wants and doesn't want before starting to shop for a bird. A wise bird dealer doesn't sell a Moluccan cockatoo to somebody who came in looking for an African grey or vice versa.

By studying the following chapters and comparing the needs and expected behavioral characteristics of each different type of parrot, would-be bird owners should be able to narrow their choices down to two or three types of birds. For example, a person who wanted a "medium large and extroverted bird that could be expected to talk" might consider an Amazon or one of the mid-sized or smaller macaws. Of course, a person with this expectation should be made aware of the downsides of both types of birds. A macaw might require more interaction than an Amazon and it might have a louder voice. An Amazon might be very independent and behaviorally stolid, but it might also develop an intrusive voice and use it more often than a macaw would.

The birds described here are all members of the parrot family, a large group called an order. The order of parrots is called *Psittaciformes*. This family is then divided into groups called genera, and each genera is divided into species or subspecies.

Each parrot has a Latin name, such as *Eclectus roratus solomonensis*. The first part of the parrot's Latin name is the name of the bird's genera or group.

The second part of the parrot's Latin name is the species. Not all genera have species. For example, *Eclectus* parrots and also *Myopsyttia monachus* (the quaker parakeet) are so successful in their habitat and so similar that they have only one species in the group.

The third word in the Latin name is the subspecies or race. Like *Eclectus,* most groups that have only one species will have more than one subspecies.[1] For the purpose of organizing this text, I have arranged the birds into three categories, Old World, New World, and Pacific Distribution, based on geographic origin.

Although it's good to have some idea about what to expect from a particular type of parrot, there is no such thing as an absolutely perfect parrot. It's not a good idea to become extremely focused on expectations, but rather to be open to whatever comes with this wonderful new experience of living with a bird. As you begin shopping, develop a rapport with the various dealers so that you can ask candid questions about what a particular bird's behavior will be like as an adult.

Shoppers' Etiquette

Baby parrots don't have fully developed immune systems. When shopping for a baby parrot, be sure to visit only one breeder or dealer each day. Bathe, and change clothing and shoes before visiting each facility. Many facilities will require you to

wash your hands before handling their babies. Be sure to ask permission to handle baby birds, as some caring dealers allow babies to be handled only with supervision. This protects the baby (and the interests of future owners) from mishaps involving mishandling at an early age.

To avoid the temptation of an impulse purchase, it's probably a good idea not to take a checkbook the first time you go to look at baby birds. Give yourself an opportunity to sleep on such an important decision. Avoid facilities that pressure you to make a quick decision.

A wise patron observes house rules when shopping for a bird. (Scarlet macaw.)

Selection

A person choosing a handfed parrot generally has the option of either choosing a very young bird (and waiting until it is weaned and ready to go home) or one that is slightly older. There are pros and cons to both. When selecting a very young parrot, the purchaser should look for an alert, robust bird. The bird's eyes should be clear and watchful. The nostrils or nares should be clean and dry. The chick should be plump and active. Smaller parrots will probably be both curious and cautious; many baby parrots will be merely curious with no observable caution. Babies showing noticeable aggression or noticeable fear should be avoided until the handfeeders work through these issues. The feathers may not be as neat as an adult bird's until the baby learns to preen itself.

If talking is important, ask the handfeeder if babies are already talking, for some baby parrots will acquire a few human words before they are weaned. Look for a vocally experimental bird who is willing to make sounds, even baby sounds, in your presence.

In most species except cockatiels, gender seems to be mostly irrelevant in the area of speech capability. Gender may affect disposition, however, with cocks being more commonly territorial and hens being more typically cautious and only occasionally territorial (with notable exceptions to this rule of thumb in several species). Now that gender can be safely and easily determined with DNA sexing, many parrot breeders and dealers have their babies sexed before selling them. This involves removing a drop of blood from a toenail and sending it in a kit to a laboratory for analysis. Persons wishing a bolder bird should look for a bolder chick without regard to gender, for although most hens do seem

to be more cautious, there are many very gregarious, outgoing hens, even some who went through a couple of very shy phases. Territorial hens and shy cocks can also be found.

Visiting the young baby whenever possible is a good idea. This allows the chick to become very familiar with its new human companions. This familiarity lends itself to the formation of the strong, mate-like bond that will occur later. It also greatly reduces the amount of stress the baby parrot is subjected to when it goes home. The baby should be eating independently before it goes to its new home. For reasons involving stress, as well as the adult bird's sense of security, wait at least a week or two after weaning to take the bird home.

When choosing an already weaned bird, more personality issues are involved. A weaned parrot chick might be more cautious than a very young baby. It might hesitate to submit to intimate contact right away. Choosing a slightly older bird requires more patience and time in many instances. Occasionally the bird will pick a person right away. While this is usually a good situation for someone looking for a parrot, it cannot be expected. In many cases the bird needs a chance to decide how it feels about the human. The advantage to selecting a bird at this age is that its inherent personality is more readily observed.

Begin an evaluation of a past-weaning-age chick by playing eye games and approaching with non-

A baby parrot's natural curiosity usually focuses on food. (Bronzewing Pionus.)

threatening posture. Don't be afraid to look at birds over a year old. Some old-time aviculturists who bought chicks before tests were available for Psittacine Beak and Feather Disease advised purchasing chicks after they successfully completed their first molt. Just because a chick is over a year old doesn't mean it's old. Most parrots can be considered young until they are about two years old. A large bird such as a macaw is still young at four.

Food-related Issues

The start each chick receives plays a large part in its ability to cope with all areas of life. A significant portion of a baby parrot's natural curiosity focuses on food. Tasting and feeling food is important in the baby's developmental processes. Whatever handfeeding method is used, it should allow the baby to get food into its mouth, not tube or gavage feeding into the crop, unless the chick is unable to swallow on its own. Solid food should be offered in a way that the baby is allowed to explore the tastes and textures while it decides to begin to wean.

Resist the temptation to hurry weaning. Each individual bird should be allowed to give up handfeeding in its own time and not be held to a schedule. While the babies are weaning, they rely on each other for support, encouragement, and a sense of security. They learn from each other how to play and how to get around in a cage, how to chew things up, and what to be afraid of. They will learn by watching older birds eat. The wise buyer looks for a dealer who is sensitive to the bird's needs during the weaning process.

The babies should be weaned onto a healthy diet. The new owner of a young parrot should not immediately subject the new youngster to the stress of changing its diet. The baby should have to endure as few changes as possible in the transition to its permanent home, and it should be offered a nutritious variety of interesting foods similar to those it enjoyed while weaning.

Environment

Too many major changes in a young parrot's environment can be stressful. The fewer things the bird has to get used to when it goes to a new home, the healthier and happier it will be. If the chick has been acclimated to its cage and toys, and is at least familiar with the new caregiver, the transition to the new home can go very smoothly.

A very young bird should learn how to use the cage that it will be living in later. The person who will be acquiring the baby should purchase a cage for the young bird to live in before it goes home. When taking home an older bird, the new keeper might try to purchase a cage similar to the one the bird has been raised in. Or the new cage might be brought to the bird and the bird given a couple of weeks to adjust before going to its new home. Parrots derive much of their sense of security from their cage. Particularly with the more sensitive species, such as cockatoos, *Poicephalus,* and African greys, and with young birds whose self-confidence is still developing, this dependence on surroundings should be respected.

Resist the Urge to Rescue

If you came to the store looking for a premium baby, it's probably best to resist the impulse to rescue a bird in need of a home. You could wind up spending lots of money on a bird that is not well-suited to your lifestyle. It could also be dangerous for other birds in the home.

Because there is this biological clock ticking away, taking the valuable baby days from the baby parrots in the store, it's only natural that a person with a baby bird to sell might say whatever is necessary to sell it. I have even heard of salespeople who have said something like, "This bird is chewing feathers and self-destructing and is to be killed tomorrow if nobody buys it today."

While rescuing a bird that seems to be in a pitiful situation can be commendable, the decision to be a hero should be made independently of looking at the birds. Being a good Samaritan isn't the same as looking for a well-adjusted baby. Unfortunately, making a purchase from an unscrupulous bird dealer to save a baby's life is helping that dealer to perpetuate abuses on additional birds. If the bird really is in trouble from the abuse or neglect of the seller, call the local animal welfare organization or animal control in your city. This situation calls for a professional.

The Totally Reliable Resource

There is another way to buy a bird. If a person is not confident in his ability to make an informed decision about a bird, he might make an informed decision about the seller or other avian professional. A first-time buyer is better off having an experienced person select a bird for him. Look for a behaviorist who will help you find a bird or a dealer who has many happy customers, many glowing faces talking about successfully adjusted companion birds. This is a typical way for zoos and trained-bird shows to buy parrots. I have seen many very fine human/avian relationships formed in this way.

The Secondhand Bird: Rehabilitating the Previously Owned Parrot

Some of the finest birds I have ever known were acquired or adopted well past one year of age. Many of them had already been removed from the first or even second home. While some of these birds were passed along to a new home because of lifestyle changes of the owners, many of them were pushed out of their homes for behavioral reasons. Some birds are sold or given away within a year or two of their purchase because humans didn't learn to accommodate the bird's needs, especially training and appropriate environment.

Sometimes a resale bird is the very best deal on a companion parrot, but buying a pre-owned bird can be a Pandora's box, including both good dreams and nightmares.

This beautiful umbrella cockatoo was rehabilitated as a teenager after being paired for many years.

Sometimes, such as in the case of a bird with an undisclosed illness, a resale bird can be the worst possible value and experience. A sick bird can communicate illness to other birds in the home and multiply problems and expenses radically.

Premium Handfeds

While many birds, especially older wild-caught or recaptured ferals, offer only limited companion potential, young adoption or resale handfed birds are good candidates to become quality companions. Indeed, some of the more traditional avicultural writers, like Dr. Matthew Vriends, often advise would-be bird owners that the best time to purchase a bird is after it has successfully completed its first molt.[2]

Radically improved behavior is possible at any age, but it's easier when the bird is younger. Generally speaking, there's a better chance to achieve glowing success similar to that in a first home with a small bird under one year old, with a mid-size bird under two years old, and with a large bird under five years old. These birds could easily be considered young. These ages approximate the arrival of breeding behaviors in these very sexual creatures. Most parrots can be rehabilitated at almost any age: new bonds can be formed, new behaviors (including new words) learned, even new feathers can be grown; but the cuddliness, docility, and trainability found in baby parrots is not usually easily recovered if the bird has achieved breeding age before socialization efforts are begun.

The best candidate for a perfect rehab bird would be a youngster that had been merely neglected rather than a bird that had been actively abused or spoiled. While a neglected bird might be either aggressive or frightened (or sometimes both aggressive and frightened), moving the bird will make a noticeable difference, possibly completely turning the behavior around. Most young parrots will probably respond favorably to being moved, and a new home is a new beginning that often brings radically improved behavior almost spontaneously.

Every effort should be made to convince the bird that it has moved to paradise. The perceived drastic changes provided by coming to a new home usually provide a window of opportunity for reinforcing good behavior during the temporary period of adjustment. This is similar to the "honeymoon period" experienced by baby handfeds coming into the first home. Nevertheless, the window of good behavior may be very brief. Work quickly and consistently to make the most of this fleeting opportunity.

Physical and Behavioral Rehabilitation

If possible, it's best to have a veterinary examination even before you commit to taking the bird. An adoption parrot may not have had the best care, so begin the physical rehabilitation process with medical evaluation and care, possibly before you ever take the bird home. If there are other birds in the home, be sure to observe appropriate quarantine procedures as specified by the veterinarian. This period will probably be at least one to three months, during which time the new parrot must be kept separated

Veterinary examination and quarantine procedures are especially important when bringing a new bird into a home with other birds. (Orange-winged Amazon.)

from established birds in the home. This period of quarantine in unfamiliar territory is an excellent opportunity to stimulate and reinforce new behaviors. If behavioral rehabilitation is not begun until after quarantine, you may have already missed the best window of opportunity to easily socialize the bird.

Ask the veterinarian to examine and update the bird's wing feather trim. This is important in training or retraining the bird to step-ups. During the first weeks in the home, provide a little extra sense of security by covering about one third of the bird's cage with a towel so that the bird has a place to hide if it chooses to do so. If there are no other established birds there, situate the new bird in the living area, but well out of traffic areas. Try to be nurturing, supportive, and consistent. Handle the bird less if it seems to tire easily, perhaps providing a little extra heat and sleep time for the first few days.

Even though the bird should have no strongly developed instincts to defend new territory, be sure to practice step-ups in a contained area outside the bird's new home territory. Be sure also to pattern the bird to step up onto a hand-held perch as well as onto hands. The bird may be reluctant to step up from the cage, so don't attempt step-ups from the cage unless the bird is first well patterned to step-ups in unfamiliar territory.

A young adopted domestic bird should be socialized exactly like a baby parrot would be. Many previously owned parrots go through a "honeymoon period" similar to the baby days (see p. 128) followed by the terrible two's (see p. 134) just like a baby bird would, but these developmental phases will be of much shorter duration with an older bird.

As quickly as possible, the bird should be socialized to enjoy the towel game (p. 153). A bird that has been mishandled may be terrified of the towel. Be sure to use a solid color towel with no stripes because many parrots for some reason fear striped or printed towels. Try to use a towel that is the same color as the bird's wings. The goal here is to replicate the feeling of security of being under mommy's wings. If the bird is initially afraid of the towel, try playing with the bird in the covers of the bed. Blankets may be less intimidating to a bird that has been roughly restrained in a towel for physical examination or grooming. Be sure not to fall asleep when playing snuggle games with the bird in the bed as the bird could easily suffocate if it crawls into the wrong position.

Diet

It's not unusual for a newly adopted parrot to prefer to eat nothing but seeds, especially sunflower or safflower seeds. This is similar to adopting a child who will eat only french fries. You want to get these birds onto a canary-based mix as quickly as possible; then you can begin mixing the pelleted diet with the seeds, gradually replacing all seeds with pellets, and eventually converting the bird to a pelleted diet.

Because of their sensitivity to being overdosed with vitamin D_3, convert *Brotegeris,* parrotlets, and mini-macaws to pelleted diet only with veterinarian supervision. Actually, it's a good idea to ask the veterinarian about that particular bird before trying to improve any bird's diet with pellets or by supplementing vitamins. If the bird has a less-than-healthy liver or kidneys, you'll probably be advised to avoid vitamin supplementation, especially with D_3, which could kill the bird. *Brotegeris,* parrotlets, and macaws, especially mini-macaws, are particularly susceptible to D_3 toxicity.

It is better to improve the diet with real food: fresh fruits, vegetables, pasta, and a quality commercial diet (see p. 200). Almost any food—quality whole grain toast, pasta, or oatmeal—served warm should seem like "love" to a previously handfed parrot that has been neglected. A parrot that is responding to the love inspired by warm food will probably want to feed humans, other birds, toys, or furniture. The sharing of masticated (already swallowed) food by parrots, called allofeeding, is a gesture of affection, sometimes of courtship.

The Aggressive Juvenile

If the bird is reported to be aggressive, but can be handled during that first window of opportunity, hold it as much as possible, usually in a snugly fluffy towel, during the first 48 hours in the new home. If it can be accomplished productively, work on step-up patterning (p. 153) for as long as you and the bird can stand to do it. Don't forget that in all socialization processes, the bird's enjoyment of the interaction is the most important part.

Consider the possibility that diet may play a role in the behavior of a truculent youngster. Consult an avian veterinarian, a behaviorist, or a nutritional consultant about improving this particular bird's diet.

The Attention-demanding Parrot

A parrot that has not developed independent play and other interests, but rather is totally emotionally and behaviorally dependent on humans, will develop annoying attention-demanding behaviors. Attention-demanding screaming is a famous component of behavior that can be described as "spoiled" in companion parrots.

Early development of attention-demanding screaming stimulates homelessness or home changes in many conures, cockatoos, and Amazons. Screaming is probably the most common reason for home changes in these birds. Early implementation of the techniques described in the sections on Forgetting Foul Language and Other Nuisance Sounds (p. 165) and Extreme Screaming (p. 169) can turn these birds around quickly if they are young enough and if they are not kept in groups. A screaming parrot, especially a famously loud one such as a mealy or *Farinosa* Amazon, introduced into a home with other established companion birds can ruin the whole group by causing the development of screaming habits.

The Shy Parrot

Many parrots have a natural or learned inclination to be cautious, and changing homes can be unsettling for cautious creatures. However, an extremely shy bird can be the most significant behavioral challenge encountered in companion bird rehabilitation.

Every effort should be made to help the bird feel safe. It's probably a good idea to leave a towel or blanket (careful of strings that might trap little toenails) over at least half the cage for the first few days. Try situating the cage at chest level first, and if the bird seems nervous, try either raising or lowering the cage until the bird seems most at ease.

Step-up patterning can also help a shy parrot to understand what is expected and to increase its confidence by enabling the bird to do what is expected. However, if the bird is too shy to cooperate with step-up practice, what do you do? Try the 12-step program on pages 20 and 21.

Older and Wild-caught Parrots

Most of the last legal wild-caught parrots entered the United States in 1992 (a small contingent of quaker parrots was allowed in 1993). If some of these cockatoos, Amazons, and macaws live as long as humans, then there will be older wild-caught parrots occasionally in the marketplace in the United States through the first half of the next century. Wild-caught parrots will probably continue to be available outside the United States, although the trend in industrialized nations is to limit both exportation and importation of birds hatched wild.

These birds, although they're older and possibly were never before socialized to human touch, occasionally offer good companion potential for a patient person. These birds require the same veterinary examination and quarantine, and they experience some of the same stages of behavioral development as a domestic baby parrot as they acclimate to the new home. The same socialization processes as with handfeds are used, but changes and advances must be made much more

Wild-caught parrots such as this gray-cheeked parakeet have not entered the United States since the early 1990s.

Twelve Steps to Making Contact by Playing Games

Some companion birds enjoy actual physical contact or are well patterned to cooperate. Other birds might be just as interactive, but simply prefer to interact passively, with eye games and body language and with no physical contact. Especially in the case of shy birds, it's a real advantage to know how to connect emotionally without actually touching the bird.

1. Some birds react fearfully to two eyes the same size. This might appear to the bird to be the gaze of a predator, an animal with both eyes in the front of its face. Look at a cautious or unfamiliar bird in the nonthreatening manner of a prey species (a species that serves as food for other animals), with only one eye at a time, as would a creature with its eyes on the sides of its head.

2. Any eye contact may be threatening to a shy bird, so don't maintain eye contact; look away if you catch the bird looking at you. Close your eyes, turn them away, or otherwise break eye contact until the bird is comfortable looking at you and letting you look back.

3. Try to be absolutely motionless when you first see the bird. Many birds freeze when they see a stranger. If you freeze when you see the bird, you are saying, "I'm not sure about you. Are you going to eat me?"

4. Try to be shorter than the bird, crouching over so that your entire head is lower than the bird's body. Because of the desire to achieve the highest status in the flock, a bird's natural instinct is to try to dominate the territory by being very high. If you try to be very short, almost any parrot will find this absolutely baffling and will often come down from where it is to see what on earth you are doing.

5. Play the blinking game. A frightened animal will not blink while maintaining eye contact. Demonstrate that you are not afraid by blinking while maintaining eye contact from a distance. An interested, interactive parrot will close its eyes or blink back to show that it is not afraid. If the bird is still afraid of you, it will not blink back.

6. Play peek-a-boo around any interesting corner, reading materials, towels, or clothing. Try combining this with the blinking game and the I-can-be-shorter-than-you game.

7. Mimic the bird's body language. When you see the bird stretch a greeting by extending one or both wings, try to show the bird that you feel the same way it feels by exhibiting the same body language.

8. Mimic simple sounds from across the room or around a corner, including tapping or knocking when you hear the bird tap or knock. If your bird plays with a bell and rings the bell, try ringing a bell in response. Try to entice the bird to respond to your response.

9. Share food with the bird. If the bird is cautious and has never taken food from you before, it might drop the food without eating it, or throw it. The bird can often be persuaded to take the food if you play this game (also called "Keep Away," see p. 130): Offer the food for a few seconds, then drop it or take it away. Wait a minute or two, then offer the food again, again dropping it or taking it away before the bird can take it. By the time you play this game the third time, the bird will probably take the food and eat it.

10. Play the drop-the-toy-and-pick-it-up game. This is probably the game most frequently initiated by parrots with humans. It's the bird equivalent of fetch, only the human does the fetching. The bird drops the toy or the spoon or the grape; the human picks it up and hands it to the bird. The bird flashes its eyes, puts beak to toy, then suddenly drops the toy again; the human picks it up.

11. Arrange to have old glasses, small wooden or plastic toys, or bird-safe jewelry that the bird can steal. Play with your toys, or have your spouse play with your toys, or wear them and allow the bird to steal them.

12. Demonstrate the joys of touching with other humans, pets, or birds. Find a cooperative friend who loves to be hugged and touched and petted, and demonstrate the joys of hugging, touching, and petting for the bird. This game resembles Dr. Irene Pepperberg's model/rival method of speech training in that it often stimulates the bird to compete for human attention.

A parrot has eyes on the sides of its head and examines things curiously with only one eye at a time. (African grey parrot.)

slowly, with this exception: A new handfed baby parrot should be actually held *for limited periods only*, guiding it with side-by-side interactions to learn to play alone (develop independence). In order to build and improve the human/parrot bond with an older, unbonded or wild-caught parrot, the bird could be held *for long periods of time* if it is reacting well to being held.

Rather than beginning with touching and holding, however, the new owner should begin befriending an untamed parrot with games and passive interactions (see pp. 20–21) here; also see Barron's *Guide to a Well-Behaved Parrot,* pp. 17–21). It is best to establish contact with the bird first with games involving no eye contact and progress to games involving limited eye contact. Offer food from the hand, play the towel game, and sleep in front of the bird before hand contact is attempted. Again, if the bird won't tolerate the towel game, try playing peek-a-bird with a blanket, bedspread, or quilt.

Some tamed wild-caught parrots bite less than some of their domestic cousins. Tamed wild-caught parrots sometimes fail to acquire human speech, but they can be charming companions in a different, wilder way.

Wild-caught parrots may occasionally be available through adoption programs with aviculture clubs. In many cases, the only way to differentiate a resocialized wild-caught or feral parrot from a resocialized handfed is by the split USDA steel band placed on its leg at importation.

Recaptured Feral Parrots and Their Offspring

There are occasional opportunities to rehabilitate parrots that have been found living wild. There are pretty dependable supplies of wild-hatched baby quakers in Florida and Texas, and occasionally observed hybrid Amazons captured by animal control in southern California. Some may argue that established feral parrots are happy living in their wild state and should be left alone.

No matter where feral species come from, free-flying non-native birds represent a danger to themselves, to domestic agriculture, and to the local environment. The birds might be living in an area where they would be subjected to extreme or adverse weather conditions. They consume food and occupy nesting sites that will be taken away from native species in the area. They might be in danger of being exterminated to protect farming operations in areas where they might proliferate. There is no protection for these non-native species birds, no reason why a citizen, especially a farmer, couldn't simply kill them.

While a recaptured feral parrot has the least potential to become a talking companion, some of them adjust well to life in the living room. Since the bird was able to survive wild, it was probably a wild-caught bird or the offspring of a wild-caught bird. A recaptured feral parrot will probably prefer seed and will probably require taming to learn the step-up interaction.

As with wild-caught parrots, begin befriending an untamed parrot with games and passive interactions. Again, start with games involving no eye contact and progress to games involving limited eye contact. When it has calmed somewhat, take the wing-feather-trimmed bird to a small restricted area such as a bathroom, closet, or hallway. Begin the first day by sitting on the floor on a towel with feet drawn up and knees up. Put the bird on a matching towel on your knees and spend an hour or so reading out loud to the bird. The second day, spend less time reading, and begin socializing with the towel game (p. 153), progressing as quickly as possible to the step-up command.

Aviary Birds

Just as there are birds that prefer to live with humans, there are birds that prefer to live with other birds. This is more common among wild-caught birds, recaptured feral birds, and parent-raised domestics than in handfed domestics. A bird may be so bonded to its wild roles, so intent on its own personal motivations, that it is completely unable to live with humans. Every moment in the company of humans can represent life threatening stress to such a bird. This is a maladaptation only in captivity. Every effort should be made to provide the bird with as natural an environment as possible, with an attempt being made to shield this bird from contact with humans. Of course, a breeding situation would be ideal, but some birds of this type are unbreedable individuals that are past breeding age, incompatible with available mates, mate abusive, or infertile. Large flights of similar type birds are desirable for keeping these birds happy.

When a Parrot Survives Its Owner

When a parrot survives its owner, there will probably be a period, usually no more than a few weeks duration, of silence or withdrawn behavior. A parrot that loses its owner may stop eating. The bird might call or continue looking for that favorite person. Likewise, a parrot might mourn, call, or seek out a recently deceased household pet. A few extremely bonded parrots may have a difficult time surviving their owners, while

Parrots kept in pairs may not relate well to humans. (Plum-headed parakeets.)

most birds adjust with relative ease to a gracious and welcoming new home.

If the bird is having a difficult time adjusting, try finding clothing or eyeglasses that resemble the former owner's appearance. If the bird is showing no interest in eating or interacting, show the bird photos of the deceased and talk soothingly of the lost friend. If the bird is exhibiting overt stress reactions such as feather or skin mutilation, don't show photos, but rather try to divert its attention to different activities (see p. 200).

Of course, the prevention of bereavement problems is easier on the bird. The existence of a second or foster home that is willing to become a permanent home is ideal. If the bird is already familiar with the new permanent humans and new permanent home, the transition will be much easier. The bird's diet and routine should remain as close as possible to what it was before the loss. To make the transition easier, owners should provide a written record of the bird's customary diet, preferences, dislikes, vocabulary; information about the bird's veterinarian, groomer, behavioral consultant, pet sitter, boarding facility, or other service providers; and any other idiosyncrasies that might affect the bird's happy adjustment in a new home. Owners who want to know where their birds will go if anything happens to them should make arrangements in advance and keep that information updated. If there is no established foster home or no provision for the bird in the owner's will, the bird might be placed through an adoption service or wind up in a shelter.

If a parrot's owner is ill, elderly, or otherwise homebound and lives alone, it's a good idea to establish a daily check-up system so that someone knows that all is well in the house every day. Not only is this good for the solitary owner, it also ensures that the bird will be found should the owner fall ill or die. Because it takes only a short time for a bird to die of thirst, a check-up system is necessary to ensure its survival. A check-up service for the elderly might be provided through a church volunteer organization or other in-home service provider; it is a noble and worthy project occasionally available through local bird clubs.

Selecting and Training a Talking Parrot

" 'Nothing that does not speak will come into this house,' he said.
. . . he never imagined that this hasty generalization was to cost him his life."[3]

And so Gabriel Garcia Marquez foreshadows the story of love of a talking bird and how it brings death to a prominent physician. Frequent parrot stories throughout Marquez' Nobel Prize winning work are a testament to the international popularity of talking birds.

Science tells us that humans talk to their companion birds more than we talk to any other pet. History and literature tell us that birds that talk back are among the most treasured of all companions. Indeed, fascination with avian talking ability is often the catalyst that entices us to bring that first bird home.

Choosing the Species

While most types of domestic handfed parrots can learn a few words, my intent here is to guide new bird owners to individuals that can be expected to learn to say many words and will learn to use at least some of them appropriately. Getting the right bird is more than half the battle, for most baby domestic parrots of the species discussed in the following paragraphs will learn to talk with very little extra effort on the part of humans. That is, a healthy, well-socialized baby parrot of a good talking species will usually acquire human speech if humans merely talk to the bird, interact with the bird, and talk to each other in the bird's presence.

In over two decades of observing parrot behavior, I find that budgies, quakers, African greys, and certain Amazons (yellow-heads, yellow-napes, blue-fronts, and blue-crowned Amazons) demonstrate the most dependable, easily accessible talking ability. I hear incredible stories about talking ringnecks, Jardine's, and lories. I've seen some exceptionally good-talking macaws, especially blue-and-golds. I have also seen fre-

A mature yellow-naped Amazon is more likely to talk than to snuggle.

quent talking ability in individual ringnecks, lories, conures, *Eclectus,* cockatoos, and male cockatiels; but I consider the first group listed to be most likely to consistently produce individuals with large vocabularies.

Gender plays an occasional role in talking ability. I sometimes get the notion that hen African grey parrots, especially hen Timneh grey parrots, talk more than males of their kind. Both genders of grey parrots talk well, however, often acquiring large, constantly growing vocabularies. They're smart, but there's a downside to the grey parrot: they're so smart, that they sometimes encounter developmental difficulties during the first year. In the case of the African grey parrot, it might be a good idea to purchase a well-socialized bird that is over one year old or has already completed its first molt.

Except for budgies, cockatiels, grass parakeets, and cockatoos, I believe both male and female birds have approximately equal ability to

acquire speech. Although I occasionally encounter talking hen budgies and sometimes even talking hen cockatoos, I don't expect hen cockatiels or grass parakeets to talk at all. In most species with good reputations as talkers, a more demonstrative, experimental, exuberant bird of either gender is more likely to be motivated to communicate than a shy, withdrawn bird.

Younger birds are more likely to learn human speech than older ones, but "young" is a matter of definition. Some birds, especially the smarter birds like the African grey parrot, don't acquire words until past a year of age. According to a *Bird Talk* survey a few years back, readers reported that the average time it took for an African grey parrot to say its first word was 14 months. That means, of course, that probably about half the birds took longer than 14 months to acquire their first word.

Additionally, birds are not dogs. You can teach an old bird new tricks, and older birds, even teenagers and beyond, who move into a new home are often so stimulated by environmental changes that they begin acquiring words.

Finding the Right Baby

Much of the research into local availability of good-talking species can be done at home. Check newspapers, yellow pages, and favorite bird magazines for breeders or dealers in your area. Call ahead to inquire about availability of chicks of the age and type you desire. Some aviaries require an appointment to see birds.

A pet parrot can be an extremely expensive, (occasionally) invasive, and long-lived acquisition. Don't rush into a decision. Dealers who care most about the quality of homes their babies go into are likely to have done a thorough and effective job all around, including crucial early socialization and weaning. Some dealers require applications from potential owners and strict requirements that the new owner will have to meet. This might include reading the industry standard, *Guide to a Well-Behaved Parrot,* or it might include requiring that the new owners attend classes before being allowed to take a bird from that facility.

Observe shoppers' etiquette, as discussed on p. 11. Don't visit multiple stores or aviaries in one day. If possible, bathe, and change clothes and shoes between each facility.

Politely observe house rules for handling baby birds, which may include asking first to handle a particular baby, washing or disinfecting hands, and stepping through disinfectant to minimize possible disease transmission. Don't provoke the birds by waving fingers in their faces.

Ideally, look for a young bird that is eating independently. If gender is germane to talking ability in the type of bird you are buying, ask to have the baby's gender confirmed by DNA testing. This process is minimally invasive, requiring only a drop of blood from a clipped toenail.

Look for a bird that is interactive, interested in sights and sounds. Look for a baby that expresses interest and attention by puffing out its head and neck feathers, stretching its wings (singly with a leg out or both shoulders stretched straight up), bobbing its head up and down solicitously, or quickly wagging its tail from side to side. These easily observable happiness behaviors are indications that the bird is interested in what is going on. Look for a bird that responds to your voice with these behaviors, especially if the bird is so young that the feathers are not completely opened. If the bird is old enough and has light enough eyes to be able to see iris movement in contrast to the pupil of the eye, look for one that frequently demonstrates excitement by narrowing the pupils. This is called pinpointing or flashing, and I believe it is an important indicator that this particular bird has the interest and motivation to talk.

A new owner may feel most confident about the bird's age and socialization during handfeeding by actually selecting a baby before it is weaned and visiting frequently, usually once a week, to handle and interact with the bird. Speech training can begin before the bird is weaned, although I prefer—for the health and safety of the bird—to have the baby weaned by experienced professionals.

Speech Training

In the past, it was thought that one-on-one interaction, including much out-of-context repetition, was the best way to teach parrots to talk. Many birds throughout the ages have acquired human words this way, but I believe these birds are more likely to merely mimic the sounds of the words. Modern parrot fanciers are more excited about the prospect of talking rather than mimicking parrots, and so our ways have changed.

The work of Dr. Irene Pepperberg, a Harvard-educated cognitive ethologist (one who studies the evolution of thought), astounded the world and the aviculture community by opening our eyes to possibilities that were often previously ignored or disbelieved. Noting that there were scientific studies underway to demonstrate talking abilities in apes and dolphins, Dr. Pepperberg began her research 19 years ago with Alex, a presumed-to-be-average African grey parrot purchased from a pet store.

Amazingly, Dr. Pepperberg's research not only taught us about avian speech capacity, it also evaluated techniques for speech training. Her studies demonstrated, for example, that attempts to train her grey parrots with audio and videotapes were useless. In another study by a different scientist, the birds learned only the sounds of human staff coming in to start the tapes, and not what was on the tapes themselves.

In Dr. Pepperberg's lab, Alex learned to identify and describe objects, even learning to use some nouns as adjectives, hence "rock corn" for dry hard corn kernels and "cork nut" for almonds. Alex developed his abilities to speak with understanding through use of the model/rival method wherein one bird interacts with two humans who demonstrate the behaviors (words and identification) that are being trained. One trainer questions the other human about colors, shapes, and objects. This person is the model for the parrot's behavior and the parrot's rival for the attention of the trainer. The model answers the question, receives a reward, then the roles of the model and the rival are reversed.

This technique probably resembles the way young parrots learn to communicate with their flock—by listening to older birds "duet" or talk back and forth. Although it is best to include humans or other talking birds in this process, if the bird is young and not too distracted or if the baby parrot is properly conditioned, the rival might even be one of those stuffed, talking parrot plush toys.

A baby parrot needs a tremendously stimulating environment. For the first two years, the baby parrot's environment should look a little like a nursery school, with lots of toys and interesting things that the bird can use to learn to entertain itself. Repetition is important, but speak to the baby parrot just as you would speak to a human infant, expecting it to learn the words it hears most. Use words in context, just as you would use them with a human baby. The bird doesn't have to be held during speech training, for much of the baby parrot's first communication efforts will probably be used to induce you to pick it up.

Try talking a little "baby (parrot) talk," for your first step to success might be in baby parrot language. If you can make a sound the bird is known to make, and the bird repeats the sound, the bird can then be rewarded with praise and affection, and you will have established the pattern by which the bird will acquire words. Use soothing, cooing sounds if the bird is a little shy. Avoid hissing or "shhh" sounds as these are made by the bird's natural enemies, and they might make the baby nervous.

Use lots of single-syllable words at first like *what, hi, ciao, bye,* and *night, night.* Use the words in context, just as you would use them with a human infant. While the bird will not usually be immediately able to repeat a word, early signs of progress include the bird sitting around muttering or babbling incoherent sounds. The bird will pick up the cadence of human language first, with understandable words and phrases following after much practice.

Early phrases that are easily acquired include "What 'cha doin' " and anything with "itty" sounds such as "pretty bird" and "here, kitty, kitty, kitty." Once you start combining words into phrases, mix them up, like "pretty kitty" and "What's kitty doin?'"

Many baby parrots, especially Amazons, will learn to talk in high-pitched feminine voices. It is not unusual for African greys to acquire deeper male voices. The voice the bird mimics can tell us which human the bird is most bonded to. The greys, especially, tend to mimic the voice of the perceived human rival for the affections of their favorite person.

Singing loudly almost directly into the bird's head is an excellent way to get its undivided attention. Many birds will stop dead still and sit there flashing their eyes as long as you will sing to them, perhaps joining in or practicing later what they have heard.

Modeling whistling is probably not a good idea for most good talking types of parrots. Since birds have no vocal cords, the mechanism by which they speak resembles structures used by humans for whistling. Whistling is probably easier to accomplish than speech, and the bird might choose to whistle *only* rather than use words. Whistling might be a good transition for teaching a type of bird not known for talking ability. Cockatiels and conures,

for example, that might not acquire more than a few words can often become accomplished whistlers. Try "Colonel Bogie March" or the theme from "The Andy Griffith Show."

Be sure to include the baby in daily activities: eating, sleeping, showering, and expressing affection to other humans and animals. These activities replicate the feeling of being part of the flock and should stimulate the baby parrot's natural instinct to communicate with other members of the "flock." If there is no problem with aggression, it might be helpful to allow the baby parrot to sit higher than anybody else during speech training.

A baby of a good talking type of bird will learn the most exciting words it hears—words that are spoken with the most gusto and enthusiasm. Therefore, profanity and angry words might be learned with only one repetition if the bird is really tuned in to humans in the household.

There's an old saying, "Live as though you could sell the family parrot," for second and subsequent owners will hear from the bird the words it heard in its first home.

And by the way, if you want to avoid the doctor's fate in *Love in the Time of Cholera,* be sure to keep your bird's wing feathers trimmed. But that's another story.

The Older Talking Parrot

Sometimes, even though the species is known to talk and the owners have done everything possible to encourage the bird to talk, it

Blue-and-gold macaws are occasionally exceptional talkers and can acquire new words at any age.

doesn't. Every bird is an individual, and not every individual wants to communicate with language.

The only way to be absolutely guaranteed a talking parrot is to acquire a bird that is already talking. Sometimes this means looking for a young talking bird; sometimes it means acquiring a parrot that is already mature. Because teaching human speech to a parrot is an inexact science and because it is inherently time-consuming, many trick-bird shows prefer to acquire older birds that are already talking.

When transferring an older bird into the home, be sure to see the veterinarian and observe appropriate quarantine protocol. Try to make the bird feel as though it has just moved to paradise. Keep a few familiar toys, but don't be afraid to make improvements in housing and activities.

Some birds react unfavorably to being quickly forced into radically different housing. Entice the older bird to choose the new cage by placing the old cage on the floor beside the new one, moving food and water bowls to the new cage, and waiting while the bird explores and begins eating in the new cage. An exciting new home and an exciting new environment often bring new words and happy new behaviors into a mature bird's routine habits.

[1]Jupiter, Tony, and Parr, Mike, *Parrots: A Guide to Parrots of the World,* New Haven, CT: Yale University Press, 1998, pp. 17–18.

[2]Vriends, Dr. Matthew, *Lories and Lorikeets,* Hauppauge, NY: Barron's Educational Series, 1993.

[3]Marquez, Gabriel Garcia, *Love in the Time of Cholera,* New York, NY: Viking Penguin, 1989.

Chapter Three

What to Expect of the Old World Parrots

The African Grey Parrots

For centuries, the African grey parrot has been known for its extreme intelligence, its ability to reproduce words, and, some say, its ability to use words with understanding. It's treasured for its bright, intelligent eyes; pastel grey scallops; and, often, bright red tail. The grey parrot breeds readily and is usually available almost anyplace in the world where parrots are kept as companions. Little wonder that the African grey begins the new century as the most popular mid-sized hookbill in the United States.

There are two subspecies, the larger African grey parrot (commonly called the Congo African grey or the red-tailed grey in the United States) and the smaller Timneh African grey parrot. There are some color variations between individuals that may be light silver or almost black depending upon the point of origin of their ancestors, as the birds become gradually darker and smaller as they occur toward the west coast of Africa. While they are not considered a separate subspecies, the smallest and darkest of the red-tailed greys is sometimes called the Cameroon or Ghana African grey, indicating its source in western Africa. The red-tailed bird's beak is solid black, and the usually smaller Timneh subspecies can be easily identified by its horn-colored maxilla. Both subspecies possess equal talking abilities, with some individuals exhibiting exceptional mimicking and communication skills.

A curious, confident young grey parrot.

The sensitive African grey temperament sometimes leads to feather chewing.

What's in a Name?

As president of the African Parrot Society, I am in constant communication with aviculturists from other countries. I try very hard not to use the term Congo grey. In other countries, zoos, taxonomists, and ornithologists do not approve of the common (street) names we give our animals here. When I refer to the Timneh grey, I always say "Timneh" or "Timneh grey." President of the African Parrot Society Jean Pattison reports that the bird commonly called a Congo grey in the United States is correctly called the African grey.

However, because of its extreme intelligence and sensitive temperament, the African grey parrot develops a surprising diversity of both wanted and unwanted behaviors. The grey parrot is so very intelligent that very creative, neurotic-seeming behaviors can appear almost spontaneously. As a companion parrot behavior consultant for over 20 years, more than half of my regular ongoing case load was sometimes represented by cases involving African grey parrots. This behavior is unquestionably linked to the bird's great intelligence, which is often reflected in its talking ability.

The grey's reputation for intelligence might also be linked to the bird's reputation as most opinionated bird; for even if a grey does not talk, it will be exceptionally capable of communicating its preferences, for African greys are famous finicky eaters, behavioral martinets, and gender chauvinists.

Like other intelligent species—humans, chimpanzees, elephants, and whales—the baby grey's intellectual and behavioral development requires a relatively long time. Likewise the grey parrot's talking skills develop a little more slowly than those of some other parrots. Like other parrots, the grey parrot learns to talk without vocal cords. Sounds are produced when the bird forces air across the top of the trachea, a process that resembles blowing across the top of a bottle. Sound variations are produced when the bird changes the shape of the trachea.

This requires practice. A baby grey is learning to talk when it rehearses quietly, muttering or whispering, until it is confident enough to produce the sounds it likes loudly. While a particular baby parrot might learn a few words before it is weaned, the average grey acquires its first word at about 11 months. This might be at about 11 months of age, or it might be at 11 months in the new home.

The Smartest Parrot

Until the work of Dr. Irene Pepperberg was recognized, parrot authorities were careful to use the word *mimic* rather than *talk* when referring to a parrot's abilities. It took a Harvard-educated Ph.D. to convince the world scientific community of what many bird owners knew all along: African grey parrots can, indeed, use words with understanding. For over 19 years, Dr. Pepperberg has studied and statistically analyzed the African grey's speaking abilities.

Working first with a secondhand, wild-caught African grey parrot named Alex, Dr. Pepperberg evaluated the bird's abilities to answer questions regarding familiar objects: their shape, number, substance, and color. But Dr. Pepperberg didn't just evaluate talking parrots; she also documented methods by which the birds acquire human speech. She has observed that grey parrots learn best when competing against a rival for the attentions of a favorite person. Therefore, although a grey parrot can and will talk in the voice of the favorite person, the African grey most often appears to prefer to speak in the voice of the rival (for the attentions of the favorite person). This tendency is the basis for some of Dr. Pepperberg's most famous work, her model/rival method, in which competition is used to stimulate language use in the African grey parrot.

In spite of its reputation for being a great talker, the red-tailed grey is often reluctant to talk in front of strangers or in unfamiliar surroundings. This previously accepted assumption has recently been shattered with the appearance of talking African grey parrots in public performance settings.

Baby grey parrots have black eyes. Expect to treat a baby grey

Baby Timneh African greys build coordination and confidence on easily gripped perches.

Suggested wing trims for African grey parrots. Wing trim (A) is for particularly good flyers. (B) is for adults. (C) is for juveniles.

almost exactly as you would treat a child. Never punish the bird, especially with hitting, squirting, or dropping. Even "the evil eye" and "time outs" can be too frightening for an extremely sensitive grey parrot.

Ginger Elden, a long-time breeder of African greys, reports that baby greys that are already talking will sometimes take a few days, weeks, or months to begin talking again as they adjust to their new homes. Grey parrots bred for stolid disposition and talking ability are changing the way we see grey parrots. Biologist and breeder Jim Murphy reports that in his selective breeding program grey parrots are not retained for breeding purposes "unless they are sweet and talking by four months old."

Baby African grey parrots benefit from starting out in smaller cages with smaller perches to prevent falling during the period in which their personality develops. If a baby African grey parrot is put immediately into a very large cage with slick, large-diameter perches, the bird's essentially cautious nature could combine with bad luck to produce a fearful, panicky bird. Baby grey parrots benefit from having sharper than normal toenails that combine with the easily gripped perches to prevent falling and to help build coordination and confidence.

The African grey must be protected from learning unpleasant human sounds such as squeals, squeaks, screeches, burps, belches, and worse. Likewise the bird must be protected from learning profanity, for the bird will probably outlive the household and will say in its next home what it heard in the first. Greys must be protected from learning screaming from other parrots, barking from dogs, and (this is extremely important) car alarms. Curiously, although they often talk, greys seldom develop a screaming problem like Amazons or cockatoos. While they are entirely capable of making and are often willing to make some very obnoxious, attention-demanding sounds, they simply do not achieve the volume of their larger New World and Pacific Distribution cousins. An African grey parrot can drive the humans in the home crazy with annoying sounds, but the annoying sounds will seldom be loud enough to bother the neighbors next door or down the block.

Behavioral training is especially important in companion greys, for they must learn cooperation, acceptance of change, and independent play in order to fully enjoy life in the living room. This is done with patterning, sensitivity, and environmental manipulations as described in my first book, *Guide to a Well-Behaved Parrot*. While tendencies toward aggression are expected, normal, and somewhat desirable, developing fearfulness must be treated immediately, for this can lead to unwelcome stress reactions such as feather shredding.

The African grey parrot is an undomesticated animal. It might respond to violence with violence. The bird must be patterned to appropriate behaviors by modeling and reinforcing, practice, and repetition. Fortunately, this is usually easily accomplished in a normally experimental, well-socialized handfed baby grey. During the first three to six months in the home, a handfed baby grey should be curious and eager to please. This is the juvenile developmental period sometimes called the honeymoon period. It is a time during which confidence gradually turns from approval-seeking to independence and the instinct to dominate. According to Elden, the honeymoon period is an especially good time to avoid corporal punishment, for like human children, the African grey parrot has memory and is perfectly capable of holding a grudge.

The Grey Parrot Subspecies
African Grey Parrot *(Psittacus erithacus erithacus).* The larger of the subspecies, this bird has a clearly red tail and a solid black beak. The African grey parrot is known worldwide for its accurate mimicking abilities and extreme intelligence. With that intelligence, however, comes a responsibility to carefully and sensitively socialize the bird in order to avoid the development of unwanted behaviors such as extreme fearfulness and behavioral feather chewing.

Timneh African Grey Parrot *(Psittacus erithacus timneh).* The tail of the Timneh African grey has a brownish wash over the red, sometimes giving it a maroon appearance. The Timneh has a black-tipped horn-colored maxilla and a solid black mandible. They are usually more active and behaviorally stolid than their larger cousins. Timnehs may learn to talk earlier than Congos and may be more inclined to talk in front of strangers. Timnehs suffer a lesser tendency to develop feather chewing disorders than the African greys.

Poicephalus: Undiscovered African Treasures

Dianalee Deter and I have been accused of being "gushy" about this family. As a behaviorist dealing with potentially homeless companion birds, I feel this gushy attitude is justified, because I believe this family is the most likely of any parrot except the budgie or cockatiel to successfully remain in the first home throughout its lifetime.

Poicephalus babies are sometimes overlooked by potential companion bird owners for their more outgoing relatives, the cockatoos, Amazons, and macaws. This is unfortunate, since the small African parrots are every bit as enjoyable as any of these showy alternatives. Poicephalus are usually more behaviorally dependable than cockatoos, much quieter than most Amazons, and more easily housed and accommodated than most macaws.

In our living rooms Poicephalus are acrobatic little clowns who like to lie on their backs and chew their toenails. They are adept escape artists who can break out of (or into) even the most bird-proof enclosures. Because they love to explore drawers and snuggle into small enclosures, they are occasionally accidentally smashed or suffocated.

They are tenacious excavators who can empty a large wooden cavity in hours. They are avid collectors who like to store any loose toys or other objects in their food or water bowls. If a Senegal wants to be petted, it might fluff up its neck feathers, cock its head to the side, close its little eyes, and pet its own neck.

Poicephalus species are reputed to share similar sensitive temperaments. They also share a reputation with the African grey parrot as the quietest (read here, "least loud") of the larger parrots. Their talking ability often outpaces their reputation as modest talkers, with occasional individuals developing large vocabularies.

Poicephalus respond dependably to routinely established stimulus-response scenarios. They enjoy redundancy and routine. They are easily guided away from overbonding, and they learn independence, especially independent play, easily. They are crazy about swings and other acrobatic toys.

Formerly described as skittish, it is said that Poicephalus parrots' temperaments were much more fragile ten years ago when the majority of these birds were wild-caught imports or the offspring of imports. But modern domestic-raised Poicephalus parrots are quite a bit different from the first few domestic clutches raised from newly arrived wild-caught parents only a decade or so ago, according to Jean Pattison. Although they are sometimes totally fearless in the face of grossly larger creatures, they are also often terrified of the most mundane, non-threatening inanimate objects such as rolled wrapping paper, balloons, or unfamiliar headgear.

Members of this group are an excellent choice for people who are intimidated by larger birds. They are a good choice for someone who might be considering adding more birds later. They are less likely to be ignored when a new, bigger bird is added than some of the less complex small parrots might be.

When good behavior is properly maintained, the companion *Poicephalus* is usually a charming little imp that both loves to manipulate favorite humans and seeks to please them. We say "usually" here because any autonomous creature can have an occasional cantankerous moment. Appropriate socialization is required to minimize or eliminate those out-of-control impulses that can ruin a human/parrot bond. Either member of this equation can be easily traumatized so that the bond between human and bird is lost.

While many, probably most, of these birds only pinch or tease humans with annoying "beaking" behaviors rather than painful, intentional bites, some also learn to bite. Although a *Poicephalus* probably can't do much, if any, permanent damage to an adult human hand, an intentional bite from a naughty *Poicephalus* can be surprisingly painful.

Behavioral Development

A well-maintained *Poicephalus* parrot can retain enjoyable companion behaviors for many years. Human companions remain delighted and intrigued by their *Poicephalus* parrots' normal capacity for aggression, tendency to cautiousness, and potential to initiate active (at times annoying) interactions with humans and pets. Due to their intelligence, new, unac-ceptable behaviors can appear quickly.

Poicephalus parrots have a reputation for developing heightened reactions, behaviors that can be expressed as either fearfulness or fearlessness. This behavior is probably the result of an exceptionally well-developed fight-or-flight response in this prey species. This behavior is also seen in many other parrots, especially smaller parrots. Fearfulness is a potentially prominent part of *Poicephalus'* instinctual behavior patterns, as many of these birds seem to go through both nippy and fearful stages before becoming fully independent. A *Poicephalus* is more easily guided to use behaviors that come under conscious control before they have begun to rely on the automatic fight-or-flight response. The response

The Senegal parrot is the most common Poicephalus parrot in captivity.

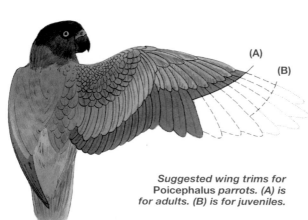

Suggested wing trims for Poicephalus *parrots. (A) is for adults. (B) is for juveniles.*

not to even giggle at unacceptable behavior, for these birds can quickly learn to nip, then curse or squeal in imitation of human pain, followed by mimicking the laughter that reinforced the behavior. This "maniacal" behavior is also often reported in other types of parrots, especially the yellow-naped Amazon.

Poicephalus parrots are humorous, inventive, and intelligent, but, as with other hookbills, behavioral problems can develop as the baby birds mature. *Poicephalus* parrots remember past incidents. They are said to hold grudges.

The Common *Poicephalus* Parrot Species

Senegal Parrot *(Poicephalus senegalus).* Behind the African grey, the Senegal is the African parrot most commonly bred in captivity. These brightly-colored clowns are known for acrobatics, mischievousness, passion, and panic. They are, perhaps, the most intense in both color and disposition in this occasionally intense family.

The Senegal parrot's head is gray, topping a mostly green body with a breast and belly ranging in color from lime-yellow to deep orange. The body markings form a shallow or deep "V" pierced by a green point running down the breastbone.

Senegal hens seem to be noticeably shyer than most cocks. However, aggressive hens are not uncommon, nor are shy cocks. As with many other species, the differ-

can be controlled with early patterning, sensitive and consistent handling, lots of loving reinforcement, balanced bonding, appropriate social modeling, and planned environmental manipulations.

A companion *Poicephalus* must be handled daily so that it will not become obsessed with controlling the immediate environment, toys, and cage. Affectionate practice of the step-up command, cuddling, and playing in a towel will acclimate the bird to intimate and restrictive interactions. Not all handfed companion *Poicephalus* like to be petted on the neck like so many other parrots, but most like to be hugged or snuggled. Seldom does any other baby parrot like to play on its back as much as a baby *Poicephalus* parrot.

Like other parrots, the *Poicephalus* parrot is often accidentally reinforced with laughter. This can happen easily. The owner must be very careful

ences are often less noticeable than the similarities. The safest, most dependable way to identify gender is with the use of DNA sexing.

Although these birds speak in adorable little doll-like voices and are well known for lacking the volume of most other parrots, the intensity of a Senegal's "whistle/alarm" call can cause pain to some sensitive human ears. Indeed, many companion Senegals obviously enjoy making annoying attention-demanding whistles and beeps (the phone, the microwave, the alarm clock).

Senegals go through a nippy stage and may also go through a fearful stage before reaching emotional independence at about two years of age. These birds may not form a strong bond with a permanent favorite human until after the nippy and fearful stages are past.

Meyer's Parrot *(Poicephalus meyeri)*. These birds have a reputation for being very, very sweet, although they are probably not as uniform in behavior from bird to bird as the cockatiel. They can also be strikingly beautiful. The head, neck, back, wings, upper breast, and tail are taupe brown or warm gray with yellow at the crown, thighs, bend of wing, and under wing coverts. Rump and underparts can range from bright bluish green to almost pure bright blue. The beak is gray. The adult bird's eyes are bright red-orange; juveniles have brown eyes.

Like Senegals and Jardine's, Meyer's are famous for lying on their backs and doing silly things with their feet. Dispositionally, the Meyer's parrot might be called a "mellow, laid-back" Senegal.[4] The right Meyer's or brown-head parrot can be an excellent choice for homes with sensitive, trainable children.

The Meyer's parrot is commonly said to be more exploratory and more experimental than the Senegal parrot. Where Senegals have a tendency to be a one-person bird, Meyer's are reported to more easily maintain balanced interactions with multiple individuals. They're more interested and willing to meet new people and explore new things. They're less likely to stay on or in the cage when not supervised. The Meyer's parrot's moods are more constant. It doesn't usually express such extreme aggression or such extreme shyness as a Senegal parrot.

Meyer's parrots have a reputation for being both acrobatic and a little accident-prone. Because a frightened companion Meyer's will often learn to dive down under things, it's sometimes in danger of being stepped on in uncontrolled settings.

Meyer's parrots are not known for exceptional talking ability, although they will pick up a few words and quite a few other sounds. They may have a predisposition to become more accomplished whistlers than talkers. These birds make almost exclusively pleasant sounds. They are the epitome of the "quietest parrot," with individuals seldom acquiring even annoying whistles.

Red-bellied Parrot *(Poicephalus rufiventris)*. With the widespread

This female red-bellied parrot is subtly colored with a wash of iridescent red over the sea-foam green belly.

use of modern handfeeding techniques, the red-bellied parrot's popularity has skyrocketed. Hen red-bellies, especially, enjoy a loud, vocal following of loyal fans. Jean Pattison, however, who has raised more than 40 clutches of red-belly babies in nine years, sees little difference between hens and cocks as companion birds. Pattison confirms that the red-bellied parrots we see today are quite a bit different from the birds that were available 10 to 15 years ago. Early clutches of wild-caught red-bellies were often extremely shy. Later clutches, even from the same pairs, show that the parents' adjustment to captivity over the years has resulted in calmer, bolder, more interactive birds with all the advantages *Poicephalus* has to offer, and more. The red-bellied parrot is enjoying a growing reputation as, perhaps, the best talker of the group.

Red-bellied parrots possess brownish gray upper parts with green lower parts and a wash of blue over the rump. They are sexually dimorphic, with cocks having a deep orange breast, abdomen, and underwing coverts. Hens have a delightful wash of iridescent red highlights over green in these parts. The beak is completely black. Cocks have a wash of orange on the cheeks. The adult bird's eyes are bright red-orange; the juvenile's eyes are brown. Some juvenile red-bellies resemble hens, the majority resemble cocks, and some juvenile red-bellies have dimorphic colors in their fledging feathers.

Possibly because of their extremely shy natures, red-bellies are reported to especially enjoy the advantages of a hide box. This might simply be a towel over one end of the cage, or it might be one of those little translucent fabric tents.

Brown-headed Parrot (*Poicephalus cryptoxanthus*). This could be the most undiscovered of these "undiscovered African treasures." Of the *Poicephalus* parrots available in captivity, the brown-head, *Poicephalus cryptoxanthus,* is sometimes both the least available and the least expensive member of this mostly modestly priced group. This bird is so rare in captivity that even some seasoned aviculturists, when shown the baby birds, are unable to identify them. But the lack of bright colors might accompany a very desirable, mild manner.

The bird has a grayish brown head and a mostly green body with bright yellow under the wings. The brownhead looks a little like a Senegal or a Meyer's parrot without the yellow or turquoise. The upper mandible is gray; the lower mandible is pale beige. The adult bird's eyes are yellow, but not always bright yellow. The juvenile bird's eyes are brown; the change to yellow is sometimes subtle.

These birds are usually easily patterned, especially to the towel game. Although they have a well-deserved reputation for calmness, brownheads are still *Poicephalus,* and individual birds may retain and exhibit all common types of *Poicephalus* behavior including coyness, clownishness, defensiveness, and a well-developed fight-or-flight response.

Jean Pattison describes brownheads as being "very close to the Meyer's in personality." They enjoy a reputation, among the few who know them, as more predictable members of a group that is only occasionally unpredictable. This bird might be the most adaptable member of this generally adaptable group.

Jardine's Parrot *(Poicephalus gulielmi).* Virtually unavailable as a companion bird only ten years ago, the Jardine's has enjoyed a steady rise in popularity, probably due to its improved accessibility, its intelligence, and its temperament. These birds are said to be capable of large vocabularies and of grey parrot-like

The brown-headed parrot may be both the least expensive and the least available of the Poicephalus family. (Jardine's, Senegal, and Meyer's parrots.)

accuracy in mimicry. Jardine's are said to share the Senegal's reputation for a love of mimicking annoying sounds with great enthusiasm. They are said to be gifted whistlers.

Although Jardine's are famous for motionless calm, their play has been described as lorie-like or caique-like. The Jardine's mood can turn in an instant from absolutely still (except perhaps for a bouncing, pinpointing iris) to tumbling rowdiness. Jardine's enjoy a reputation for loving bath time. They easily learn to enjoy human-provided spray baths. The real, human shower is often too forceful and scary for any *Poicephalus,* including the Jardine's, but the bird might enjoy sitting on a high perch in the shower and being sprayed with a water bottle or other spraying device as humans shower.

Jardine's enjoy a reputation as most stolid of temperament, being reportedly less inclined to the fight-or-flight response than some of their cousins, notably the red-bellied parrot. However, Jardine's parrots can learn to bite with enthusiasm. They can be stubborn and extremely focused on their own individual needs and interests.

Jardine's are said to go through a "teething" or nipping stage (during the first year in the home) during which the beak-on-skin activity has sometimes been described as mild beaking and sometimes as excruciatingly painful. However, even one bird that was called a monster during its nippy phase ultimately learned more productive "love sponge" behavior.[5] Usually, consistent handling and ignoring the nipping will cause the nipping to disappear. Jardine's should be handled by all adult family members in all phases of development, with the use of the towel game (see p. 153) if necessary.

(see p. 153)

Jean Pattison reports that the Jardine's may be the most nurturing of siblings, with a reputation for feeding almost anything they recognize as a juvenile. Babies sometimes revert to begging when stressed, such as when they go to a new home. On the other hand, Pattison also reports that her Jardine's seem to have more sibling aggression than any other type of parrot she breeds, especially the African greys, which have virtually no sibling aggression.

Like other *Poicephalus,* Jardine's are given mixed reviews regarding their suitability for children. Some children do extremely well with them, some do not. It might be best to separate the bird and the children if either are going through difficult transitions, such as the bird experiencing a predictable "teething" or nippy phase.

Cape Parrot (*Poicephalus robustus*). Uncommon as companions at this writing, Cape parrots are the largest of the *Poicephalus* family. A wash of color over the neck gives the bird its common name, the brown-necked parrot. Females are slightly brighter with a well-defined area of poppy on the forehead. Males may have some less-defined poppy on the forehead. The adult bird's eyes are dark brown like the juveniles.

As companions, Capes have much in common with their smaller *Poicephalus* cousins. Like their smaller cousins, they love playing upside down, hanging and swinging, and lying on their backs in their owner's hands and on the floor. They are sometimes fascinated by their feet. Like other *Poicephalus* parrots, Capes are crazy about nuts.

The Cape parrot's enormous beak is well-suited to breaking hard nuts.

Dianalee Deter has observed that a cautious male Cape boarded in her shop made a sort of all-purpose beep when soliciting attention in apparent stress mode. Stationed near a middle door near the rear of the shop, he seemed to use the call in a sort of nervous way. He was much quieter when he could be closer to the activities in the front of the shop. This Cape's preferred position was behind a bird-safe plant near the front door where he could see everything, and yet not be noticed.

Although most individuals are rarely noisy, the Cape parrot can be very loud. Jean Pattison reports that Capes are, unquestionably, the noisiest of her exclusively African collection. Pattison also reports that the Cape disposition is quite dependable, with individuals rarely forming the problematic, excessively strong bonds that African parrots are famous for. She reports that they change hands and bonds easily.

The Companion Lovebird

A companion lovebird bonds more easily to humans than to another bird. In many respects, this arrangement works very well because the relationship between two lovebirds can turn hostile in a blink. The smallest of the short-tailed African parrots, lovebirds have long been bred in captivity both in Europe and in the

United States. Numerous color mutations have been developed from the nine species.

By the early 1980s, I had begun to research lovebirds by reading everything available about them. Expert after expert reported that it was cruel to keep a solitary bird. No one had ever taken the time to explain to me that there are many ways to live with birds, and there are two divergent schools of thought on this in the United States. Keeping one lovebird leads us to the human-interactive companion bird and keeping two lovebirds to bird-identified aviary birds. Their socialization is different. Their behavior is different.

At that time, and even today, most books and articles on the subject of lovebirds were written for the hobbiest or would-be breeder. I didn't understand that my objective differed from that in the books. Standing against the storm of misinformation, my personal experience and that of my associates had repeatedly advised against the addition of a second lovebird. As with most other

Companion characteristics can best be maintained by keeping only one lovebird. (Fisher's lovebird.)

parrots, the addition of a second bird of the same type, more often than not, adversely affects human relationships with the first companion bird.

Buying a Companion Lovebird

Genetics, environment, and socialization are major factors in the development of lovebird behavior. Many lovebird breeders specialize in producing birds for particular genetic goals. Some produce companion lovebirds for disposition. The former lovebirds are usually parent-raised; the latter are usually handfed by humans.

Many breeders believe that lovebirds are best removed from the parents before their eyes open. Sensitive handfeeding is a must. Ideally, babies are kept singly both during handfeeding and after weaning. When purchasing a baby lovebird and waiting for it to wean, resist the temptation to ask that weaning be hurried along. As with larger parrots, deliberate abundance weaning is more likely to produce a bird that stays tame. Healthy, well-handled baby lovebirds usually wean between six and ten weeks old. Birds that take longer to wean appear to have a better chance of remaining tame as adults. Handfed lovebirds probably have the best chance to remain tame if they go to their new homes within a month after weaning.

Toys are not optional. If the bird is to remain tame, it must fill its hours with appropriate activities, not sit around storing up energy to make everybody nuts. A generous number of diverse, lovebird-sized toys, both destructible and indestructible, give a companion lovebird opportunities to blow off steam (express energy that might otherwise come out as aggression).

The bird must have opportunities to play alone, developing confidence by engaging in self-rewarding behaviors. If a human is the only toy a lovebird plays with, we are on our way to territorial behaviors, to bonding-related aggression, and to other problems. Especially, the lovebird must have a toy to beat up. This toy, often a bell, sometimes becomes both a surrogate enemy and mate, being the object of the bird's most hostile and most intimate aggressions.

Lovebirds often form inappropriate bonds or adversarial relationships with inanimate objects. Watch for aggression or unusual fixations on toasters, hair dryers, baskets, dolls, and knickknacks. Balancing bonding to avert the development of too strong bonds will remain a part of the bird's behavioral environment throughout its life.

A companion lovebird must be handled daily so that it will not become overly bonded to toys and cage. Love, cuddling, and playing in a towel will pattern the bird to intimate and restrictive handling. Some handfed lovebirds like to be petted on the neck like so many other parrots, but some do not. Most lovebirds like to be hugged or snuggled. This can be problematic as many of the lovebirds are cavity breeders that love to crawl inside clothes, laundry, furniture, or bedclothes only to be squashed or suffocated.

As with larger parrots, daily practice of the step-up command (see p. 51) maintains the bird's patterning for cooperation and establishes humans as the dominant member of the relationship. Many long-time devoted lovebird owners pick up their mature lovebirds with hand-held perches only, not hands.

Prevent the bird from developing chasing behaviors by removing it from the cage to service the cage. That is, whenever feeding, cleaning, or changing accessories, first remove the bird to a chair back or play perch. If a lovebird learns that hands will jump or run away when they are bitten and chased, the bird might learn to create drama by chasing other pets and humans. If a lovebird charges, with head feathers ruffled and beak open with obvious intent to bite, it must be distracted from the attack, possibly with a loud "Hey!," clapping, slapping a rolled newspaper on a table, or creating a barrier between the bird and the victim. Then some appropriate behavior may be stimulated, possibly step-ups with verbal reminders to "Be a good bird."

As with all parrots, positive reinforcement of appropriate lovebird behavior, not punishment for inappropriate behavior, is the only effective means of ensuring long-term cooperation. While yelling "No," "Don't," or "Stop" can momentarily interrupt a behavior, reminding a bird to "Be a good bird!" more effectively prompts appropriate behavior that can then be reinforced.

If a lovebird is becoming too territorial at home, try rearranging and moving the cage and play areas. Occasional outings where the bird is handled by sensitive, astute strangers can be used to manipulate bonding behaviors, improve patterning, and lower territorialism.

Trick training is an excellent means for continuing to reinforce cooperative behavior and preventing the development of inappropriate behavior. Any activities that are not annoying to humans, unsafe, or unhealthy for the bird may be reinforced to fill the behavioral environment with appropriate behaviors. Bathing, searching for hidden food (foraging), and chewing wood and paper can approximate some of what the bird would be doing in the wild.

Water and Other Hazards

Because of their curiosity and activity level, lovebirds are notoriously vulnerable to accidents in the home. Drowning is a particular hazard, as lovebirds are big drinkers. Lovebirds have been observed to drink more water than other small parrots such as parakeets. They like to bathe and play in water and often fill the water bowl with trash. They are inordinately subject to accidents involving water: drowning in a toilet, half-full glass, or undrained tub.

Lovebirds are fascinated by any tiny space they can crawl into, so they are also prone to accidents

Suggested wing trims for lovebirds. (A) is for adults. (B) is for juveniles.

involving enclosed spaces such as drawers, dryers, and microwaves. They are especially happy to crawl inside coat sleeves, and more than one hapless lovebird has been taken home from a party in a coat left in a pile on a bed.

As with many other small companion parrots, lovebirds probably tend to die more often in household accidents, especially those related to flying, than from illness. Meticulous, up-to-date wing-feather trims are an absolute necessity if a companion lovebird is to live to a ripe old age. A bonded companion lovebird wants nothing more than to be next to that favorite human. They have a tendency to follow too closely, making them easy to step on, sit on, roll over on, or slam in a door or drawer. Flighted lovebirds are often struck down by ceiling fans and also suffer danger of escape as well as danger of being fried, flushed, "nuked," or "yoga'd."

There is no cavity too small for a lovebird to try to explore, no enemy too large to be challenged. These are definitive behaviors of this incredible little feathered dragon. They are a major part of the mystery and enchantment of the love-bird. Discerning owners of companion lovebirds both correct for and exploit these behaviors daily for happy effect.

Oxymoron

Some people say that the name lovebird is an oxymoron, a word that contradicts its own true meaning. The development of strong bonding behaviors in lovebirds is often accompanied by the development of aggression, abandonment anxiety, breeding stress, and other difficult behavioral issues. In pairs these tiny parrots are everything that their larger cousins are: territorial, defensive, and able to inflict painful damage to both human and avian skin. In particular, lovebirds seem to become easily fixated on an individual, object, or location and to defend such with excessive devotion. This tendency to extreme bonding can also work to the disadvantage of a pair, for bonding or attempts to bond are sometimes accompanied by spousal abuse.

The Common Lovebird Species

Peach-faced Lovebird (Agapornis roseicollis). The active little peach-faced lovebird likes to perforate the edges of paper, fabricating little streamers that it stuffs likes flags into its rump before flying homeward. According to Arthur Freud, author of *The Complete Parrot,* this is a remnant of their wild behavior, for like the quaker parakeet *(Myopsyttia monachus),* the peach-faced lovebird is a nest builder rather than a cavity breeder. The largest and usually the heartiest of the lovebirds, the peach-faced lovebird has a reputation for being the easiest to keep tame.

Fisher's Lovebird *(Agapornis fischeri).* These brilliantly colored birds are quite recognizable by their white eye rings and bright red beaks. Fisher's are neither as hearty nor as large as peach-faced lovebirds. They have a reputation for being more aggressive, and, in a companion setting, a Fisher's has been known to kill a peach-faced.

The Ringnecks

Another of the birds previously considered aviary birds, the ringneck parakeets have gradually worked their way indoors. In the last 20 years, we've seen an amazing influx of these elegant birds handfed and introduced to the living room. From the beginning, reports of companion ringnecks were glowing, with a surprising number of even first generation handfeds learning huge vocabularies. Their voices are said to be clear; they are beautiful, charming, and breed readily in captivity. Although they are not yet common in most parts of the country,

with proper management, ringnecks just might turn out to be one of the most popular companion birds of the next millennium.

Although the rose-ringed species, the most common, have a reputation for easily changeable personalities, we hear more uniform stories about other members of the family. Especially common these days are stories of Alexandrine ringnecks, their mostly gentle nature and uniform treatment of humans. This is not a bird that will attack all but the chosen human. While a ringneck may exhibit an obvious preference for a particular human, this nonpair bond species easily develops relationships with

The ring-necked parakeet is more likely to enjoy flirtatious postures than actual cuddling. (Indian ringneck parakeet.)

Immature Indian ring-necked parakeets share the coloring of a mature female.

Cochise

Cochise, an Indian ringneck hen, came to us in 1998. Her favorite toys are those little cat toy balls with bells in them. She not only loves them, she "worships" them!

After arranging her balls along the edge of her play gym and properly bowing, cooing, and clucking at them, she ambushes them like a child knocking off toy soldiers! She then jumps up onto the edge of the gym and looks down to make sure she "killed" the balls.

When given those "dead" balls back, she picks them up with either foot or beak and beats them into submission before placing them on the edge of her play gym to start the "worship-and-kill" game all over!

Betsy Lott
Parrot rescue and adoption worker
San Francisco, CA

multiple humans, making it an excellent family bird. A ringneck is more likely to jealously defend a territory than to defend a person.

Nancy Newman, owner of Sky Dancers Aviary, reports that a ringneck is not a good choice for someone who does not have a lot of time to spend handling and cuddling the bird, for in order to remain trusting of humans, most ringnecks must be handled consistently most days. Although ringnecks do not typically enjoy petting, they often very much enjoy posturing and enthusiastic face-to-face interactions. Most ringnecks don't like to have anybody or anything touch their long, elegant tails. Indeed, it can make a ringneck quite skittish for people to be constantly trying to touch its tail (unlike some macaws who actually seem to like some types of tail play).

With their long graceful tails, smooth, glossy feathers, and delicate markings, ringnecks might be called the most elegant of parrots. Well, elegant is a relative term when applied to a bird, for even these most ornamental of parrots can be goofy, too.

Ringnecks like dancing and "mugging" and communicating with body language rather than with actual physical contact. They will posture and stretch and crane their necks in approximate mimicry of humans playing passive posture games with them.

Ringnecks usually develop neither bonding nor territorial aggression, though they may be "fear nippers" or "annoyance nippers" who apply beak to flesh only with the intention of getting the flesh to go away. Indeed, the ringneck personality can be cautious to the point of skittishness. Most companion ringnecks prefer some kind of readily available shelter, whether that accessible safe place is a cage with the door open, a little tent or hide box, the favorite person's shoulder, or maybe a plant or huge toy to hide behind. A ringneck might consistently turn its back or keep a visual barrier between it and a person or situation it dislikes.

Ringnecks are swift and agile flyers; they are especially sensitive to loud sounds like firecrackers, and must have wing feathers trimmed to prevent household accidents. It's a good idea to keep the windows and curtains nearest the ringneck's cage closed during times when fireworks might be expected. Ringnecks have occasional night frights like cockatiels and benefit from being covered and having a night light.

Ringnecks are visually dimorphic at sexual maturity, usually two to three years. Newman reports that both sexes make good companions, although I see these birds as sort of resembling *Eclectus* and lovebirds in that females can be expected to be at least as aggressive as males.

Ringnecks can be accomplished talkers, developing large, understandable vocabularies. Many ringnecks will easily talk in public and around strangers.

Suggested wing trims for ringnecks. (A) is for adults. (B) is for juveniles.

The ringneck's long tail makes it necessary to have a larger cage than might otherwise be given to a bird of this weight. The bird must be able to avoid hitting its tail on the side of the cage every time it turns around. Also, a ringneck should have enough room to comfortably sit on the bottom perch without its tail touching the bottom of the cage.

The Common Ringneck Species

**Rose-ringed Parakeets or African and Indian Ringnecks *(Psittacula krameri krameri* and *P. k. manillensis).* The rose-ringed parakeets are best known for their bright red beaks and for the ring of red or pink edged in black and pale blue that encircles the mature male's neck. The rose-ringed species has a reputation for being the most difficult ringneck subspecies in which to maintain human interactive behaviors.

(left) The African ringneck is smaller and has a different color beak than the Indian subspecies.

(right) The companion Alexandrine enjoys a reputation as an outstanding talker.

Alexandrine Parakeet *(Psittacula eupatria)*. The Alexandrine is a generally docile bird with the potential to develop a large vocabulary. This bird can make very loud noises and this is usually an indication that the bird's needs are not being met; Alexandrines are not prone to screaming for the joy of it. They are large for a parakeet and have extremely long tails. They need a large cage; a cage that is at least 24 inches (62 cm) wide by 24 inches (62 cm) deep is necessary to comfortably house this bird.

Plum-headed Parakeet *(Psittacula cyanocephala)*. The plum-headed parakeet is about the size of a cockatiel. The male has a purplish-red head while the female and juveniles have a grey/violet head. This bird has a reputation as staying more easily tame than the rose-ringed parakeets. The plum-head's voice is pleasant, chattery. This species is not as loud as the larger members of this group.

[4]Jean Pattison, Interview, 1997.
[5]"The Jardine's Parrots," Rita Shimniok, *Bird Talk,* April 1996, pp. 62–74.

Chapter Four

What to Expect of the New World Parrots

The Magnificent Macaws

With their long tails and delicately ornamented faces, the macaws are often called both majestic and comical. And, of course, both descriptions are absolutely accurate, for few creatures even approximate the hyacinth macaw in either beauty or comical nature. Possessing both elongated tail and wing feathers, macaws are spectacular in outdoor flight and cuddly in the living room.

These birds have the most massive heads and the most massive beaks, relatively, of any of the parrots. The huge head is necessary to attach the enormous beak, which is necessary to break open the hard-shelled nuts these birds consume in the wild. In our homes, macaws love to use those giant beaks to disassemble things, especially nuts (the metal kind), bolts, and cages.

Part of the comical appearance of most macaws is provided by the bare face that clearly shows the remnants of feather trails, the lines

of circulation where feathers grow. Like human fingerprints, the pattern of facial feathers is unique to each macaw.[6] This bare patch on the face, usually white, leather-like patches, probably evolved to keep oil, resulting from the birds' usually high-oil diets, from damaging feathers. It provides us with an interesting insight into the emotions of birds, however, because it shows us that humans are not the only animals

Macaws are often called both majestic and comical. (Greenwing macaw and hyacinth macaw.)

51

that blush. Macaws blush when embarrassed, excited, or otherwise physically stimulated.

Macaws are famous for being extremely adaptable, for learning new behaviors, and for teaching them to each other. Only in the last 400 years, since the introduction of cattle to their native range, did hyacinth macaws develop a symbiotic relationship with cattle. Now hyacinth macaws follow the cattle to harvest nuts with predigested hulls from the cattle droppings.[7]

Because they are so prolific in captivity, I have included several uncommon (at this writing) macaws in this list of common macaws. If present trends continue, these birds—including the red-bellied macaw, the red-fronted macaw, and the hyacinth macaw—will be appearing more often in the birds-for-sale columns and in stores.

Common Companion Macaw Behavior

Macaws love to be included in things. If they are not properly contained, macaws will seek out humans in the home. This can be dangerous should other animals also have access to the same space. Many macaws love cuddling and snuggling, and because they are such adorable babies, it's easy for a young macaw to develop dependent and manipulative behaviors if it is not well patterned to cooperate from an early age. Step-ups, fetch, and active play involving wing flapping rather than constant snuggling will help the bird to develop

confidence rather than obnoxious attention-demanding behaviors.

Bird behavior consultant Liz Wilson reports that macaws love to lunge at people, rarely biting at first, but rather bluffing to observe human responses. If a bird can be allowed beak on skin, the bluff is called. If humans act afraid, a macaw will sometimes take over the household. These birds love drama, and few things tickle them more than making their humans angry enough to yell. A macaw that is allowed to develop these behaviors is at risk of spending its life in a cage, so consistent and effective socialization is the key to a successful life in the living room for a macaw.

Exercise is especially beneficial in maintaining the health of the skin. I have seen facial feathers regrow on older macaws that were put on conditioning programs that included daily flapping exercises. The birds were encouraged to hold on to their humans' hands and flap until they were just slightly winded, a condition that in macaws is accompanied by blushing. As the birds' condition improved, tiny new feathers began to re-line the once almost-bare face patches.

Chewing is both an exercise and a natural expression of sexual behavior to the macaw, a cavity breeder. Unfortunately, chewing also is one of the most frequent reasons for a macaw to lose its home. Every macaw must have wood to chew up every day in order to keep the beak and the disposition strong and healthy. This is not optional. If a macaw is denied access to destructible chewables, it must find destructible chewables, or it will soon learn to destroy its own feathers.

Special care must be taken when introducing branches with bark to macaws, as I have come across two vastly separated reports of macaws being extremely sensitive to different parts of the oak tree. The fruit (acorns) and bark of the oak tree are documented toxins, and I personally know of the loss of two mature male blue-and-gold macaws that died of eating oak bark. Additionally, breeder Kashmir Csaky reports that "It is possible that many hyacinths may be allergic to the pollen of some species of oak trees. I know of hyacinths housed in flights under oak trees in Florida that pulled all the feathers from their own heads and their eyes were swollen shut when the oak pollen began to fall. These were six unrelated birds. It may be possible that they would be allergic to pollen of other oak trees to varying degrees." The description of allergic reactions to naturally occurring toxins is confirmed by Alicia McWatters, MS, in her book *A Guide to a Naturally Healthy Bird* (Safe Goods, 1997).

Loudness is probably the behavior that most often costs a macaw its home. The larger birds, the hyacinth and the greenwing, have booming voices that have been described as able to wake the dead, Liz Wilson reports. However, some of the louder macaws are actually less-frequent screamers than some of their smaller cousins.

Status in the Wild and in the Living Room

Although almost all the larger macaws are threatened or extinct in the wild, several macaw species are rumored to be overpopulated among companion populations. Indeed, most macaws appear to reproduce more frequently in captivity than in the wild. At this writing, macaw prices, relative to personal income in the United States, have never been lower. Parrot rescue volunteer Carol Darezzo says, "Especially, because of their availability and reputation as a 'first time macaw' for just about anyone, blue-and-gold macaws often wind up in homes where their loudness, destructiveness, and behavioral needs all come as a shock to their new human companions. Many would-be owners are not properly prepared for the demands and needs of a large macaw, let alone for the commitment of being responsible for any creature for half a century."

Like the large cockatoos, the macaws are potentially the longest living of all companion parrots. It's a mixed blessing. A bird that can live more than half a century will certainly require multiple homes during its lifetime. And while most macaws adjust easily to home changes, there seems to be a growing trend to more birds than homes available for them. The macaw's adaptability can benefit this situation, for no other bird can be more easily and effectively resocialized at a later age. I have seen very old macaws that had not interacted with humans in decades settle in to become treasured household companions. The macaw is the epitome of the adage: "You *can* teach an old bird new tricks."

On Wings

Wing flapping is important to macaws, and flapping is a flying substitute, of course. In companion settings where household dangers lurk at every turn, wing feathers are usually best kept trimmed and absolutely up to date. Because macaws are so large, it's easy to forget that under the right conditions, macaws can fly with all flight feathers trimmed. Flyaways are common in startled birds that owners didn't know could fly. However, even macaws with full wings can adjust to harnesses.

Because of the dangers posed by flying, we're starting to see variations on wing feather trims designed to more effectively ground the birds

This modest wing trim is not enough to ground a macaw. (Military macaw.)

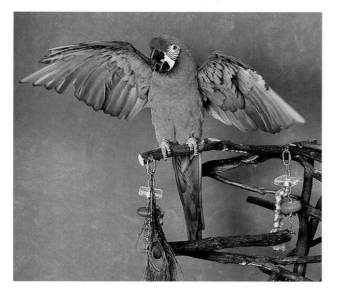

while providing balance for flapping. A macaw's wings are huge relative to the body, and the power each wing provides is quite impressive. Macaws especially suffer if only one wing is trimmed, for it then becomes very difficult for the birds to do flapping exercises. Pet store owner Ginger West reports great results from a suggested wing trim, which provides an outlet for air that might otherwise be utilized to gain flight.

The Common Macaws

Hyacinth Macaw *(Anodorhynchus hyacinthinus).* The hyacinth is the largest of the companion macaws. At this time, I would not call the hyacinth a common companion parrot, because they are still extremely expensive, both to purchase and to maintain. The hyacinth, as well as the rarer members of the genus *Anodorhynchus,* the almost extinct Lear's and glaucus macaws, are the only macaws that have neither a bare face patch nor a uropygial gland, according to avian veterinarian Margaret Wissman.

Hyacinths are natural acrobats. Ginger West reports seeing more than one doing somersaults. Kashmir Csaky reports that hyacinths love to run along the ground and hop; also, Dazzle, one of her baby hyacinths, is the only bird she has ever seen that will chase her own tail. Like greys, hyacinths are sometimes seen to dig in corners. Because of their extreme size and strength, hyacinths need specially fabricated caging (be sure a particular cage is guaranteed for a

On Outdoor Safety

Liz Wilson reminds us that whether the bird's wings are trimmed or not, no feathered companion should be outdoors without a carrier or a harness. She tells this story:

"It was a lovely July day, almost 30 years ago. I'd just gotten my blue-and-gold macaw's wings clipped, so I felt comfortable taking her outside with me. The groomer had done a severe clip, cutting all Sam's primary and secondary flight feathers, and besides, everyone always said, 'Clipped birds can't fly.'

"What I didn't realize was that Sam had not read the same books and had her own opinions. So I wasn't prepared when a firecracker exploded a few feet away. With an ear-splitting scream, Sam leaped into the air and flew—45 feet up in a tree, at a 45 degree angle—*with not a single intact flight feather.*

"I cannot describe the sensation in the pit of my stomach as I watched her go, but I remember it vividly. But I was one of the lucky ones. Sam sat in the tree and laughed while I borrowed a 45-foot ladder, climbed up and retrieved her. Sam taught me well—under the right circumstances, any bird can still fly, no matter what.

"Look for directions for training a parrot to wear a harness on the Internet at *http://www.birdsnway. com/wisdom/ww25e.htm and http://birds.miningco.com/.*

"For more information on 'clicker training,' a similar type of operant conditioning that can aid in teaching a bird to wear a harness, see *http://www.geocities.com/Heart-land/Acres/9154.*"

hyacinth, not just for a macaw). A hyacinth macaw also needs a veterinarian with hyacinth experience.

Greenwing Macaw *(Ara chol-roptera).* The greenwing is the largest macaw that can reasonably be called common. It has a reputation for an easy disposition, good talking ability, great beauty, and for being mechanically inclined (it can completely dismantle some cages). Especially appealing are the delicately traced lines in tiny red feathers on the white face patch. So appealing are these lines that in art, especially commercial and product art, when we see from the facial feathers what is supposed to be a scarlet macaw, it's often a greenwing macaw with the green patch on the wing depicted in yellow.

This giant bird needs lots of exercise, lots of chewing materials, and lots of handling to maintain good disposition. The greenwing macaw can be a surprisingly active bird as well as a willing talker. It has an extremely loud voice, and will use it when necessary. Disposition may be maintained with little difficulty in young

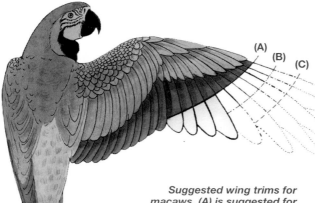

Suggested wing trims for macaws. (A) is suggested for particularly good flyers. (B) is for adults. (C) is for juveniles.

birds and during the breeding years, but these birds have a reputation for being really nice when they are much older.

Blue-and-gold Macaw *(Ara ararauna).* This is the most prolific of macaws, the most common, and the least expensive of the large macaws; and what a dollar value it is! This macaw is, perhaps, the most evenly disposed of this family. It has a reputation for clear talking ability as well as occasionally developing extremely large vocabularies. A good talking blue-and-gold macaw can rival a yellow-naped Amazon in terms of clarity, size of vocabulary, and ease of acquiring new words. I have heard more than one story of blue-and-gold macaws apparently learning a word and using it on the spot.

While we see occasional extroverted birds and occasional shy birds, for the most part, the blue-and-gold macaw's personality can usually

be easily guided to develop both interactive and independent habits. This reputation for extreme dependability of disposition is rivaled only by the greenwing and hyacinth reputations.

Blue-and-gold macaws adapt easily to their surroundings and easily become comfortable enough to breed.

Increased availability and resulting low prices have combined to occasionally place these birds in a category called an impulse purchase. It's not unusual for a bird to be added to a home that is totally unaware of the length of commitment necessary to provide for the lifetime needs of a full-sized macaw. While many blue-and-golds go into homes where they stay for generations, many others are passed from home to home even though they may have few or only minor behavior problems. Opportunities to adopt older blue-and-golds are great, and as has been said previously, these are not dogs. The blue-and-gold macaw has a reputation for being easy to socialize or resocialize at almost any age.

Scarlet Macaw *(Ara macao).* Underrated and misunderstood, the scarlet macaw's reputation is for unpredictability. Whether this is a matter of nature or nurture is still highly debated. Liz Wilson reports that many "people are so fearful of scarlets that they react differently" around them. These birds are highly intelligent and aware that they can intimidate people immediately. When they become nippy, it's probably due to inadvertent reinforcement that the bird received. Unfortunately, this can lead to the bird being abused or neglected.

Parrot behavior consultant Layne Dicker has often advised that these birds benefit from an extremely rich environment. Understimulation, especially an understimulating environment with an unexciting routine, can contribute to the development of aggression in the scarlet macaw.

Military Macaw *(Ara militaris).* The military macaw is probably the most highly underrated and underappreciated of the commonly available macaws. For this reason, in addition to being extremely inexpensive, there is often a choice of birds: a very favorable situation for one looking for a particular disposition or a special rapport. The disposition of the military macaw varies but could probably be placed somewhere between the blue-and-gold's relatively even temperament and the scarlet's frantically exploratory temperamentalism. And, like the scarlet macaw, the military macaw can go through nippy periods if boredom is allowed to persist or if minimal needs for interaction (handling most days) are not met.

Red-fronted Macaw *(Ara rubogenys).* This macaw is not especially common, but reports of its fine qualities are being passed around. Sometimes it is called the "most gregarious" of the macaws. Dave Flom of Minnesota reports that baby red-fronts in the brooder wrap their little bodies around each other like yin

The red-front is sometimes called the "most gregarious macaw."

and yang. Other baby macaws just slump over and sleep wherever they are, whether near a sibling or not. Probably the easiest place to see a red-fronted macaw is at a Rainforest Cafe.

Chestnut-fronted or Severe Macaw *(Ara severa).* My favorite, the severe macaw is a charming size, maybe 12 to 16 ounces (350–450 g). But the severe macaw is just as much fun and exciting to live with as its larger cousins, and due to its smaller size this bird is usually quite a bit easier to care for than a large macaw. With a reputation a little like a scarlet macaw, this intelligent little bird needs lots of exercise (including showers), environmental stimulation, and consistent handling to remain a good

companion. In spite of its small size, this bird may not be the best choice for families with children. The severe macaw has a shrill voice that may be more annoying than a larger macaw.

Hahn's Macaw *(Diopsittaca nobilis).* This smallest macaw, which enjoys a reputation as potentially the best talker of the group, might be said to resemble a blue-crowned conure. In fact, the easiest way to tell the Hahn's macaw from a blue-crowned conure is by the bare face patch. Unsuspecting tourists have been, in the past, sold blue-crowned conures with plucked facial patches as Hahn's macaws. The difference in the value of the birds is great, with a typical

Hahn's macaw usually selling for at least twice the cost of a typical blue-crowned conure, and being well worth it. Domestic blue-crowned conures are in fact quite brilliant, even as public performers,[8] but they are not considered in the main to be as smart or as talkative as the darling little Hahn's macaw.

Breeder Heike Ewing reports that the Hahn's macaw is "more cuddly" than some of the larger macaws. Playful, active, and acrobatic, these birds are curious and, like their larger cousins, require interaction and environmental stimulation in order to avoid boredom-related feather chewing.

Yellow-collar Macaw *(Prophyrrhura auricollis).* Perhaps the most popular of the smaller macaws, the yellow-collar is a fine choice for one who loves all the qualities of a full-sized macaw without the huge maintenance demands. Yellow-collar macaws can easily develop or be guided away from attention-demanding behaviors. They tend to form strong bonds with their favorite people. Yellow-collars can be good talkers, acquiring a ready variety of understandable words. They can easily learn to talk to get attention rather than scream for it.

This is one of the highly underrated macaws. These birds, like full-sized macaws, can learn new things, including new vocalizations and human words, at almost any age.

Red-bellied Macaw *(Orthopsittaca manilata).* This darling bird is small and generally possesses a pleasing disposition. Although still unusual in companion settings, this is one of the few macaws that is well populated in the wild. The natural calls of the red-bellied macaw sound a little like a small child. They have sweet voices and are great talkers. Red-bellies are cuddly, and not so rowdy as most other macaws.

Survivability was poor in early captive populations because of misunderstandings about diet. Ginger West reports that Howard Voreen first identified the palm fruit that comprises the total wild diet of the red-bellied macaw. Red-bellies have a greater need for vitamin A (in the form of beta carotene) and a lesser need for oil in the diet than other macaws. With increased understanding about their diet and special needs, expect to see more of this charming bird.

The Amazing, Dependable Amazons

The quintessential parrot: Amazons, with their short-tailed heavy bodies, are the epitome of what most people think a parrot is. Were it not for the Amazons' loud voices, I would be tempted to call them the "most perfect" parrots. Intelligent, charming, beautiful, playful, they are well suited for those who like a little "vinegar" in their greens. They are behaviorally predictable (sometimes unpredictably so), and usually behaviorally stolid.

The tiny yellow-collar has all the majesty and goofiness of the larger macaws.

The red-bellied macaw is expected to become more numerous in captivity.

The Amazon parrot is often predictably unpredictable. (Yellow-headed Amazon.)

Any reasonably observant human usually knows exactly where she stands with an Amazon.

These primarily green birds are talkative, adaptable, and rarely shy. Few birds relish rainfall (provided in the shower by caring humans) more than Amazons; as I have frequently observed, an Amazon enjoying a shower will get sillier as it gets wetter. Indeed, Amazons that are denied access to rainfall frequently become truculent, as disposition and feather quality decline.

Amazons are recreational eaters and are plagued by the problems related to obesity probably more than any other health problem. Overweight older Amazons suffer cardiovascular problems, foot problems, and feather disorders as they become increasingly sedentary.

Amazons, more than any other companion parrot, should probably not be free fed; rather they must learn other activities besides eating for daily entertainment. I fought a weight problem in my yellow-naped Amazons for years until Dianalee Deter taught me about scheduled feedings. Now my less-overweight Amazons receive an abundant offering of varied fresh foods in the morning and the exact recommended amount of Harrison's Bird Diet in the afternoon. They are slimmer and seem happier and more active. Their feet and toes seem less pudgy, and Portia has a few yellow feathers on his nape again, after about eight years with not one yellow feather on his fat little neck.

No other family enjoys such a widespread reputation for universal talking ability. These birds are extremely attracted to high-pitched feminine voices, including singing voices. Those who read my first book may recall that my 20-something Amazon, Portia, is crazy about opera and the artist formerly known as Prince.

An Amazon will usually let humans know, in no uncertain terms, when something is wrong, either with its voice or with its disposition. A bored Amazon might scream for attention and then bite when it is picked up. This may not be aggression, but rather simply little punishments for neglect. A screaming, nippy Amazon will often show easy benefit from a program to improve handling and improve the environment.

Of all the parrots, Amazons seem the most adaptable. They can probably tolerate more of most human imperfections than most companion parrots. Especially, Amazons are said to tolerate neglect better than macaws, greys, and cockatoos, who can emotionally self-destruct. That is not to say that Amazons should be neglected, but rather that they may require less actual face-to-face interaction in order to stay sane than many other parrots.

In the past, when wild-caught birds were common, most of the Amazons except older yellow-heads and overly sensitive blue-fronts were extremely easy to tame. Today, since the time of wild-caught birds has past, the baby Amazons come tame and may be more easily maintained tame than most other parrots. However, the Amazon parrot's developmental period may be more noticeable than any other parrot: unpatterned birds often suddenly decide to take over, transitioning through a nippy period at about nine months of age. With careful socialization, including prepatterning to step-ups, hand-held perches, and towel games, this terrible-two's-like behavior may be virtually unnoticeable or might pass quickly. Diana Holloway reports that domestics mellow out usually by ten years of age.

The Common Amazons

Orange-winged Amazon *(Amazona amazonica).* This most common of all Amazons in the wild was once called "the poor man's Amazon," being the least expensive and most easily accessible of the Amazons imported into the United States. They are charming characters with unique, adorable mannerisms, especially shadow boxing, in which the feathers of the neck and cheeks are held erect in a hawk-head-like position while the bird stabs at a shadow on the wall or other imaginary enemy. During the times that these

I truly believe that if we could read the mind of a typical Amazon it would sound something like, "Hmmmmm, what should I do now? Eat or bathe? Eat or bathe? Eat? Bathe? This is not easy!"

—Layne David Dicker
"The Parrot Ambassadors"
Bird Talk, November 1998, p. 56.

Suggested wing trims for Amazons. (A) is for adults. (B) is for juveniles.

Hens seem generally less extroverted and quieter than cocks. White-fronts share a reputation with yellow-napes for mischief, noise, and a willingness to nip. Like the blue-fronts, the white-fronts have a reputation for being a little more reactionary. They are active and benefit from the exercise provided by a larger than usual cage or flight, according to Holloway.

White-fronts more typically enjoy head scratches and petting than the typical yellow-head or blue-front. Males will nip from time to time, mostly during breeding season. Females, even wild-caught, tend to be docile. They are more prone to screaming than a yellow-head, but their screams are not nearly so loud.

I have seen little feather chewing and only a little true aggression in this family. They can be easily provoked and reinforced to nip. Although behavioral complaints are unusual, the two problems I most often encounter with white-fronts are screaming and failure to learn human speech.

Blue-fronted Amazon *(Amazona aestiva xanthopteryx* and *A.a. aestiva).* There are two subspecies of these, the most reactive of Amazons. *A.a. xanthopteryx,* the more common subspecies, is brilliantly colored, possessing bright yellow and poppy ornamentation at the shoulders; *A.a. aestiva* has more extensive blue on the head.

The blue-fronted Amazon's reputation probably resembles that of the

birds were imported, they were not known as great talkers, and since the 1992 ban on avian imports, the availability has plummeted.

Domestic birds should be both good talkers and of even temperament, although all parrots pursue their own agenda from time to time. The orange-winged Amazon has a reputation for being especially good with children.

White-fronted Amazon *(Amazona albifrons).* The smallest of the common companion Amazons in the United States, the white-front is sometimes erroneously called the spectacled Amazon in the United States. This is also the only common Amazon that is observably sexually dimorphic to humans. Most male birds possess red feathers in the area of the wing known as the alula; the alula of the female white-fronted Amazon is usually green.

little girl with the curl in the middle of her forehead, for when they're good, they're very good, and when they're bad, they're horrid. I have seen full flighted blue-fronts that were docile and well meaning. I have seen immature blue-fronts that were aggressive before weaning. Most, however, seem to resemble their African relatives, *Poicephalus* and *Psittacus,* with an observable degree of cautiousness sometimes contributing to aggression in some birds' personalities.

Females are probably slightly less likely to develop extreme territorialism than males, but extremely territorial females are sometimes seen.

Yellow-headed Amazon (*Amazona ochrocephala*). Known for their great beauty and talking ability, the yellow-headed Amazons are highly prized. Yet prices should remain relatively low, for the yellow-headed Amazons reproduce well in captivity, adjust easily to new homes, and can remain problem-free for their lifetimes. I have seen birds that were confined to the same small cage for decades blossom under the efforts of new owners who began to include the birds more extensively in daily activities.

Famous for their vocal abilities, these birds love high female voices. Especially, yellow-headed Amazons are fascinated by opera, and can easily pick up arias, though both the words and the melody may be well improvised, and much poetic license taken.

Actually, the primary behavioral problems seen in yellow-headed

Amazons are screaming and biting. Biting is easily managed with step-up drills. It's especially important to pattern these birds to hand-held perches, as cooperation skills can be easily maintained with hand-held perches even if the bird is too cranky to allow handling by human hands.

As mentioned, the yellow-headed Amazons can be temperamental, sometimes deciding to attack all but the most favored human. Females can be as excitable and protective of

The red alula differentiating the male white-fronted Amazon is just barely visible on the two babies in the center and to the right of this photo.

The blue-fronted Amazon is exceptionally beautiful, but is often temperamental.

their mate/human as males. This tendency is much more easily controlled than the same tendency in yellow-napes.

Yellow-naped Amazon (Amazona ochrocephala auropalliata). Considered by some to be the *crème de la crème* of this very desirable family, living with a yellow-naped Amazon might be a little like living with a feathered dragon. Most of them can breathe a little fire every now and again. Holloway reminds us that these birds are feisty. They can seem smarter than their humans, and they really need owners who are as intelligent as they are, or they simply take over. Females are sometimes less aggressive than males and might not be quite as territorial, but this can vary and aggressive females are not at all unusual.

Mealy Amazon (Amazona farinosa). Mealy Amazons are the largest of the common companion Amazons. Their Latin name *farinosa* means flour. They are often called gentle giants, being somewhat more difficult to provoke into biting. Like cockatoos and African greys, a healthy mealy Amazon will have powder on its feathers. They have a reputation for being both the loudest and the mellowest of the Amazons. This species includes the mealy (which usually has red or yellow on the head), the plain-colored Amazons (which are mostly green), blue-crowned and *Virinciteps* Amazons (which feature a varied wash of blue and lavender over the crown). Several of the mealy family birds have a famous characteristic donkey-like "bray."

The Red-lored or Yellow-cheeked Amazon (Amazona autumnalis). This stocky, mid-sized Amazon has a good reputation in most areas as a companion, with the notable exception of the loud volume of its calls and a potential for problem screaming. Curious and energetic, domestics have a reputation as good talkers. As with the mealy Amazons, the red-lored's disposition is often so good that the volume doesn't matter. Deter suggests that domestically raised red-loreds are not as noisy as their imported predecessors. Both male and female birds are cuddly, almost never refusing a head rub. Males are more aggressive in the spring.

The red-lored Amazon has a reputation for being very loyal to humans in its flock, although the number of humans accepted by the bird may be limited.

Red-loreds sometimes require more beak maintenance than other parrots, as this is the only common companion Amazon with a tendency to malocclusion of the mandible and maxilla called scissor beak. Holloway reports that this may be a genetic predisposition that is being bred out as more domestics than imports are available. This may be a seasonal problem occurring primarily during breeding season.

Green-cheeked Amazon (Amazona virigenalis). Smaller and slender bodied, this Amazon is sometimes called the Mexican red-head, a name indicating its source.

Although the green-cheeks resemble the lilac-crowns physically, these birds are more active and playful. They can be extremely affectionate and interactive, but they have a reputation for dominating younger or shorter family members. However, in my experience, the green-cheeked Amazon is just as likely to decide that the youngest, smallest kid is the best person in the family, and to treat everybody else like a rival. There is a wide variety between the dispositions and personalities of this Amazon species.

Lilac-crowned Amazon *(Amazona finschi).* With achingly-beautiful colors, this bird looks a little like a differently colored green-cheeked Amazon. But the lilac-crown personality is generally considered to be quieter, gentler, and less exuberant than the green-cheek. The voice is described as softer all around, including both calls and occasional language.

Diana Holloway describes the lilac-crown as an "exceptionally expressive" Amazon. She describes a characteristic head-fluff greeting that she calls a "Poof." Actually, this bird has also been called the gentlest Amazon; but like "quiet," "gentle" can be a very subjective and variable adjective. The lilac-crown is an Amazon, after all. It can be good, and sometimes not so good, with children.

The Conures

Unlike their wild-caught predecessors, handfed conures are highly

Allofeeding (sharing masticated food) is a common courtship ritual in Amazons. (Green-cheeked Amazons.)

verbal, less noisy, often larger and heartier than their sometimes half-starved, wormy, imported predecessors. From an agricultural pest that generated little interest to a "star" of

Today's domestic lilac-crowned Amazons more easily learn human speech than their wild-caught ancestors.

the pet trade, conures are the epitome of the slogan "You've come a long way, baby." Since the banning of imports into the United States in 1992, few other parrots have demonstrated such improved adjustment to life in the living room as the conure. Blue-crowned and mitred conures, especially, have gone from among the most commonly abused and neglected birds to treasured companions who talk in front of strangers, sometimes professionally!

There is the case of Squawk, Tani Robar's blue-crowned conure, who stood the parrot world on its ear by performing in Robar's highly regarded trained-bird show, including speaking on command. Old timers who knew only wild-caught conures couldn't believe the loud, clear voice and the obvious twinkle of great intelligence behind those white-ringed eyes.[9]

Aritinga conures like this Wagler's conure often develop surprisingly loud calls.

The movie *Paulie* depicts the life and travels of a blue-crowned conure. Paulie is from New Jersey, and he has to make it across the country to Los Angeles to be reunited with his very favorite person. It's a charming story and beautifully told. It accurately depicts some of the brassiness this smallish parrot is capable of.

Unfortunately, because the acting done by the bird consists of the work of 14 actor birds and a legion of computers to enhance the bird's actions, it's pretty easy to get the idea that conures are little geniuses in feathered bodies. Maybe some blue-crowned conures are little geniuses in feathered bodies, but most of them are just birds. It's probably better to have minimal expectations of these charming creatures. When you're expecting the bird to mug like Jim Carrey, dance like Madonna, and articulate like James Earl Jones, remember what old-time parrot trainer Kevin Murphy said: "Be patient, it's only a little bird. Your parrot will most probably reward your patience handsomely."

In these families of parrots there is quite a wide range of intelligence. Generally, however, most humans probably underestimate how much the bird can learn. In this group, to an even greater extent than in other parrots, you get out of the bird what you put into it. Like many other parrots, conures are probably more prone to becoming bored than becoming overstimulated.

Conures are extremely well suited to life indoors. Even many wild-caught specimens adjust superbly, sometimes to the extent of becoming the dominant creature in the household in much less than a year. While they are vocally expressive, domestic specimens are not as loud as larger parrots, although they do scream more frequently than larger birds. Because they love the stimulation of lots of attention and interaction; conures do very well in storefronts, and I have seen them adjust successfully to several different types of small businesses.

Suggested wing trims for conures. (A) is for adults. (B) is for juveniles.

Much of the conure's previous reputation as a poor pet can be related to its negative monetary value in its native lands. Because so many of the conures were considered agricultural pests, and because there was local pressure to capture all the birds rather than carefully harvesting only the babies, many older conures were trapped and sold into the pet trade. It meant that these older birds were especially poor candidates to become companion birds, and many of them, especially Nandays, were never socialized and were not considered good pets. These birds were often quite noisy, often came carrying a worm load, sometimes didn't tame down, and didn't have a particularly bright future. Many of them, however, wound up in breeding programs, and their domestic offspring are now teaching us what conures are all about.

There was once an agricultural pest conure in the United States. The Carolina conure *(Carolina carolenesis)* was the only parrot that occurred only in the United States. It was said to be numerous in the early 1800s and was considered extinct by the second decade of the nineteenth century.

I often wonder what would happen if farmers suddenly had the means to exterminate pest conures. Would developing Central and South American nations follow the United States model in decimating these parrots? Captive populations of some conures might join the captive populations of macaws, some cockatoos, and lories in the class of birds that are more numerous in captivity than in the wild. Indeed, domestic conures show every sign of being potentially better companions for humans than several of the cockatoos.

The Common Conures

Blue-crowned Conure *(Aritinga acuticaudata)*. Blue-crowned conures have a reputation for being extremely affectionate and loving when properly nurtured and socialized as babies. Although intelligence and talking ability vary greatly, some individuals can be extremely intelligent and learn to talk easily.

Like all conures, blue-crowns relish bath time. They will bathe in any water dish if humans don't provide showers or other water for bathing.

Newman reports that, "In my experience, most blue-crowned conures seem reluctant to bite hard and will, instead, either push your hand away with their beak or take it gently in their beak and move it away. But seldom will they bite hard. This anomaly has been confirmed by other breeders and owners. Even parent-raised

The sun conure is, perhaps, both the most beautiful and the loudest of the Aritinga *conures.*

blue-crowned conures will usually tame quite easily."

The blue-crown is a personable little bird that suffered in the past from a reputation for being extremely loud. Handfed domestic babies don't have nearly the loud learned language of their wild-caught ancestors, but they can still get the message across when their needs aren't being met.

Cherry-headed Conure *(Aritinga acuticaudata)*. This bird has a reputation as the best talker in this group. Even imported birds often develop large vocabularies. Unfortunately, the cherry-headed conures also have a reputation as frequently tending to bonding and territorial-related aggression.

Sun Conure *(Aritinga auricapillus solstitialis)*. These beautiful little conures have more than once gotten themselves into situations where an appreciation for visual beauty far overrode the humans' abilities to tolerate their voices. This is the domestic conure most likely to wind up homeless, for even though the wild-caught Nandays had a worse reputation for noxious sounds, the domestic sun conures carry a heavy reputation for making far more noise than anyone would imagine from such a small bird.

Mitred Conure *(Aritinga mitrata)*. During the import years, I believe the mitred conure was one of the most likely birds to be bounced from home to home. They were so inexpensive and often very large and pretty, but they didn't seem to be especially interactive, especially vocally. New parrot owners often seemed to have expectations that the mitred would be Amazon-like or macaw-like, and they were often disappointed.

Things have changed. Today's handfed domestic mitred conures are talkative, interactive, bright-eyed, and beautiful. They are not as common as one would hope, considering that they probably have an excellent chance of remaining for a lifetime in their first homes. Modern domestic handfed mitreds tend to be pushy, and require lots of hands-on interaction to maintain their sweetness, according to Newman.

Nanday Conure *(Nandayus nenday).* Nandays have a reputation for being very beautiful and very sociable, and if sociable means communicative, then Nandays are certainly that. Few birds this size can make anywhere near this much noise. They are not suitable for apartments or condos or for persons with sensitive hearing. However, if noise is not an issue, these are beautiful and amusing birds for a tiny price. Because of their natural sociability, Newman says Nandays make a good choice for multi-bird households.

Patagonian Conure *(Cyanoliseus patagonus).* Few birds have such a well-deserved reputation for screaming as Patagonian conures. This bird's voice can even make other birds uncomfortable. This is a bird for a person with an estate. But if you have a good deal of insulation between you and your neighbors and if you crave an amazingly beautiful, unbelievably intelligent, loyal com-

panion bird for a relatively low price, this just might be the bird for you. Not unlike macaws in intelligence, the Patagonian conure even has a shaped eye ring slightly reminiscent of the macaw's bare face patch.

Cliff dwellers, Patagonians are known to dive down rather than up when frightened indoors. Companion birds learn tricks and are famous for being tricksters, playing jokes on humans and pets in the home. Newman suggests that their cliff-dwelling habits also influence their living room play, which includes games like hide-and-seek and peek-a-boo.

Maroon-bellied Conure *(Phyrrhura frontalis)* and Green-cheeked Conure *(Phyrrhura molinae).* Beautifully marked with delicate scallops on the breast, these birds might even be called an ideal conure, because *Phyrrhuras'* small size make them ideal even for small living

The Patagonian conure is amusing, charming, and a good talker, but unquestionably the loudest of all the conures.

The Phyrrhura *family enjoys a reputation as the "quietest" conure, having the least loud voices and a less frequent tendency to scream. (Maroon-bellied conure.)*

spaces. The maroon-bellied and green-cheeked conures are identical in almost every way, except that the green-cheeked conure's tail is mostly red and the maroon-belly's tail is mostly green.

Often called the quiet conures, this *Phyrrhura* family is highly treasured among conure lovers. Don't forget that quiet is relative and that even a quiet conure makes noise. This bird is reported to have a lower volume call than a cockatiel.[10]

Quakers: Terrific Talkers for a Tiny Price

When naming the best-talking parrots, African greys and yellow-naped Amazons often head the lists. But these are pricey, long-living species involving a large initial investment and a couple of generations of planning and commitment. For a sturdy bird with a more reasonable price and life expectancy, many who fancy a talking bird are now turning to the quaker parrot.

At first glance, the quaker or monk parrot *(Myopsyttia monachus)* does not appear to be particularly compelling, but its plain colors and unimpressive size mask a truly exciting personality. Among other things, it's not unusual for this intelligent little bundle of energy to use human words with understanding before it's six months old. In my study of talking quaker parrots, published in *Bird Talk,* October 1998, I found that it is not unusual for baby quakers to learn human speech at six weeks of age. While most talk by ten months, it's not unusual for a quaker parrot to learn to say its first human word after it is one year old.

No baby parrot, including the quaker parrot, can be guaranteed to talk merely because it is of a particular species. One of the most exciting aspects of the talking capabilities of the quaker parrot is the sheer number of words these birds can acquire. In my studies, quaker parrots over one year old averaged between 50 and 60 words. However, quaker parrots are not known for being especially easy to understand.

Many of these birds had learned both to use words with understanding and to sing word songs. The latter use of language probably more accurately resembles bird song, and for the purpose of my work, the number of words in songs was not included in the total number of spoken words.

Many quaker parrot owners reported that their birds used an average of 15 to 16 words in ways consistent with their meanings, and some owners of talking quaker parrots report that their birds speak *only* with apparent understanding. That is, these birds do not merely repeat any old word at any old time, they use *all* words *only* with the apparent intent of conveying appropriate meaning at the appropriate moment. Most of the birds in this group spoke an average of about eight words.

Selecting a Talking Bird

While no baby parrot can be guaranteed to talk merely because it's a baby quaker, an experienced hand-feeder can usually guarantee that a particular individual baby quaker will talk. This is because baby quakers usually begin trying to mimic, often actually making understandable sounds, by the time they are fully weaned. But even if a baby quaker has not talked by the time it weans, a bright eyed, interested bird that vocalizes and seeks interaction at ten weeks will probably have at least a few words by the time it's a year old. In this group, the average age at which a quaker parrot spoke its first human word was four months.

Quaker parrots are especially prone to accidents in the home, including flying away. Wing feathers

The quaker has been called both the "best" and the "worst" parrot.

must be trimmed at least a couple of times a year to prevent drowning in the toilet, burning up in the skillet, or crashing into the ceiling fan. Tame quakers that fly away in urban areas are usually easily recovered.

Most Commonly Reported First Words* of 55 Talking Quaker Parrots

Hello	15
Step-up	7
Peek-a-boo	5
What	3
Hi	3

These words also appear to be most commonly repeated in a manner consistent with their meaning.

*Other first words were unique or unknown.

Quaker parrots are especially prone to accidents, including drowning, in the home.

Because they are famously territorial, quakers have special behavioral needs. Like humans, if quakers do not learn cooperative habits and limits of acceptable behavior by the time they reach sexual maturity, they may be completely out of control. It's best for quaker parrots to learn cooperative behavior just after weaning in order to prevent the development of early aggressive behaviors during the developmental period called the terrible two's (which usually appears sometime between 9 and 18 months in quakers).

Most behavior is comprised of a series of habits that are routinely reenacted. A bird that learns to habitually cooperate will be less likely to try to dominate humans in the environment. In order to create good habits and to establish a pattern of cooperation in the bird's behavior, we practice a couple of interactive exercises—step-ups and the towel game—most days in neutral territory.

What to Expect

Because of the quaker parrot's instinct for territorial aggression, it's important not to service the cage with the bird in it. Just open the door, let the bird come out to the top of the door, then step the well-practiced bird up to a hand or hand-held perch and put it on a play pen. Then food, water, toys, or perches can be safely changed, and the bird will not learn how much fun it is to chase hands and other human parts.

A well-adjusted quaker parrot is too busy to be noisy. If the bird is making lots of unpleasant sounds, it may be unhappy. Try to find out why. Much chronic noise-making is a habit, like any other. First assess and improve the environment, then guide the bird to replace habitual noise-making behaviors with more appropriate behaviors.

Suggested wing trims for quakers. (A) is for adults. (B) is for juveniles.

These little green feathered dragons are never spayed or neutered for behavioral reasons and, therefore, they may be expected to demonstrate several diverse forms of sexually-related behaviors. In this group, approximately half of the birds over one year old masturbated. While a little more than half of those birds seemed to prefer the pleasure of a toy, a little less than half seemed to prefer their favorite person's hand. One of the birds in this study was reported to pleasure itself frequently "with anything handy while saying 'peek-a-boo' the whole time."

Like cockatiels, the genus of *Myopsyttia* has only one species. While there are subspecies of quakers, they are seldom identified to the consumer, and there are no reported behavioral differences among the subspecies.

The Clownish Caiques

Caiques might be called the closest thing to New World lories. Playful and exuberant, they are animated little clowns, always on the go. Whether they're hopping in enthusiastic display, making a beeline across a table to examine an unfamiliar object, screaming in anger and disbelief as you put them back into the cage, or leaf bathing in a visiting politician's hair, the clownish caiques seem almost an exercise in self-parody. Caiques love hugging and towel games. Beware: They are in danger of suffocation when they seek out the folds of quilts and afghans just for the fun of it.

Like lories, caiques develop extremely strong feet and legs. Even caiques with full wings appear to prefer to hop and climb around a lot rather than to fly, according to Sally Blanchard, editor of *Pet Bird Report.*

The caique's personality can be extremely complex, with the same bird sometimes exhibiting both aggression toward and fearfulness of the same individual. A caique might suddenly exhibit fear of an inanimate object, especially a new one. Like the scarlet macaw, a caique might be sweet as pie when picked up only to bite fiercely when being put down. A caique can react intensely to a new hat, hair color, or garment.

Black-headed caiques are swaggering little clowns.

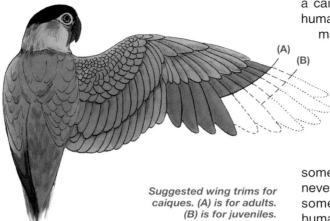

Suggested wing trims for caiques. (A) is for adults. (B) is for juveniles.

Like the scarlet macaw, caiques are known for their extreme intelligence. It's always a challenge to stay one step ahead of these smart little birds. Each day will differ, as these birds will always be looking for new ways to have fun by frequently improvising new behaviors.

The caique's love of bathing is well reported. Like lories, they will sometimes play their water away. Because they love to play in water, caiques benefit from having water changed more than once daily and from having a tube if they are left for long periods. Caiques even love "leaf bathing" as Spikey LeBec, Sally Blanchard's celebrity caique, loves to demonstrate in his adoring fans' hair.

Caiques are not known for exceptional talking abilities, nor are they known for great volume. Their voices are not loud. Most caiques probably prefer mimicking sounds to mimicking human words. Like one of the small African parrots *(Poicephalus),*

a caique might enjoy trying to drive humans in the home to distraction by making ear-splitting sounds.

A caique will seldom get you kicked out of your neighborhood, but it can be very annoying inside the home. Sally Blanchard reports that the acquisition of obnoxious sounds varies greatly from one bird to another, and that some owners report that they have never heard that shrill alarm call that some caiques are known to abuse humans with.

Caiques can be stubborn and difficult to distract from whatever quest they're currently pursuing. They can exhibit bonding-related aggression and have been seen to stalk family members disfavored by their favorite person. Frequent outings and handling by multiple individuals are especially beneficial to the gregarious caique personality. For example, if one family member is often attacked by the bird, then that family member will probably benefit the most from being the means by which the bird goes to the veterinarian or groomer. Even if the less favored human never actually handles the bird, sometimes being carried around in a carrier in strange places by the less favored person will restore at least some harmony to a disharmonious caique/human relationship.

It's not unusual for a caique to take advantage of any opportunity to chase in its home territory. Although Spikey LeBec is pretty nice to most people on his many outings, he can be a little tyrant at home. Sally Blanchard reports that "the minute somebody acts like they're afraid of Spike, well, there he is, 'all over them.'"

As with quakers, lories, and other small birds that tend to develop chasing, it's important not to allow humans to intentionally or unintentionally provoke a caique. It's a good idea, both for immediate practical reasons and for long-term behavioral benefit, to remove the bird before servicing the cage.

The Caique Species

Black-headed Parrot *(Pionites melanocephala).* These are popular pets in Venezuela. They eat seeds, fruits, and flowers in the wild. They also favor insects in captivity.[11]

White-bellied Parrot *(Pionites leucogaster).* Described by some as a single species with the black-headed caique, this bird appears to be just about the same bird without the black head. It is suspected that these two species hybridize in the uppermost regions of the Amazon where the river that separates their ranges is narrower.[12]

Pionus Parrots

The *Pionus* parrot family is another wonderful bird, like *Poicephalus,* that is often overlooked in favor of larger, showier birds. *Pionus* babies are not as flashy as some other birds in the medium-size parrot family. Adults develop colors ranging from the muted white front, to delicate pastel

shades of the bronze-wing, to the dazzling cornflower blue and pink of the mature blue-headed *Pionus.* Companion *Pionus* have a reputation as cautiously calm and graciously interactive, with a normally subdued volume.

The white-bellied caique is very much like the black-headed species.

Pionus usually tolerate well the presence of humans, pets, and other types of birds in the home. Indeed, *Pionus* are known more for ignoring disliked humans than for attacking them. If a *Pionus* doesn't like someone or something, it will often sit with its back to the offending party, according to Ginger Elden.

Pionus love baths and are vigorous bathers. Because they are not as high-energy as the *Poicephalus* family members, many older humans enjoy *Pionus* for the noninvasive companionship they usually provide. *Pionus* learn to play with toys easily, may even tolerate servicing the cage without being removed, and love interaction just as much as any other parrot, Betsy Lott reports.

Pionus are known more for their stolid dispositions, undemanding personalities, and subtle beauty than

for their talking ability, although they can pick up a few words in a little robot, computer-like voice, Elden says. *Pionus* parrots are not typically loud birds, and so they often do well in apartments. These little birds, especially the females, have shrill calls and can use them, although there is usually something wrong in the environment when this kind of behavior appears. The *Pionus*' fear response sounds a little like it might be asthma, but this must not be confused with a health problem. Look for something that the bird is afraid of, advises Elden.

Cautious is the word that best describes young *Pionus* babies, who would rather snuggle than explore. After three months, however, these inquisitive youngsters begin exploring and can be in danger of household accidents like being stepped on if they are not properly contained, Elden warns.

At around two years old, a *Pionus* will begin testing the limits of the behavioral environment. This typical behavior is an expected developmental phase that passes with consistent handling and continued interactions. Strong flyers and strong-willed individuals benefit from well-maintained wing trims. A flighted *Pionus* can develop extreme territorial tendencies and might decide not to let people into the house at all. To prevent the development of adverse reactions to grooming, these sensitive little birds should be groomed early and frequently throughout their lifetimes, as they can come to fear towels excessively if towels are not a part of the birds' ongoing experience (see the towel game, p. 153).

(A)

(B)

Suggested wing trims for Pionus *parrots. (A) is for adults. (B) is for juveniles.*

The Companion *Pionus* Species

Blue-headed *Pionus* (*Pionus menstruus*). Very dependable of disposition, this bird will affectionately select a favorite person, but will seldom abuse others because of the strength of the bond with the favorite person.

White-crowned *Pionus* (*Pionus senilis*). Not so brightly colored as some other members of the family, this bird's personality is far from colorless. They are beautiful, and this may be the most active of this generally placid family. Elden reports that hen white-crowns are especially treasured companions, but that doesn't mean that the males can't be really sweet also. White-crowns have a reputation for being both the most aggressive and most territorial of the *Pionus* species.

Bronze-wing *Pionus* (*Pionus chalcopterus*). Possessing stunning, subtle colors, this bird is usually a noninvasive addition to even the smallest living room. I seldom see behavior problems in these birds, although they can be sensitive to grooming and exhibit a great deal of towel stress. Young birds should be well acclimated to the towel and towel games should be continued throughout the birds' lifetimes.

Scaly-headed or Maximilian's *Pionus* (*Pionus maximiliani*). Perhaps the most docile of this generally docile group, Maximilian's *Pionus* is more subtly colored than others. With proper socialization on both sides, these birds often adjust easily to handling by children.

The "Pocket Parrots": *Brotegeris* and Parrotlets

Two families of New World parrots are often referred to as the "pocket parrots": *Brotegeris,* a sturdy little bird that has a reputation for being "born tame," and *Forpus* or parrotlets.

Brotegeris

These birds were so popular during the days when they were available, in the 1980s, that their prices were observed to first double, then triple. They are not sexually dimorphic, and some of them, like the gray-cheeked parakeet, have proved more fragile than expected. These birds were more common during the days of importation, as they appear

Maximilian's Pionus has a reputation for a docile demeanor well suited to children.

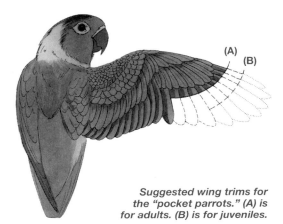

Suggested wing trims for the "pocket parrots." (A) is for adults. (B) is for juveniles.

habits, it was easy to allow a gray-cheeked parakeet to live at liberty in the home. However, it is very easy for these little guys to develop extremely territorial behavior. Gray-cheeks and bee-bees, especially, had a reputation for forming excessively strong bonds with chrome appliances. This meant that there were quite a few of these little characters who wouldn't let certain people into the kitchen or bathroom. I have personally treated several cases of overbonding to a toaster in this family.

These birds require just as much careful patterning and maintenance of behavioral limits as a larger bird like a caique, for they might be called caique-like or lory-like in their ability to focus on a frightened human and pick on them. I found that one of the greatest dangers to *Brotegeris* in the home was their tendency to attack other companion animals—one of the leading causes of *Brotegeris* death in the home is the bird harassing a dog until the dog turns on it.

The second most common behavioral complaint, behind inappropriate territorialism, is noise. In spite of their small size, the *Brotegeris* voice can be both loud and abrasive. Prevent the development of screaming behaviors by providing an appropriate location where the bird is a part of things, and lots of access to interactive toys and destructible chewables.

If you have an older *Brotegeris* parrot and want to switch it to pellets, proceed cautiously. See the veterinarian first. If the bird has a weak

more difficult to breed than parrotlets, lovebirds, *Poicephalus,* and cockatiels.

During the time when these birds were exported, reports were widespread that this entire group had for centuries been harvested in the manner of a renewable resource by indigenous peoples like those seen in the "Spirits of the Rainforest" video. This Discovery Channel production shows Machiguenga girls of Yomuibato, Manu spitting chewed banana into the beaks of baby golden-winged parakeets *(Brotegeris crysopterus).*

Although the gray-cheeked parakeet had the best reputation of the group, even the commonest bee-bees seemed to come tame. However, even though the *Brotegeris* parrots practically all came tame, that didn't mean they were easy to keep tame. Because of their small size and relatively modest chewing

liver or kidneys, a diet change might be too hard on the bird. Also, be careful supplementing vitamins for *Brotegeris,* especially if pelleted diet is fed, as they are little birds and can be sensitive to vitamin D$_3$. Feed whole fresh foods instead of supplementing vitamins for *Brotegeris.*

Parrotlets

Forpus, the family of tiny parrots called parrotlets, are sometimes called the South American lovebird or blue-winged lovebird. Breeder Sandee Molenda likes to say, "Although they are the smallest parrot, they don't know it." They are everything one would expect of a "real" parrot. I have never been asked to do behavioral intervention on a parrotlet. In the days when wild-caught birds were traded, *Forpus* parrots were managed by indigenous peoples like *Brotegeris,* according to Matthew Vriends.

The most common companion parrotlets in the United States at this writing are the green-rumped, Pacific (celestial), and spectacled parrotlets. These birds, which cannot quite be called common, are not yet produced in numbers enabling them to be found in the typical pet store. The best places to find parrotlets are parrotlet breeders, specialty bird stores, and bird shows.

Parrotlets don't require daily handling in order to remain tame. Vriends reports that they seem naturally tame, are quiet, and are not messy. The parrotlet's voice is charming, chattery, and seldom invasive in the slightest. Even the scream of an angry parrotlet usually falls way short of obnoxious.

Sandee Molenda reports that they may be temporarily angry after you've gone away for a while. They have obvious memory and are loyal to their favorites from the past. Parrotlets bond strongly to their favorite person and sometimes abuse spouses. They can be extremely cage territorial and, like a quaker, probably benefit from being removed from the cage to change toys, food, and water so that they do not develop chasing behaviors. It's important to keep the parrotlets well socialized to towels (see p. 153) and to hand-held perches (see p. 5) for handling when they're in a cranky mood.

Molenda also reminds us that everybody benefits when the companion parrotlet's wing feathers are kept consistently trimmed. In the parrotlet personality, the feelings of power stimulated by flight can create playfully and territorially aggressive behaviors. Additionally, this careful keeping of trimmed parrotlet wings will help to ensure the bird's safety, for these little birds are so curious and exploratory that they much more frequently die in household accidents than of illness.

The Common *Brotegeris* and *Forpus* Species

Gray-cheeked Parakeet *(Brotegeris pyrhopterus).* During the 1980s when gray-cheeks were coming into this country frequently, Freud says they had an almost universal

The celestial parrotlet is even smaller than a budgie.

reputation for gentleness. Indeed, I saw docile, interactive, charming birds step right out of the crates from the import stations during the 1970s and 1980s.

Canary and White-winged Bee-Bee *(Brotegeris versicoloris versicoloris* and *B. v. chiriri).* Sold by the thousands through chain stores, these birds had a loyal and very vocal following through the 1970s and 1980s. Even wild-caught birds

had a reputation for easy interactions with humans and many long-term, successful bee-bee/human relationships were forged.

Pacific or Celestial Parrotlet *(Forpus coelestis).* The Pacific parrotlet has had a head start in the pet trade over the other species of *Forpus,* but they can be more aggressive. They will take advantage of an opportunity to boss people around. If someone backs off, the bird will be convinced it can chase them and will try harder the next time. This might actually be playful behavior, as these birds, like other parrots, love to improvise interactive games, according to Vriends.

[6]"Spirits of the Rainforest" video, Discovery Communications, Inc., 1993.
[7]"Parrots: Look Who's Talking," Thirteen/ WNET and BBC-TV, 1995.
[8]Tani Robar, "Fantastic Performing Parrots" video, Robar Productions, 1994.
[9]"Fantastic Performing Parrots" Video I, Robar Productions, 1994.
[10]"Phyrrhuras: The Quiet Conures" video, The Feather Tree, 1997.
[11]Juniper and Parr, *Parrots, A Guide to Parrots of the World,* New Haven, CT: Yale University Press, 1998, p. 503.
[12]Juniper and Parr, *Parrots, A Guide to Parrots of the World,* New Haven, CT: Yale University Press, 1998, p. 504.

Chapter Five

What to Expect of the Pacific Distribution Parrots

Budgies: The Most Popular Parrot

The common parakeet or budgie (short for *budgerigar,* a native Australian word meaning "good to eat") is the most popular caged bird in the world. Their size, ease of reproduction, modest physical requirements, and predictable dispositions have earned *Melopsittacus undulatus* respect in all sectors of aviculture. They are the darlings of homemakers and Ph.D. geneticists. They are beloved by town and country dwellers, wealthy and fixed-income owners of all ages, religions, and social persuasions. Except for the cat (and if you don't count fish), they are probably the most common pet.

Anyone who knows parrots will see everything they expect from a large hookbill in these tiny bundles of energy. In some ways, parakeets have twice as much energy as a large hookbill because they do everything twice as fast. They are fabulous talkers, but because they double the speed of everything they say, unless you speak half as fast when you are speech training, you might not be able to understand them. They mature very quickly, so especially good attention must be paid to step-up practice during the time of rapid behavioral development (two to six months).

The budgie is the world's most common companion parrot.

One of the most delightful aspects of owning a budgie is their extreme availability. There is probably no community of more than a thousand people that does not have at least one budgie breeder. They are readily available all over the world, mostly at very low prices. They apparently command the highest prices in places like the United Kingdom, where a large and active show culture exists. In 200 years of captive breeding, domestic aviculture has produced hundreds of dazzling color variations.

When selecting a budgie, look for a very young bird. An experienced budgie dealer can advise you on the physical characteristics to look for in a young bird: perhaps some dark spots still on the beak, perhaps lines on the forehead coming all the way down the cere (the raised area around the nostrils), perhaps a very smooth, pale cere. I prefer to buy from a dealer who allows me to handle or tame the bird in the store.

Start by having the dealer trim the wing feathers so that the baby bird can be easily taught to step up from finger to finger. Be sure to specify a "training clip" with no long feathers left at the end of the wing to be bumped or get caught in cage bars. This procedure must be maintained three or four times a year if the bird is allowed to be at liberty in the home. A flying budgie in a home with cooking pots, toilets, ceiling fans, and common poisonous plants, among many other dangers, will not enjoy a long life, and might be maimed by any number of accidents caused by flight in the home.

Find a quiet corner, maybe a closet or bathroom, and sit on the floor with the baby budgie nestled loosely in your hands. Spend a few minutes talking quietly (not whispering, for they have a natural aversion to the hissing sounds made by their predators, the snakes) and making humming sounds directly into the bird's head. Be careful not to move your hands or head when you talk. Gently place the baby bird on the top of an index finger and speak soothingly until it remains still on the finger. If the bird flutters off, it has only a very short way to fall because you are sitting on the floor. Gently pick the bird up and place it back on the finger.

After the bird has become accustomed to sitting on the finger, you can begin slowly approaching the

(A)
(B)

Suggested wing trims for budgies. (A) is for adults. (B) is for juveniles.

feet from below (not from in front of the face) with the opposite index finger. Slowly, gently lift the tip of the toes of the foot nearest the tip of the index finger the bird is sitting on with the opposite index finger. When the foot is lifted successfully off the finger the bird is sitting on, slowly, gently push back with the top hand and lower the (back) hand the bird is sitting on. After a little practice, the bird should easily step up onto the front (top) hand. As the bird transfers weight to the new hand, give the command "step up."

Within a very few minutes, a young, untraumatized bird should easily understand what it is you expect and cheerfully comply with the step-up command. This step-up practice will become a daily part of your routine, for good discipline with any parrot is maintained with daily practice of this exercise. The daily step-up practice is similar to prayer or meditation in that it gives the bird (and owner) a behavioral and emotional baseline in which the bird knows exactly what is expected and exactly what will happen. In the future, if the bird becomes angry, or jealous, or fearful, those emotions can be calmed with the practice of the step-up command.

Housing and Care

Especially if the bird is to spend a great deal of time in the cage, be sure to purchase an adequately sized cage. Be sure that the bird has at least three dishes, one for the regular diet, one for water, and one for daily soft foods such as hard-boiled egg (mashed with shell on), broccoli (they like the little balls on the tops), toast (without butter), grated cheese and carrots, and whatever healthy fare you regularly consume. Budgies are especially fond of cooked rice, quinoa, and pasta.

Probably the only downside to budgie ownership is the possibility of a short lifetime. Since they come from the dryer parts of Australia, they appear to prefer seed. If they eat only seed, budgies can develop a couch-potato-like syndrome including many diet-related health problems, such as fatty liver disease, and suffer a reduced life expectancy. The new pelleted diets should help to prevent these diet-related problems and are readily available from pet stores, veterinarians, and other avian suppliers.

The Budgies

American Budgie. In the United States, a thriving trade in pet budgies at popular prices created a demand for many different colors of birds. The resulting plethora of color variations appear in birds that are smaller than their United Kingdom cousins.

English Budgies. The British show circuit, with its huge following and show standards for large parakeets, has produced a genetic line that is much larger than the common pet bird usually available in the United States. These birds are much more expensive than their American cousins and have a reputation for a shorter lifespan.

Those Cuddly Cockatoos

They have names like Sugar, Honey, Peaches, Angel, Baby, and YumYum, describing their sweet, interactive natures. They also have names like Kaiser, Napoleon, Caesar, Alexander, and Hillary, depicting their strength and majesty. Occasionally, I run into cockatoos named Sarge, Killer, Dikembe Mutumbu, Dracula, and Nosferatoo. The most common cockatoo name I've heard is Houdini (for their incredible talents as escape artists). With such diversity, you must know that the companion cockatoo has a reputation for being as unpredictable as springtime in the Rockies.

The Goffin's cockatoo is a famous escape artist.

Many things set cockatoos apart from other birds and from other parrots. Especially, cockatoos are among the only birds with a mobile crest, rather than a crest that merely identifies species or gender. Indeed, a cockatoo can completely cover its beak with the facial fan feathers. Cockatoos have the most expressive faces of any bird; indeed they have moveable crests, "face fans," and auricular feathers around the ears. Cockatoos can express extremely complex emotions with those head and facial feathers. Jim Murphy sent me a photo of a Moluccan cockatoo in full display showing that his facial display (obviously the most important part of the display) was fully one half of his total body height!

Common companion cockatoos come mostly in white with pastels, the most common Australian species being mostly white with various shades of yellow crests. One of the Indonesian cockatoos, the umbrella, has the Latin name *Cacatua alba,* meaning literally "white cockatoo." Breaking from the mold are the pink cockatoos: the rose-breasted, the Goffin's, and the Moluccan. Rarer cockatoos also come in black, some with red or yellow markings.

The crests of the various species of cockatoos are said to be recumbent or recurve. The most common crest, the recumbent crest such as that of the Goffin's cockatoo *(Cacatua goffini),* lies flat on the head when not in use. The recurve crest, like that of the sulphur-crested cockatoos *(Cacatua sulphurea),* sweeps back up and away from the back of the head. Although there are no studies to confirm this, author Jim Murphy suggests that the recurve crest has more signaling capacity than the recumbent type.

Cockatoos have soft body feathers covered with powder, which is an indication of good health. Cockatoos have large, strong feet; large, strong beaks; and sensitive, expressive faces. Most companion cockatoos love bathing, including human-supplied showers. Cockatoos are frequently known to make and use tools: sticks for scratching and tapping and displays for mates.

Cockatoos are cavity breeders who love to chew. When a companion cockatoo is chewing up the clock or the Queen Anne chair with joyful abandon, it's not expressing anger or discontent. The bird is demonstrating its nesting skills. A cockatoo who is chewing up wood is expressing a sexual behavior, saying to favorite humans and anyone else who will notice, "Look what a good mate I would be. I could carve a darling nest cavity for you!"

Cockatoos possess some of the most "human" of all characteristics found in parrot-type birds. They are (serially) monogamous, although perhaps not sexually exclusive. They copulate for reasons other than procreation. They utilize "birth control" by refusing to raise chicks that can't be supported by the environment. The male parent takes an active part in the rearing of offspring. And, also like some humans, cockatoos suffer from a tendency toward spousal abuse. Cockatoos obviously have memory.

Cockatoos might be called the most (domestic) catlike of all parrots. A cockatoo might suddenly decide that it wants to be held by the only person in the room who doesn't want to touch it. One companion cockatoo might be inclined to absolutely smother you to death all the time, or another might become positively apoplectic if forced by chance or circumstance to have any physical contact with a human. Of course, there is also a great deal of middle ground.

Imported cockatoos were generally less talkative than their imported New World cousins, the Amazons and macaws, being more inclined to imitate movement than sounds.[13] Now that all new baby cockatoos in the United States are domestically raised, we are hearing many exciting and amusing stories of cockatoo talking ability. Although most cockatoos are known more for cuddling than for talking, there are certainly some outstanding talkers in the bunch. Common expressions for cockatoos to pick up early and easily are "What 'choo doin'?," "Step up," "Gimme a kiss," "I love you," and "Nite, nite." Although they are not, generally, extremely verbal, many cockatoos—perhaps most cockatoos—can be loud, at least occasionally. Cockatoos are known sometimes even to scream in the dark.

But even though we can only occasionally expect outstanding talking ability, we can always expect an incredible penchant for acrobatics and stunning mechanical ability. If lories are the "puppies" of the parrot family, then cockatoos are the "monkeys." Cockatoos love all kinds of simple mechanical devices: nuts and bolts, and carabiners, including many cage door-fastening devices.

The cockatoo bite has the potential to be the most penetrating of all parrot bites, because most cockatoo beaks possess three very pronounced points: one on the maxilla (upper mandible or beak) and two on each side of a razor sharp chisel-shaped cutting edge on the mandible (lower beak). Not only are the beaks relatively large, they are often very sharp. A cockatoo beak can puncture the skin in three places and slash with the lower mandible all in one movement. Fortunately, most domestic cockatoos are lovers, not fighters. However, even the most romantic "Romeo" will occasionally attack a perceived rival or try to browbeat a beloved companion to get his way. This aspect of the cockatoo personality is probably the most problematic part of a long-term relationship with a cockatoo. The occasional tendency to sudden aggression is managed with vigilance and with continued good step-up practice, the towel game, and other patterning rituals throughout the bird's lifetime.

Although some cockatoos may be absolutely trustworthy regarding bites, this varies with age and with individuals. This family has been called emotionally incontinent. A truly trustworthy teenage cockatoo may be unusual: In my experience maybe no more than 10 to 15 percent of mature companion cockatoos could be called completely trustworthy. Like many exotics, most sexually mature cockatoos are pretty dispositionally uneven and may exhibit frequent or occasional aggression. This will usually show itself in a cycle twice yearly, spring and fall. This may or may not be gender-related, with males being the most combative in most, but not all, species. I have seen some very aggressive cockatoo hens and some very docile cocks, but watch those facial feathers for emotional cues, for the cockatoo mood can change with amazing swiftness. Julie Weiss Murad, founder of the Gabriel Foundation, reports that the mature male cockatoo is one of the birds most frequently surrendered to shelters.

Special Needs

A cockatoo should definitely not be an impulse purchase. I do not recommend cockatoos to individuals with antiques or with respiratory or dust sensitivities (because of the abundant powder they exude), to anyone with sensitivity to loud noises, to homes with extremely active or irrepressible children, or to individuals of quick and fiery temper (the bird might provoke anger in such a human).

Cockatoos are sometimes called codependent because of the extremely strong bonds they can form, sometimes rendering them totally emotionally and behaviorally dependent on a chosen human. This can lead to attention-demanding and other neurotic behaviors, as the bird may seek to fulfill its desire for 100 percent control over the favored human, or the bird might react to a realization of lack of control. A cockatoo that is addicted to attention can drive humans crazy demanding it. The same bird can go crazy if it doesn't get the attention it demands.

In addition to the large amounts of powder produced, the cockatoos' loud voices and frequency of using those loud voices make them prime candidates for failure in their first homes. It's easy to underestimate how much that powder and voice will affect all members of the family, and human incompatibility with cockatoos can destroy families as loyalties are formed, reformed, and broken. Usually, however, it's the bird that's out of a home when its needs can't be accommodated by the humans who chose it.

Caging requirements for a cockatoo are great. The larger species must have especially strong welds and bars, as these birds love to exercise their huge, strong beaks on the cage, and an insubstantial cage will simply be dismantled. Because of their extreme curiosity and mechanical ability, cockatoos cannot be left alone outside a well-designed cage or bird-proofed environment. Colorado avian veterinarian Dr. Jerry LaBonde says, "If it's been in an accident, it's probably a cockatoo."

The most common reason cockatoos lose their homes, however, is neither powder nor destructiveness. Cockatoos most commonly lose their homes because of their loud voices. While an African grey, *Poicephalus* parrot, or lory can occasionally drive humans to distraction with their loud vocalizations, those birds' voices seldom carry beyond the home where they reside. The voice of a cockatoo, on the other hand, can carry well beyond most city lot limits; indeed, the voice of a cockatoo might offend someone down the block. A cockatoo scream can be a true behavioral emergency wherein humans may be at risk of losing their place to live. If there's concern that your neighbors are sensitive to loud sounds, be especially sure to avoid the Moluccan and umbrella cockatoos. If a cockatoo is still in order, maybe a rose-breasted cockatoo would work out.

Cockatoos do well with humans who are fully capable of setting limits

Cockatoos lose their homes most frequently because of their loud voices. (Moluccan cockatoo.)

early and enforcing them. I recommend cockatoos to people with a great appreciation for playfulness, a love of nature, and a tolerance for the ebb and flow of destructible possessions. I recommend cockatoos to those who are willing to take great care designing their bird's environment for behavioral effect. Most of all, I recommend cockatoos to people with a longing for great beauty in their lives. A cockatoo is like a special child to cherish and protect from its own very emotional nature. If you think you would enjoy living with a gorgeous flower with an occasional temper, chances are you would treasure a 'too.

The cockatoos' extreme needs and sensitive temperaments put them at risk for feather chewing. (Goffin's cockatoo.)

Acquiring a Cockatoo

When buying or adopting a cockatoo, be sure to check for powder on the feathers by rubbing a broad feather between thumb and forefinger. If a particular cockatoo has no easily observable powder on the feathers, don't buy it without a full veterinary workup to ensure that it does not have Psittacine Beak and Feather Disease (PBFD), an incurable disease that can be communicated to other birds.

There are many wonderful opportunities to adopt older cockatoos. These birds probably come with a behavior problem or two, but older cockatoos can often be relatively easily and effectively resocialized. I have seen truculent older birds who could be handled by almost anyone who knew how to use the towel, although many mature male cockatoos may be untrustworthy without a towel or hand-held perches. The ability to be resocialized later in life is one of the cockatoo's most attractive traits, for these are among the most long-living of parrots.

Longevity isn't always an advantage, however, as there may be many more older companion cockatoos than there are homes available for them.

The "Cockatoo Identity"

Sybil Erden of Oasis Sanctuary says that often cockatoos who come to her sanctuary with emotional and behavioral problems are vastly improved by the company of birds of their own kind. That is, she sees ben-

efit to keeping more than one cockatoo so that the birds retain a sort of
"cockatoo identity." She tells the story
of a Goffin's hen cockatoo in her
care who came in self-mutilating
and soon learned appropriate
play habits merely by watching the bird in the next
cage. Erden reports that it
doesn't seem to matter
whether the birds like each
other. It must also be
observed that birds that
come into a sanctuary may
have been in unhappy cir-
cumstances and in less-than-
ideal environments and that the
addition of cockatoos was not
usually the only way the bird's life
changed. Jim Murphy adds that cockatoos that are not raised around
other cockatoos can lose the ability to
learn necessary life skills, including
independence and the very ability to
raise offspring.

Suggested wing trims for cockatoos. (A) is for adults. (B) is for juveniles.

The Common Cockatoos

Sulphur-crested and Citron-crested Cockatoos *(Cacatua sulphurea).* This family of four sub-species features a bright lemon or cab yellow crest that curves forward and an otherwise white body with occasional touches of yellow. These birds are comical, acrobatic, and mechanical. They are often highly prized in companion settings even though they are exterminated as agricultural pests in their range.

Medium Sulphur-crested or Eleanora Cockatoo *(Cacatua eleonora).* In this larger bird, which

The sulphur-crested cockatoos have a lemon-yellow crest.

The citron-crested cockatoos have a deeper, cab-yellow crest.

possesses more pleasing proportions than some of the lesser-sulfurs, the crest feathers are noticeably longer in proportion to the head than the lessers. The Eleanora cockatoo

The rose-breasted cockatoo is known as the "quiet cockatoo."

is known for amazing acrobatic antics, often including full upright-crest displays while perched absolutely upside down. There's not much in the world that's cuter than a baby Eleanora that uses exactly the same posture whether upside down or right side up.

Greater Sulphur-crested Cockatoo (*Cacatua galerita*). This bird has the reputation for being the calmest of the sulfur-crested cockatoos, although it must be noted that the word *calm* here is used relative to cockatoos only, and "calm cockatoo" is sort of an oxymoron. At this writing, the greater sulfur is relatively difficult to find outside of Australia. We are hearing reports that the companion greaters available in the United States are "smaller than they used to be." Whether this is the result of stunting or crossbreeding with Eleanoras is unknown.

Rose-breasted Cockatoo (*Eolophus roseicapillus*). The rose-breasted cockatoo is said to be a usually cautious bird, often with a well-developed fight-or-flight response. The calls of the rose-breasted cockatoo can be loud, but are usually infrequent. This bird is often called the least loud of the common companion cockatoos. They are high-energy creatures that require a larger cage than some of the larger cockatoos. Rosies don't need extremely strong cage bars and welds like a Moluccan or umbrella cockatoo, but they can outsmart some of the most sophisticated door-locking mechanisms.

Ginger West reports that rosies commonly speak their first few words before weaning and have clear, distinctive voices. Most rosies seem to limit their alarm calls to dusk and dawn or when excited. The tightly knit feathers shed less feather dust than most other cockatoos. Indeed, West reports that their feathers are similar in texture to that of the grey parrot and that a typical rosie probably sheds about as much dust as a typical grey parrot (which is still more than most other parrots except for cockatiels).

This cockatoo and the hen umbrella probably have the best chance for successful adjustment to the first home. Wing trims are extremely important, as a full-flighted rosie may develop a stronger fear response than other cockatoos and therefore will be more difficult to maintain as a companion, West reports. These little cockatoos are more prone to obesity than their larger cockatoo cousins.

Major Mitchell's or Leadbeater's Cockatoo *(Cacatua leadbeatri).* At this time, this is an uncommon bird, but highly prized and sought after. A cautious bird, the Leadbeater's cockatoo is known for great beauty and for loud, infrequent calls. These birds have a reputation for being ill-suited as companions for humans, although occasional individuals, including handfed handicapped or imperfect handfed birds have successfully maintained companion status.

Salmon-crested or Moluccan Cockatoo *(Cacatua moluccensis).*

Major Mitchell's or Leadbeater's cockatoo is not known for good companion qualities.

Often said to be the loudest and most long-living of the common companion cockatoos, these birds have magnificently resounding voices and a reputation for using them with great frequency. Unlike most other companion parrots, this bird will scream even in the dark.

These birds are gorgeous and showy, but probably require more space and patience than almost any other bird. Successful Moluccan owners are probably deserving of special awards for patience, for these birds have a poor likelihood of success in their first homes. Because they are also so long-living, Moluccans are often available through adoption organizations.

Umbrella Cockatoo *(Cacatua alba).* The umbrella is the next most-commonly-called-loudest of the cockatoos. It can be especially loud in breeding settings, with the hen's solicitation for sex sometimes being deafening. We are now seeing many good talking umbrella cockatoos. The cocks have a reputation for becoming aggressive and behaviorally uneven during breeding cycles whether there's a mate present or not. This behavior is seldom seen in the hens, and I believe, therefore, that the hen umbrella cockatoo is the most desirable of the common companion cockatoos. Like many parrots, the umbrella cockatoo can become obsessed with floor control, including attacking human toes, feet, and other body parts encountered on

The bare-eyed cockatoo has a good reputation as a human companion.

the floor. Limits and watchfulness are necessary when a cockatoo shares the floor with children or even adults who are unfamiliar with the need to block cockatoo toe attacks.

Goffin's Cockatoo *(Cacti gof-fini).* Goffin's cockatoos are known to scream in the dark. They also scream during sex. They are cautious, reactionary birds with a tendency to form extreme and unpredictable bonds that can foster neurotic habits. When these birds were being imported in huge numbers, they had a reputation as a poor pet with a huge failure rate as a companion. I have probably helped to place more free homeless Goffin's cockatoos than any other bird. Even handfed Goffin's can be difficult to manage behaviorally. This bird is not for everyone, but the ones who do adjust well in homes that adjust well to them are among the most beloved of all companion parrots. Goffin's cockatoos might be smaller than most other common cockatoo species, but they are extremely active and need a cage that is at least as big as that required by an umbrella or Moluccan cockatoo.

Ginger West observes that the Goffin's cockatoos she knows seem best suited as only birds and that behavior problems often appear in these little love sponges only after additional birds are added to the household. I have seen only birds develop behavior problems as a result of being left alone in dual career households where owners spend long hours working away from home. If another bird is to be added, try adding another cockatoo, as Sybil Erden suggests that the Goffin's cockatoo benefits from the presence of another cockatoo.

Little Corella or Bare-eyed Cockatoo *(Cacatua sanguinea).* This little Australian parrot is more behaviorally stable than the Goffin's cockatoo, although some say that with its bare, puffy eye rings, it looks like a depressed Goffin's cockatoo. Don't be fooled by appearances; this mischievous bird is well known as a charming companion with excellent ability to mimic human speech. Freud says they have been called the "most intelligent of the white cockatoos."

Long-billed Corella or Slender-billed Cockatoo *(Cacatua tenuirostris).* This bird is even more behaviorally stolid than the Little Corella. It shares the Corella's reputation as the best-talking cockatoo. Indeed, a pudgy slender-bill is quite the "star" of the popular video "Parrots: Look Who's Talking."

Once considered to be on the verge of extinction, this bird is now considered a major agricultural pest in its native Victoria. Laws protecting the birds have vastly increased their numbers. These birds are opportunistic, expanding with the growth of agriculture, Freud reports.

The Perfectly Charming Cockatiel

The cockatiel is, in fact, a miniature cockatoo, including the cocka-

The long-billed Corella is an uncommon companion bird in the United States.

too's mobile crest and facial fan. But the cockatiel is vastly less work, amazingly less expensive, and usually a much less troublesome housemate than a cockatoo. The cockatiel is almost universally regarded as the most docile of all companion parrots. There are no species or subspecies in this genus. Additionally, there is more uniformity in cockatiel personalities than in those of other parrots. Few handfed cockatiels are dispositionally uneven, undependable, or otherwise undesirable as a pet. The genera *Nymphicus* is so specialized that it has only one species, *Nymphicus hollandicus.*

Cockatiels are beautiful, gentle, and a pleasure to be with—everything a parrot should be. They make excellent first birds and last birds, for the cockatiel will try human patience less than any other hookbill. Betsy

The pearl hen cockatiel.

Lott reports that the cockatiel makes an excellent family bird that seldom nips even the smallest and wobbliest of humans in the home. Cockatiels love to whistle, and males will learn a few human words. They are one of the few companion parrots that will usually live their entire lifespan in one household.

(A)
(B)

Suggested wing trims for cockatiels. (A) is for adults. (B) is for juveniles.

Cockatiels are some of the few parrots that show gender in the coloration of their feathers. Adult male birds bear bright orange circles on the cheeks; hens' cheek patches are less brilliant. The male birds are famous for their beautiful, melodious courtship songs.

Cockatiels, like many of the larger parrots, come in a variety of color combinations. Although not flashy like the green, red, and blue larger parrots, they have wonderful coloring and bright personalities. Cockatiels become devoted household members when given plenty of love, proper nutrition, and care. Diane Grindol, author of *The Complete Book of Cockatiels,* reports their life expectancy as 15 to 20 years, although she has known of a cockatiel that lived a reported 38 years.

Cockatiels require wing trimming, but not for reasons related to aggression prevention, like other parrots. Cockatiels are flyers, not fighters, so a frightened bird can easily break its neck on a window it knew very well was there and would normally avoid. Grindol suggests a progressive wing trim involving a couple of wing feathers every few days so that chicks learn to manage their bodies and develop landing skills. Severely clipped chicks often land awkwardly and break their tail feathers.

Grounding an adult cockatiel with a wing feather trim is absolutely impossible. No cockatiel, even one with every primary feather trimmed, can be trusted outdoors without a harness or carrier. They are simply so light-bodied that they can be blown away by a brisk wind.

One of the most striking anomalies affecting cockatiels and almost no other birds is known as "night frights." It's not unusual for these sensitive birds to thrash in apparent fear in the darkness. It's not unusual for a cockatiel to be so frightened in the night that it knocks out all its tail feathers, or maybe all the feathers on one wing. Grindol suggests the presence of a small night light and advises that if thrashing is heard, the room light can be turned on and the bird calmed with soothing words. This might have the effect of showing the bird that all things are as they should be and there is no danger. The light can be turned off when the cockatiel is feeling calm again. Night frights are more common in the lutinos and the newer color mutations than in the normal gray cockatiels.

The love song of the male cockatiel can be achingly beautiful. At about four months old, even before it acquires its adult male markings, little boy cockatiels start strutting, hopping, and whistling. It's the easiest way to know which are the little boys—to listen before you look. The female cockatiels will, for the most part, retain the monosyllabic chirp of the juvenile bird rather than acquiring words, songs, or whistles. My own cinnamon pearl cockatiel, Pearl, is quite the lady, never uttering a sound except her feminine call most of the time. The single exception is when she masturbates: She whistles what I

consider to be the second most common male cockatiel courtship song.

The Exotic *Eclectus* Parrots

Their beauty can take your breath away. The first time most people see a hen *Eclectus,* they literally gasp in awe at the uncompromising brilliance of a bird that looks like it's made of red and purple velvet. However, the *Eclectus* parrot isn't named for its beauty, but rather for the eclectic nature of its coloration and behavior.

Both behavior and color usage in *Eclectus* parrots vary significantly from that of almost all other parrots. For one thing, a hen *Eclectus* parrot is colored quite differently than the cock, and this isn't just a matter of a little less orange on the crown and shoulders as in the case of the Jardine's parrot *(Poicephalus gulielmi).* The female bird is colored almost

This mix of normal, pied, and pearl cockatiel babies have a good chance to live their entire lives in one home.

completely differently than the male bird, including almost all parts except, usually, the mandible (lower beak). Most of the female birds are red and purple (some also have yellow) with a black maxilla (upper beak), while the males are mostly green and blue with a light or bright orange maxilla and a black mandible.

Many people refer to the female *Eclectus* as more brightly colored than the male. This is somewhat misleading, as the females are generally darker reds and purples that would provide camouflage in dark spaces. Reds are more difficult to see in the dark. The male bird's coloring is generally a very bright, almost "electric," green that would blend in with new foliage.

And coloration is only one of their differences. *Eclectus* parrots have been observed to molt more gradually than other parrots who shed large numbers of feathers only in the summer.[14] *Eclectus* parrots produce and shed less feather dust than many other parrots. These eclectic birds may be a good choice for anyone with dust sensitivity, because their feathers more naturally resemble lory feathers than cockatoo or African grey feathers. The *Eclectus* parrot's contour feathers have a hair-like appearance rather than the broad flat leaf-like appearance of other parrots' feathers. That is not to say that the feather structure is different, but rather, the barbs do not cling as tightly to each other, leaving each barb coming off the central shaft or rachis in an individual strand. This gives the *Eclectus* parrot its famous fur-like appearance.

Possibly because of this feather peculiarity, *Eclectus* parrots have a reputation for being more physically standoffish and enjoying actual touching of the skin (but not, necessarily, the feathers) much less than cockatoos and macaws. While many companion parrots of other types enjoy an occasional head or neck scratch inside the feathers, *Eclectus* parrots prefer a different style of petting. They do not like to be petted against the direction of the growth of the feathers but often enjoy petting in the direction of the feathers as a furred pet would. Even older, said-to-be-ornery *Eclectus* can usually learn to enjoy the towel game (see p. 153) because it seems to be an extension of their great love of being hugged.

The differences between the many subspecies are more readily observable in the female than in the male birds. Additionally, the sexes have a reputation for tending to reverse the gender-related personality traits commonly assigned to parrots. That is, instead of the male being the more aggressive bird, humans can expect a companion hen *Eclectus* to often seem more aggressive than the cock.

This aggression factor in hens is often observable even in baby *Eclectus* parrots, with the males tending toward caution and the hens tending toward boldness or even, occasionally, aggression. Some baby hen *Eclectus* parrots expressing aggression are demonstrating direct response to a stimulus or exhibiting a transitional behavior that will mostly be left behind. This is a time for immediate behavioral intervention with socialization to towel play (to prevent accidental reinforcement of nips and stabs) and step-up practice with towel-covered hands, rather than step-up practice with bare hands.

This young Eclectus parrot, called a chimera, shows colors of both genders.

The bird will benefit from step-ups with hand-held perches and bare hands (once she has obviously left the nips behind). Special care must be taken to ensure that accidental reinforcement of nips does not take place, and the very best way to do this is with consistent handling with techniques designed to prevent the bite in the first place. The *Australian Birdkeeper's A Guide to* Eclectus *Parrots, Their Management, Care & Breeding* suggests that aviary-raised hens might be less aggressive "on the nest" than hand-reared hens because of "the fear factor."

Companion *Eclectus* parrots have a reputation for extremely diverse personalities, although most *Eclectus* parrots probably tend to be a bit cautious. When confronted with a new person, situation, or garment

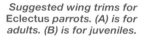

Suggested wing trims for Eclectus parrots. (A) is for adults. (B) is for juveniles.

(*Eclectus* are reportedly very sensitive to color), this bird can hold completely still, and often does so. The bird might be absolutely motionless, except that careful examination might reveal wildly bouncing, pinpointing eyes revealing the intelligence within as the bird appears to be concentrating on what to do next.

Eclectus parrots are known to reproduce human speech in softer, sweeter voices than their distant Amazon relatives. The *Eclectus* version of human speech has been said to sound seductive, but *Eclectus* screams can be deafening. They have very big voices, but, for the most part, *Eclectus* parrots don't usually choose to use them, or at least don't use them frequently. But when they do, watch out! Dianalee Deter describes the *Eclectus's* characteristic call as an "air raid siren."

Even the diet of the *Eclectus* parrot must differ, for this bird's intestines are much longer than those of any other parrot. *Eclectus* have a greater

need for vitamin A and show benefit from greater-than-normal amounts of fruit. Many *Eclectus* take great delight in eating an occasional mealworm.

Also like African greys, *Eclectus* parrots are sensitive to low calcium levels. This can have a behavioral component, as irritability has been observed in birds with low calcium levels.

Many behavior problems appearing in other types of companion birds are related to the excessively strong and protective bonds those birds form with surrogate human mates. These bonds do appear in *Eclectus* parrots, but they are neither so rigid nor exclusive in *Eclectus* as in other parrots. Maybe this is because the hen isn't as shy and reclusive as in other species. (He knows she can take care of herself?) Because these bonds differ in *Eclectus* parrots, there will be a lesser tendency to develop bonding-related behaviors such as aggression. A companion *Eclectus* will usually express an obvious preference for one human over all others, but this parrot will rarely attack non-favorite humans. An *Eclectus* parrot is more likely to try to leave than to nip.

When aggression appears, the *Eclectus* parrot tends to strike rather than stalk. This striking behavior can be observed in very young babies. It is best modified with the use of step-up practice and the towel game (see p. 153). Frequent practice of towel cuddling minimizes the bird's opportunities to strike, protects hands should the bird figure out how to strike, and eventually replaces the unreinforced behavior with a more beneficial one.

Although an *Eclectus* parrot will rarely stalk a human with malicious intent, companion *Eclectus* are famous for sneaking around, quietly making sure that they are where the action is in the home. For this reason, they must be provided with protected foraging areas. Additionally, the birds must be provided transportation to and from approved areas. Areas must be well designed to help the birds stay put, lest they be accidentally stepped on as they scoot silently from place to place.

I have seen some wonderful companion hen *Eclectus* of each subspecies that were gentle with all and handleable even by the smallest child. I have seen apparently identical hen *Eclectus* that would readily bite any human flesh that came within reach. There is much variation in disposition from bird to bird and from season to season.

The *Eclectus* Subspecies

Grand *Eclectus (Eclectus roratus roratus).* The largest of the *Eclectus* parrots, the grand *Eclectus* is said to be both well established in aviculture and thriving in its range.[15] It is probably the most common *Eclectus* in the United States, although the other subspecies are also well represented in U.S. aviculture.

Red-sided *Eclectus (Eclectus roratus polychloros).* The red-sided *Eclectus* is the largest and most colorful of the Eclectus subspecies, with

the hen birds possessing a dazzling periwinkle blue eye ring. Well represented in U.S. aviculture, both hen and cock of this race are the most colorful of this very brightly marked group, with the male bird's beak resembling a colorful concoction called a Tequila sunrise.

Vosmarie *Eclectus (Eclectus roratus vosmarie).* As with other *Eclectus* subspecies, the male vosmarie has a reputation for being gentler than the female. *Equinox@ eclectus.com* even goes so far as to report that the male vosmarie has been observed to do well in ". . . homes with small children," presuming, of course, that both bird and children are well socialized.

Solomon Island *Eclectus (Eclectus roratus solomonensis).* This bird is observed by some to have the best potential as a companion for humans. Tony Silva quotes reports describing a stronger bond between pairs in this subspecies, with breeding females reportedly being submissive to the advances of their mates. For this reason, in this subspecies only, females may be equally docile companions as males.

The Lovely, Lively Lories

There is no more vibrantly active and amusing creature on this planet than a lory. Unquestionably the most colorful of common companion parrots, they are also incredibly acrobatic. With their eye-popping

The red lory is probably the most common companion lory.

jewel-toned feathers and frantic, mind-boggling antics, lories are sometimes called feathered puppies for their exuberant, playful natures. It's not unusual to see two lories on the floor locked together, rolling over and over like growling puppies in mock battle.

Lories are bold in more than color: Behaviorally, they are among the most expressive of parrots, with astute owners always easily interpreting a lory's mood from its body language. Fast flyers and talented escape artists, they are accident-prone in the home. They are rough-and-tumble mat wrestlers who will often flip over on their backs to fight with their strong, muscular feet when frightened. This is also one of their favorite ways to play. Males are usually more territorial and temperamental than females, but that can vary with individuals and species.

Florida aviculturist Linda Greeson reports that lories are very "foot oriented," having developed extreme coordination skills in order to reach the flowers they need to eat. They must be exceptionally athletic and possessed of extraordinarily strong feet in order to climb out to the ends of very tiny, very flexible branches to eat the nectar, pollen, and buds that sustain them in the wild. Greeson also reports that her birds love to lie on their sides and foot wrestle while talking to each other.

Their domineering ways and fearless attitudes have often been painfully endured by their significant others, including significant other birds and pets. Special care must be taken to build in behavioral controls for their extreme bonding-related behaviors, for more than almost any other type of parrot, a companion lory has a reputation for abusing all but its favorite companion. This type of behavior is becoming increasingly less common, however, as advances in breeding and behavioral practice are coming to the fore.

Bold, stolid, and predictable (predictably extroverted, seldom shy) of disposition, lories are said to be the easiest birds to hand raise. However, the concept of the companion lory is relatively new to avicultural circles, for in the past, these birds were considered messy, high-strung, and unsuitable indoors. With the exception of Rosemary Low's *Encyclopedia of Lories,* published in 1998, all books previously published on the subject of lories describe their care

100

as aviary birds: birds kept only in pairs or in groups and usually maintained in flights that are at least partially outdoors.

But that was then, and this is now. With recent advances in diet, housing, and behavioral practice, lories are increasingly becoming treasured companions and confidants to humans. They are a new class of living room birds, spreading joy and laughter, and, like other companion parrots, at least a little mess in their wake. They aren't exactly common companions yet, but lories have some special advantages: they're easy to handfeed; they wean at a very young age; and they provide dazzling colors, all for a popular price.

The lory's reputation for ease of handfeeding and early weaning is unquestionably related to the bird's natural diet and to the unique structure of the bird's tongue. The brush-like tongue helps the bird to eat liquid nectar and powdered pollen from flowers, the basis of its diet in the wild. It's a significant advantage in the handfeeding and weaning process. Judging from their widespread presence in pet stores, even in chain pet stores, at this writing, lories just might be the common companion parrot of the future.

The adjustment to becoming a companion bird from being an aviary bird has not been easy in all cases. I have observed that there is an extremely short window of opportunity for teaching a young handfed lory the limits of acceptable behavior.

I have also found wild-caught lories to be less aggressive overall than handfeds who never experienced fear of humans. I lived with half a dozen wild-caught lories, handled them occasionally, and never saw one of them draw blood. In my work as a behaviorist, I am called on to modify the worst behavior. I have seen young, poorly socialized handfed rainbows who could and would bloody all but the favorite human.

Obviously, there's a difference in the ways humans socialize lories and in the ways lories socialize lories. In many ways, the lory's behavioral development and reputation in companion settings remind me of that of the quaker parrot *(Myopsyttia monachus):* they are said by some to be the best and said by some others to be the worst. Like the lovebird and the quaker parrot, lories must be carefully socialized to hand-held perches as well as to hand-to-hand step-up drills and to the towel game. Because these birds are so emotional, it's probably best to keep a towel nearby so that they can be quickly subdued if they get too wound up.

Companion characteristics are best maintained if only one lory is kept. However, these animals are so amazingly entertaining in "living room couples" (compatible birds of either different or same sexes) that the urge to include a companion lory for the companion lory is very difficult to deny. Extra care must be taken to socialize the birds well to the towel game (see p. 153) immediately upon their arrival in the new home. Like most parrots kept in pairs, they can become nippy very quickly, but this tendency seems easier to manage in lories than many other parrots. The best way to prevent the development of nipping is not to allow them to have the opportunity to nip anybody anytime.

While it will be virtually impossible to prevent most solitary companion lories from forming an extremely strong bond with one person, it is possible to teach them to allow interactions with others under most circumstances. This can usually be accomplished with daily step-up practice and towel games. Birds that are frequently reinforced for peaceful behavior are more likely to remain peaceful. Sometimes these birds are so high-strung that they must be at least occasionally step-up practiced when wet, for the exercise provided by frequent drenching showers will help these extremely active birds when living in companion settings to acceptably use up some of that excess energy. Lories must be allowed a great deal of activity to burn off excess energy that can otherwise be expressed as temperamentalism.

Lories and lorikeets have a characteristic smell, which is strong in breeding season and is quite different from that of macaws and Amazons. The family *Eos,* which includes the now nearly common blue-streak, has the strongest odor, an almost fetid floral aroma like some sweet jungle flower.

Lories do a lot of hissing, swaying, and hopping as part of their never-ending displays and postures. I remember seeing a blue-streaked lory courting a small statue on *America's Funniest Home Videos*. I was once accused of becoming a hermit when two blue-streaked lories, Heckle and Jeckle, took up residence in my living room. These birds were unbelievably amazing and amusing to watch, even for a jaded old bird person like me. For quite some time, I fought an irresistible urge to do nothing except sit and watch them.

Diet

For many years it was believed that lories in the wild were primarily nectar eaters. Indeed, lory nectar supplemented with fruit (and the inevitable insects that go with the fruit) was often said to be all they required. Modern ornithologists' studies, such as the work of Dr. Matthew Vriends, revealed that their main diet is ". . . the nectar of flowering trees, but much pollen also is devoured as well as sweet, soft fruits and berries; sometimes the soft, unripe seeds of grass and other plants are also eaten."

Dr. Vriends also reports that in the wild the lory's droppings are "well formed," but for some reason, lories in captivity have always had a reputation for runny poops. Perhaps it was because they were fed almost exclusively nectar and fruit. If captive lory droppings could go from runny to well-formed, many more homes would open up to this dazzling creature.

Increased understanding of the more solid parts of the lory's natural diet have led to the development of solid modern diets, and therefore more solid poops for lories. Tom Roudybush, MS, an avian nutritionist, suggests that humans probably unintentionally caused the lory's former reputation for runny poops by feeding a diet too high in water that stimulated excessive kidney activity. He reminds us that deficiencies in a seed diet can kill a lory more quickly than any other parrot. While some immature and sprouted seeds are tolerated, even relished, avoid especially dry, hard seeds found in old-fashioned parrot mixes from the stores. Roudybush relates that his clients report excellent long-term results from feeding powdered Roudybush dry parrot formula to lories. He suggests that lory diets be supplemented with nectar, either as a powder or diluted, two days weekly in an amount approximately equal to one half the daily volume of regular food.

Rosemary Low suggests that dry diets may be appropriate for the lories she calls omnivorous, such as rainbow, red, and blue-streaked, but not for the predominantly liquid-feeding species, such as Duivenbode's. Several lory owners and breeders reported in data collection for this book that their lories were temperamental if they did not have frequent supplementation with nectar. This is probably related to the speed of the lory's metabolism, which is dependent upon sugar. Because the dry lory diets are so new, it's important to have regular veterinary diagnostics run to ensure that the bird is receiving an appropriate, healthy diet.

Diet-related health problems in lories include liver problems caused by fat or iron, as well as candida related to sugar content in the diet. Dr. Jerry LaBonde also reminds us to avoid honey, reporting that while honey itself is fine for lories, it can carry harmful microorganisms, and that lories can develop various health-related problems if honey is fed.

Special Accommodations

The way lories eat is more like squashing something. Each piece of moist food is systematically smashed until there's only a flat piece of pulp left. Then the bird shakes its head and throws the piece of pulp out of the beak before starting on the next piece. This leaves sort of pre-dried cement-like fruit and vegetable residue stuck to anything it reaches. For this reason, it's a good idea to have Plexiglas® lining the areas of the cage where the bird eats and to waterproof walls and accessories nearby.

Because they will play with anything that isn't tied down, lories must be fed in dump-proof bowls. Because they are known for frequent water games, if they are to be left alone all day, lories should also be provided with water in a tube so that when they play away all the water in the bowl, there will still be water to drink. Breeder Michele Traugutt reports that lories also frequently contaminate their water, as they love to dunk toys and food and then fish for them. Dr. Matthew Vriends reports that most of the lory species commonly kept as companions prefer to sleep in a nest box. Perhaps this is one way these brightly colored birds avoid predation in the wild. In the living room they can be injured if startled in the dark, so some form of privacy protection is recommended, even if it's just a towel over one end of the cage. Living room lories might burrow under newspapers to sleep or hang like bats in a corner.

Companion Lory Behavior

Lories can be domineering to the point of harassing literally every living creature in a household except one (or maybe even everyone). Usually, however, if the bird is well handled during the honeymoon period just after weaning, its interactive behavior can be carefully maintained. It's very difficult to resocialize a lory that has decided it is intended to stalk anything that breathes except the primary person.

Socializing handfed lories is not unlike socializing other handfed parrots. However, they will require a little more environmental planning and extremely consistent behavioral practice from the very first days in the home, for these birds mature very quickly. The period of cooperative behavior followed by the development of the individual agendas (possessiveness, jealousy, and territorialism) is brief. A lory must *not* learn that it can get its way by intentionally causing pain. While lory beaks are softer than the beaks of other parrots and don't often draw blood, their nips can be incredibly painful.

The real secret of successfully socializing companion lories, however, is effective wing feather trims combined with socializing them to interact well with tools and providing adequate exercise. These amazing critters are so excitable that they can turn nippy in an instant. If a companion lory uses energy appropriately (flapping, playing, and bathing), there is less energy left to act up. If they are well socialized to interact with towels (see the towel game, p. 153), and if a towel is always within reach, those excited nips can be avoided and, indeed, habitual nipping will be completely eliminated or, rather, prevented. This

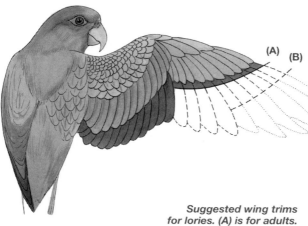

(A) (B)

Suggested wing trims for lories. (A) is for adults. (B) is for juveniles.

"tools" method of interacting includes toys as well as towels. If you always have a hand-held toy or two to stick between your hand and the bird's beak, both your hand and the bird will be happy.

One of the most closely guarded secrets about lory behavior is their reputation for very understandable human speech. Linda Greeson reports that red, chattering, and rainbow lories are "such good talkers it's scary." Their voices are sometimes described as being as accurate as the African grey, mimicking human voices so perfectly that you can tell exactly who it is that the bird is copying. Like African parrots, they are less loud in general than their New World cousins. Also like Africans, they are gifted mimics of electronic devices, sometimes learning an electronic phone ring so accurately that humans in the home don't know whether to answer the phone or to tell the bird to be quiet.

Occasionally accused of being "grudge poopers," lories have been said to squirt disfavored persons and other pets from across the room. I have not seen this behavior, in spite of living for several years with four lories in the living room and spending huge numbers of hours with those particular birds.

Although I have seen many human/bird relationships wrecked by adding a parrot companion for that bird, I have seen several charming companion lory situations in which the birds lived with a same-sex companion of the same species. These "living room pairs" were active, playful, and not usually handled by humans, except with perches or towel-covered hands. They were also fantastically amusing to watch. Rosemary Low advises that if same-species companions are to be acquired, find birds the same age and raise them together rather than run the risk of an adult or adolescent bird abusing the new baby parrot.

Lories appear to have the opposite attitudes about copulation to those of *Poicepahlus,* birds that are often so shy that they mate secretly, often in the nest box. My blue-streaked lories were much more interested in public displays of affection. Actually they were motivated by crowds, being literally exhibition copulators who preferred to mate whenever they were on display in front of large groups of people at the various shows and conventions we attended together.

Lories are fantastic flyers and gifted escape artists. They form extremely strong bonds both with other lories and with humans, and because of the strength of the bonds and the lories' gift for maintaining contact with shrill, easily audible calls, they are usually quite easily recaptured. It's easier to prevent flyaways by keeping a lory's (and especially, a lorikeet's), wing feathers meticulously trimmed and never taking the bird outdoors without a cage or carrier.

According to Vriends, some lories are long-distance flyers in the wild, even exhibiting a nomadic lifestyle. This nomadic behavior may be the reason why the companion lory's territorial bonds are stronger for the favored person than for any particular territory. Also for this reason, lories often respond well to outings as a means of fulfilling curiosity and exploration needs as well as improving bonding with less-favored humans. Sometimes just putting the lory into the carrier and driving it around in the car will help to ease the bird through a temperamental period.

The Common Lories

Rainbow Lorikeet *(Trichoglossus).* This multi-species group is known for "million dollar colors at a pauper's price." The rainbow lory is probably both the most inexpensive and the most high-strung of the common companions in this genus.

There are more than 20 subspecies of rainbow lorikeets.

Although Matthew Vriends reports that there are more than 30 subspecies of this dazzling animal, we most commonly see the green-naped rainbow lorikeet *(Trichoglossus haemodatus)* in companion settings in the United States. This bird is a well-known nomad that benefits behaviorally from safe, contained outings with both favored and less-favored humans.

Red Lory *(Eos bornea bornea).* The red lory was probably the first lory seen as a common companion in the United States. This bird is only slightly less high-strung than the blue-streaked lory, which is usually a little less high-strung than the rainbow lories. Easily tamed as wild-caughts, red lory handfeds seem more docile than most handfed rainbows. *Eos* lories respond well to food rewards.

Chattering Lory *(Lorus garrulus garrulus).* In spite of the implications of their name, the chattering lory is perceived as the quietest of the common companion lories, except possibly Duivenbode's. It's not that the chattering lories can't be loud. They can be, and their voices are at least as shrill and piercing as any other lory, but the companion chattering lory is less high-strung than its *Eos* and *Trichoglossus* cousins and doesn't usually choose to use that shrill call so often. The chattering lory, like the red lory, has a reputation as an excellent talker.

Blue-streaked Lory *(Eos reticulata).* This subspecies of the red lory is a relatively recent arrival in the

U.S. marketplace. Its beauty, ease of reproduction, ease of transitioning to new homes, and relatively low price have made it probably the most accessible lory available to the public at this writing.

I had never seen blue-streaked lories until I was given a couple of charming young imported cocks in about 1985. Why had we not seen these birds before? Why were they suddenly available everywhere? Rosemary Low explains: "Beginning in the 1980s we started seeing more unusual lories in the pet trade than ever before. Logging roads were being bored into the jungles of Indonesia, and these previously inaccessible sites were yielding previously untraded types of lories. Several glorious birds like the blue-streaked lory were suddenly as available as the corner pet store."

Blue-streaks may be the hissingest, swayingest, sexiest of this group. These birds can hardly be called secretive copulators, with some birds becoming obviously excited and sexually active when numerous humans are present, the more the merrier. A sexually excited blue-streaked lory really "wowed" the whole country on *America's Funniest Home Videos* in 1993 as it actively courted a tiny statue.

Duivenbode's Lory *(Chalcopsitta duivenbodei).* Admittedly uncommon, Duivenbode's lory has a reputation as the best companion bird in this group. This species is called the "glossy lories," and they are an exquisite treat for the eye.

Duivenbode's lory is unbelievably gorgeous and is usually absolutely meticulous about maintaining perfect feathers. In captivity, we might see baby tail and, occasionally, cage fray in adult tail feathers, but in most adults, every golden brown, yellow, and violet feather will be clean and tight.

Duivenbode's lory must be kept at human room temperature, as they are known to be intolerant of cold. Although not exactly common, Duivenbode's are occasionally available in Florida, California, Oregon, and, rarely, in other parts of the United States.

Other Pacific Distribution Parrots: Kakarikis and Grasskeets

Kakarikis, Rosellas, and Bourke's parakeets, long-time residents of the aviary, have also begun appearing in living rooms around the United States. These birds can't exactly be called common companions yet, but the potential is there, with home breeders turning out more and more handfed domestic birds every year.

Each of these birds is characterized by great beauty, especially the Rosellas and Bourke's. Rosellas, but not Bourke's, should acquire human words. Both Rosellas and Bourke's often come with truly lovely natural songs.

Suggested wing trims for grasskeets. (A) is for adults. (B) is for juveniles.

and curious, these birds love playing whistling games and noncontact peek-a-boo.

Good flyers every one, these birds must have spacious cages or flights and must be wing feather trimmed if allowed liberty in the home. They can startle easily and take flight suddenly, sometimes causing injury even in familiar rooms. They should be well socialized to step-ups both with hands, hand-held perches, and towels from a very early age.

The Common Grass Parakeets

Kakariki *(Cyanoamphus nova-ezelandaie).* These active little parakeets look a little like miniature conures. They love to climb and benefit from horizontal cage bars. Because of high activity levels and constant movement, this bird is very difficult to keep tame as a pet. What we miss in personal interaction, we gain in entertainment, however, for Kakarikis are tremendously interesting to watch maneuver about the cage. Even full-flighted Kakarikis seem to prefer climbing to flying. These birds love leaf bathing. Males tend to aggression.

Eastern Rosella and Western Rosella *(Platycercus eximius* and *Platycercus icterotis).* This is a strong, beautiful bird. Males tend to aggression when kept in pairs.[16] While these birds can have a really beautiful song, they can also be loud. They are generally well suited to humans who do not expect to handle

Most of these parakeets are considered peaceful but have a reputation for being high-strung. Many who keep them expect more side-by-side interaction, with birds and humans enjoying independent activities, rather than face-to-face interaction. A grasskeet that likes a particular human will want to sit as close to that favorite human as possible. Active

Like the Eastern and Western Rosellas, the Pennant Rosella is strikingly beautiful and develops a beautiful natural song.

them, but who appreciate them for their aloof quality and beauty.

Pale-headed Rosella *(Platycercus adscitus).* A stunning bird that is, again, well suited to humans who love to look and whistle and sing with their birds, but not necessarily touch them. Maintaining this bird on a physically interactive level with humans is difficult, but a good rapport can easily be maintained for side-by-side interactions.

Bourke's Parakeet *(Neopsephotus bourkii).* These lovely little pastel birds are reportedly active in the wild at dawn, dusk, and on bright moonlit nights. As a companion, they are said to be trusting and agreeable when not breeding. They are charming companions with virtually no tendency to chew or scream. Although Bourke's seldom learn even one human word, they are often treasured companions and highly prized for their beauty and for their pleasant, enjoyable voices.

The Kakariki benefits from consistent handling from an early age.

[13]Lantermann, Werner and Susan, *Cockatoos,* Hauppauge, NY: Barron's Educational Series, 1989, p. 5.

[14]*A Guide to* Eclectus *Parrots, Their Management, Care & Breeding,* South Tweed Heads, Australia: *Australian Birdkeeper,* 1991, p. 6.

[15]Sweeney, Roger G., *The Eclectus,* Port Perry, ON: Silvio Mattacchione & Co., 1993, p. 17.

[16]Wolter, Anette, *The Long-Tailed Parakeets,* Hauppauge, NY: Barron's Educational Series, 1992, pp. 66–67.

Chapter Six

General Care and Other Considerations

Bringing the New Baby Bird Home

Before bringing the new baby parrot home, ask the breeder or dealer to check to be sure that the

Ask for a proper wing trim. The first day in the home is the most common day for a bird to accidentally fly away. (Blue-and-gold macaw.)

bird's wing feathers are properly trimmed. The first day home is one of the most common days for an accident, especially for an improperly trimmed bird to fly into something and be hurt or to be blown away. Be sure that the baby bird has been trimmed in the manner suggested in this book (see the chapter and illustration for the specific type of bird).

Whether or not the new baby is trimmed as suggested, *do not* trust that the bird can't fly until you get to know this individual bird better. Some birds can fly with very little wing feather, and a newly purchased baby bird has no business outdoors unless it's in the cage or in a carrier.

For the first week or so, it's a good idea to keep the baby a little warmer (about 5°F) (about 2.8°C) than usual. Try to find out what temperature the bird is used to. If it's cold outside, warm up the car before taking the newly weaned baby to the car. Carry the bird in a rigid carrier that can be belted into the car for safety.

Most dealers will give a reasonable guarantee of the bird's health. Take the bird as soon as possible to an experienced avian veterinarian for a complete blood panel and any other tests that the veterinarian recommends. Some breeders, like Dave Flom and Mary Karlquist of Minnesota, go so far as to suggest the time of day to take the baby bird to the veterinarian. They say, when taking the new baby to the veterinarian, try to make the first appointment of the day so that the baby bird won't be exposed to other birds in the veterinarian's waiting room. Dave even suggests that the bottom of the bird's cage or carrier be wrapped in a plastic garbage bag if it is to be set on the floor of the veterinarian's office.

Many veterinarians suggest that the bird go to the veterinarian in its own cage. In this way, the doctor has an opportunity to examine and evaluate droppings, cage setup, and other elements related to husbandry.

Be sure to ask the veterinarian whether or not the bird's band fits properly or whether it should be removed. Some parrots are prone to band-related accidents, especially if the band it too large and fits loosely on the bird's leg. In most cases, an experienced avian veterinarian will probably recommend removing a poorly fitting band immediately.

Some bands are so loose that they can be slipped off. An experienced groomer, behaviorist, breeder, or veterinarian would be able to see if the bird's shortest toe could be positioned back through the band, and then a too-large band can sometimes be slipped off over the joint of

the other three toes (this toe-holding technique is probably the way most baby birds' bands were applied). Some bands must be cut off, a process usually involving anesthesia in the case of a stainless steel band, or a jeweler's ring cutter in the case of an aluminum band. A bird without a band can have its DNA registered for identification purposes through Zoogen, Inc. at a very modest cost.

If possible, go to an avian veterinarian who does not usually work with the dealer from whom the bird was purchased. Expect the veterinarian to recommend laboratory tests. The costs of these tests are

A too-large band can be dangerous and represent a hanging hazard to a companion bird. (African grey.)

A band this large can often be removed by slipping it carefully over the two back toes and easing it over the foot. (African grey.)

not usually part of the bird's health guarantee from the seller, but they could save much expense and heartache down the road if the baby bird turns out to be harboring unseen illness. If the diagnostic tests determine that the bird has a health problem, a responsible dealer honoring a guarantee will provide treatment. Some dealers will expect the bird to be returned to them for treatment.

Try to bring the baby parrot home as early as possible during the day so that the bird can become accustomed to its surroundings before dark. Keep a towel over about one half of the cage for at least the first few days. Provide the baby bird with a night light, maybe one of those that plugs into an electrical socket, especially if there are pets in the home that might move around in the dark. Be careful to quarantine the new bird from contact with any other birds in the home until the veterinarian says such interaction is not dangerous. Most veterinarians will probably recommend a quarantine period of at least 30 days.

Watch the bird carefully to determine whether or not it's eating. Occasionally, a newly weaned baby parrot might quit eating independently as a result of some factor related to the move. See When the New Baby Won't Eat Independently (p. 146).

Be sure to provide the diet the bird was eating before coming to this home. Additions such as warm foods like oatmeal and macaroni (no salt) can feel like love to a newly weaned baby parrot. Offer these warm, com-fort foods daily for a while to enhance your bond with the bird as well as guarantee a smooth transition to the new home. Eventually, the bird will probably refuse anything that seems like baby food. Everything most people need to know about companion parrot diet is available in Petra Burgmann's *Feeding Your Pet Bird* (Barron's Educational Series, 1993).

Parrots grow wise very quickly. They are adept at manipulating humans. In most parrots there is probably a window of opportunity of a few weeks or a few months to implement appropriate socialization practices before unwanted behaviors begin to appear. Reread the sections on behavioral development and early socialization, for the ability to introduce and reinforce appropriate behaviors during the time the bird is a baby will affect the bird's behavior for the rest of its life.

The Cage

Every companion parrot needs a cage of its own. The cage is the bird's retreat. This is where the bird can relax and feel secure. No surprises occur here. There are toys to play with and food to eat. There are no demands made and no threats.

In addition to making the bird feel safe, the cage also helps keep the bird physically safe. Birds love to explore. Left unsupervised, they are in danger of being stepped on or shut in doors. They might decide to chew on an electrical cord or a poisonous plant or to take a dive in the toilet. A typical curious parrot can get into a surprising amount of trouble in a typical human environment.

Baby's First Cage

Some baby birds can come home and go directly into a large cage that can accommodate their needs for life. Some baby birds need a cage designed especially for the periods of behavioral development they will go through during the first year or two.

Especially, shyer species such as greys and *Poicephalus* can have a bad reaction to the wrong first cage. The shy baby parrot's first cage should be small, safe, intimate. But almost any baby parrot can exhibit a poor adjustment to a first cage. An inappropriate cage for a baby parrot might be too hard to climb, with too many vertical bars and not enough horizontal bars. An inappropriate cage might be too large to provide a sense of security for the baby.

A bird that is having a bad reaction to a too-large cage might thrash, fall, and engage in multiple attention-demanding behaviors. It might revert to wanting to be handfed; it might begin chewing feathers or developing redundant fearful behaviors.

If a large permanent cage has already been purchased and the bird is reacting to the size, the bird's perception of the cage can be manipulated by providing a raised grate, making the cage seem smaller. Simply use self-locking cable ties to secure the grate or a homemade "false grate" to a higher group of hor-izontal bars. Once the baby bird begins developing confidence and independence, the grate can be lowered. If it's difficult or impossible to raise the grate, some birds adjust successfully to lowering the perches to near the bottom, then gradually raising them as the baby's coordination and confidence increase.

To increase the parrot's feeling of security, the top of the baby cage might be covered, extending down 4 or 5 inches (10–13 cm) on all sides of the cage. The bird can go up into the top for privacy in much the same way it might go up into a tree. (Such a cage cover is best placed on the cage while the baby bird is not inside.)

The Permanent Cage

Once most parrots are 18 to 24 months old, they have usually developed the confidence necessary to move to a permanent cage. A parrot that is frequently out of the cage doesn't require a cage as large as a parrot that is frequently left in the cage for long periods. If the bird is in an open play area most of the day, and the cage is used primarily as a sleeping or roost cage, then there is no real need for a larger cage. However, if the bird is expected to spend the entire day in the cage while humans work, or if the bird has to stay in the cage for extended periods when humans are on vacation, a larger cage is required.

The bird's emotional needs are also a factor in determining proper cage size. While some parrots do not feel secure in a cage that is too large, some seem almost claustrophobic in a too-small cage. Each particular bird's reaction to its cage is important, for a cage that might seem appropriate to one parrot might contribute to neurotic behaviors in another.

It's usually best to buy the largest cage feasible for the human living space. Sides with horizontal bars encourage companion birds to exercise by climbing up and down the sides. While they can certainly climb up and down vertical cage bars if they really want to, most birds must have more motivation to do so. Without horizontal bars, they will climb up and down less often and rely on walking back and forth on the perches for exercise. At least two sides of the cage (whether on the sides or the front and back) should have all horizontal bars. A cage with too few horizontal bars will contribute to sedentary behavior and failure of curiosity.

A good cage is safe for the bird and easy for humans to maintain. The easier the cage is to maintain, the longer most people will enjoy the relationship with their bird. Look for bird-proof door closures and those wonderful wing-like mess catchers that contain both the mess and the bird. Some modern cages have tear-off rolls of paper to simplify cage cleaning. Most of them are self-supporting units on wheels for easy access to cleaning, and many of them have three or more bowls for food and water. Avoid round, domed, or cylindrical cages, except in very

large cages or flights for very confident species. An arched top rectangular cage is fine for most birds.

Features

A large door is important in helping to prevent fearful behaviors as a response to going into and out of the cage. The bird should be able to sit comfortably on the hand without having to duck while going through the door.

Composition. A good cage for a companion parrot is best made from noncorrosive metal, never wood or Plexiglas®. Acceptable substances include steel, brass or chrome plate, and welded wire that is no longer shiny. Painted cages are potentially dangerous. Powder-coated cages will usually stand up to the test of a medium-sized parrot's beak and are usually very safe. A wooden cage will be reduced to toothpicks eventually no matter what kind of wood is used. Hardware cloth or shiny welded wire is usually coated with zinc, which is toxic. Welded wire can easily be made safe by scrubbing the surfaces with detergent and a wire brush or by leaving the cage outside and exposed to the elements until it becomes dull. Hardware cloth is always dangerous to chewing birds.

Structure. The cage should be structured so that there are no openings between the bars that are large enough for the bird to put its head through or small enough to catch a toe. Ornamental wires or bars are usually best avoided. Many birds can get legs or feet caught in bars that form a "V." Avoid round or cylindrical cages, as most birds feel safer with a flat back wall and corners. Square or rectangular cages offer more surfaces for climbing. Domed shapes may have bar spacing that gets progressively narrower toward the top; this is a dangerous configuration that can trap and injure parrot toes.

Quality. A good quality cage will have bars that are too thick for the bird to bend. The places where the bars join will be smooth. There will be no sharp edges within the little parrot's reach. It will not be easy to disassemble, or else the bird will take it apart. The finish should not be flaky. Remember that the bird's lifetime could be 40 years or more.

Serviceability. A cage that is easy to maintain can minimize the few unpleasant aspects of keeping a parrot. The doors should be easily opened and easily locked. Food and water dishes should be easily removed and replaced. The cage should be easy to clean, with a removable tray and, preferably, a removable grate. Some birds like to roll around on the bottom of the cage. A grate will keep them from rolling in their feces and old food, which is a disease hazard. The bars of the grate should be as close together as the bars in the rest of the cage.

Introducing the Youngster to a New Cage

While some birds can merely be removed from one cage and locked into another cage, most juvenile or baby companion parrots are best induced to choose to move to a new cage. This can usually be accomplished easily by placing the new cage in the position of the beloved old cage with the old cage beside it for a day or two. If the bird freely enters the new cage and seeks toys and food there, then in a day or so, food and water can be removed from the old cage during most of the day. By the second or third day, if the bird is eating in the new cage, the old cage can have all toys and perches removed, and can be set on the floor or laid on its back so that the bird will be more or less required to complete the move to the new cage.

Height and Location

Feelings of happiness, safety, and security should be associated with the height and location of the cage in the home. Most parrots like to be located in an area where they can experience the most interaction with their human flock members and still feel safe. A cage that is exposed on all sides will not seem secure, so avoid placing the cage in the middle of the room or against a window. A bird located beside a high-traffic doorway could experience fear reactions whenever anyone unexpectedly rushes through.

An ideal location would be against a wall and across the room from entrances and heavy traffic areas. Shelter may be important to some parrots' feelings of safety, and parrots just love peeking out from behind plants and toys.

Many birds love to spend lots of time on top of their cages holding on and flapping like crazy. The cage top should be comfortable for this activity. A flat-topped cage or one that is only slightly arched is best. If a cage-top perch is used, be sure that the highest point where the bird can sit comfortably is also easily gripped for strenuous flapping. The highest point on the cage should also be easily reached by humans needing cooperative responses for step-ups. Cage-top play can be encouraged in birds that exhibit shyness or fearfulness when they are lower; this might include cockatiels, grey parrots, and *Poicephalus.*

On the Perch

A perch is more than a place to sit. Appropriate perches build confidence, maintain beak and nails, provide opportunities for independent behavior, and prevent uneven wear on the feet. They are the most significant element in the cage environment, for a companion bird needs a place to sit every minute that it isn't hanging, climbing, or socializing with humans.

The most common perches available in stores are horizontal perches made of smooth hardwood dowel, PVC, manzanita, or, in some places, madrone. These perches are hard and difficult or impossible for most birds to chew up. They have no bark or thin bark that is not easily peeled, but they are more easily cleaned than soft wood perches. These perch materials are suitable as durable perches for larger birds such as macaws and cockatoos, but they don't fulfill all the needs of most birds, especially smaller birds.

Also available commercially are cholla wood perches, which are hollow cactus wood with many holes. They are porous, have no chewable bark, and are not easily cleaned, but they are relatively inexpensive and can be thrown away and replaced regularly. They are easy to grip and an excellent medium for preventing falls in baby birds, in birds with a weak grip, or in birds whose toenails are overgroomed.

The most desirable wood occasionally available in stores is citrus. Citrus wood has the advantage of being a little softer than the other commercially available woods, with bark that can be peeled even by smaller birds. Some other fruit woods are occasionally available, but avoid apple and other fruit woods bearing fruits with poisonous pits, as these can be toxic during certain times of the year.

Hardwood perches can be made more comfortable by wrapping them with cotton rope or twine. Cotton rope perches, stiffened with wire throughout, are now available in most places. Rope perches should be stiff, not flexible, as limp rope used as a perch is difficult to get onto and off of, and will contribute to sedentary behavior in parrots who sit on rope exclusively. The option of a climbing rope can accomplish the opposite behavioral result.

Special perches are now available for the grooming of toenails. Usually made of a coarse stone-like concrete material, these perches should not be installed as the highest perch in the cage because the bird spends so much time sleeping there and uncomfortable wear patterns could result on the feet and nails. In the wild, most parrots roost or sleep in trees on wooden branches. A more natural placement of these stone-like nail-grooming perches is beside the water source, which might be one of the only places a parrot might sit on rocks in the wild.

Perch Size

A bird sitting on approximately the same size perches day in and day out will have uneven wear patterns on the bottom surfaces of the feet. The skin may appear red or irritated as the feet wear unevenly. Dianalee Deter taught me that a patch of irritated skin across the middle of the foot indicates that that part of the bird's foot is supporting all the bird's weight on the perch and that the perch is too small. Wear on the outer pads of the toes indicates that the perches may be too large (and, of course, birds on too-large perches might fall and injure themselves or their dispositions).

Perches should be of a variety of diameters (and textures and hardness) so that some perches may be gripped tightly for flapping exercise and some may be perched upon with extended toenails contacting the abrasive bark so that toenails are subjected to abrasive wear. It's probably best to situate the largest perch in the highest place or where the bird customarily sleeps.

It's not uncommon for perches in a new cage to be much too large for the bird that will occupy the cage. This can easily occur when a well-meaning owner selects the largest possible cage for the new bird. As discussed previously, the largest possible cage is not always the most appropriate for a new baby bird, but it may be a tremendously helpful element in the successful adjustment of a resale bird. However, a large cage usually comes with large diameter perches that must be replaced if the cage is used for smaller birds. Perches should not be placed above food and water dishes as this can cause them to be fouled.

The Development of Fearfulness

Appropriate perches are the first line of defense in preventing the development of anxiety and fearfulness that can so easily progress into

Baby greys gain coordination, confidence, and stamina from gripping the perch and flapping. (Timneh African greys.)

self-mutilation in treasured young birds. Appropriate perches provide a grippable, irregular surface enabling the early development of a sure grip. Babies that fall less not only suffer fewer broken feathers, they are also more confident and less likely to express fearful reactions such as falling then thrashing about at the approach of a stranger. This is extremely important, for fearfulness may be at least as significant in the development of feather chewing as failure to develop appropriate chewing and preening behaviors.

Some behaviorists suggest that if the baby parrot is falling frequently, the grate should be either removed or padded with towels, then newspaper. This will help to prevent both damaged feathers and phobias related to getting a wing or leg stuck between the bars of the grate. My approach to this problem is to supply many interesting, forked small and larger diameter branches so that the baby can develop grip and confidence by preventing the fall in the first place. As I have mentioned previously, the grate can also be moved up to prevent injury from occasional baby parrot falls.

Providing multiple branches, even though the bird may choose to sit on or chew up only a few branches, adds to the development of confidence, as it also provides opportunities to make successful decisions. Whether a bird chooses to sit on the highest branch even though it may be almost vertical or the most horizontal branch even though it may be relatively low allows the bird to develop curiosity, evaluation, and processing skills and related mental, physical, and behavioral patterns that are normal and necessary in the living room environment.

In addition, if the indoor environment remains unchanged for long periods of time, a bird can easily develop fearful responses to any form of change: new people, objects, or situations. The periodic introduction of fresh branches in interesting, stimulating configurations helps to condition the bird to accept changes without fear or aggression, for it is stress caused by changelessness that is at the heart of many unpleasant companion parrot behaviors.

The Development of Appropriate Chewing Behaviors

The most compelling need for branches with bark, however, is to provide birds with an opportunity to learn appropriate chewing behaviors. Chewing is a major behavioral component in the day-to-day life of a normal cavity-breeding bird. It is a necessary part of sexual expression in a wild parrot. The amount of time spent chewing usually increases during the early lifetime of the bird, probably peaking during prime breeding years.

Baby parrots can learn to splinter smooth hardwood dowel. Some do, but many do not learn it easily or immediately. In addition, if a parrot learns to splinter smooth wood, then any smooth wood—the table, the window sill, the picture frame—that the bird can reach may be considered fair game. It is observably eas-ier for young birds to first learn to peel bark from branches. Additionally, the provision of identifiably different bird-chewing wood facilitates training away from the culturally unacceptable behavior of destroying the furniture and the woodwork.

Selection, Preparation, and Presentation of Branches

I like to provide a variety of textures of wood, preferring those that are neither too soft nor too hard. Apple, apricot, cherry, plum, and some other fruits may be usually or sometimes safe for birds, although they may sometimes contain cyanide in bark, leaves, and seed kernels. Apple branches have been reported to cause allergic reactions in some birds (double yellow-headed Amazons) at certain times of year. Also poisonous are boxwood, oak, yew, wisteria, black walnut, and horse chestnut. When I am gathering branches for my own use, I prefer to avoid all fruit woods; when I am buying branches from a dependable supplier, I presume their various fruit wood branches are safe.

In addition to naturally-occurring toxins, one must guard against offering wood with introduced toxins: insecticides, herbicides, and lead from auto exhaust fumes. Avoid sick looking trees that grow along freeways as they may be hydrocarbon polluted. Branches should be cleaned with bleach water (a ratio of ¼ cup (60 ml) bleach to 1 quart (1 liter) water), then thoroughly rinsed, dried, and carefully examined for insects.

(Even purchased perches should be cleaned, unless they are in sealed covers, bags, or containers.)

Branches are ideally presented in tree-like positions, with forks occurring at multiple different angles in addition to horizontal. They can be attached in tree-like positions to the sides of cages with wire, twine, tape, or plastic self-locking cable ties available in the electrical department at the hardware store. Toys may be hung from higher branches. If the branch is set in a Christmas tree stand, concrete, or situated on the floor, lower branches must be removed to inhibit roaming.

Hardness

Manzanita is probably the most common commercially available branch. In some places it may be the only commercially available branch. As mentioned previously, manzanita is easy to clean and relatively permanent; but while this hardwood functions well as a perch, several other types of branches provide more opportunities for appropriate chewing behaviors, especially for smaller birds. Manzanita is often so hard and has so little bark that it might as well be concrete (except that it has none of the abrasive properties of concrete). Manzanita is excellent as semipermanent perches for large hookbills that go through anything else in a day, but even these buzz saw birds should have access to multiple textures of perches and toys to destroy in order to combat boredom.

Woods of medium hardness are good for medium and smaller birds and birds with understimulated chewing interests. Loro Parque in the Canary Islands gives their parrots fresh pine branches weekly. I like all the members of the poplar family, because they are exceptionally peelable. The bark of birch, poplar, and aspen can be removed in a variety of interesting sizes and shapes by almost any artistic and enterprising bird.

Soft woods are good for stimulating chewing in birds with a history of attention-demanding behaviors, failure of independence, or failure of curiosity. I prefer the weed tree, Ailanthus *(Ailanthus altissima),* which, although taller, resembles common sumac. Ailanthus, an Indonesian tree, was introduced into the United States in the mid 1700s. Its name is a Moluccan word meaning "tree that grows up to the sky." These trees are commonly called "trees of heaven" in the United States. They are now common in most eastern and central urban environments. Ailanthus is frequently observed in U.S. zoos. This tree is a weed and is (in)famous for prospering even when it grows from cracks in the sidewalk (remember *A Tree Grows in Brooklyn?*).

Less substantial, but also safe, are the woods from smooth, shiny, or staghorn sumac (*Rhus copallina, glabra,* and *typhina,* respectively). These common dry-land weed trees differ significantly from their rarer marsh-dwelling cousin, poison sumac *(Toxicodendron verivix),* the leaves and bark of which have caustic effect on human skin. Both Ailanthus and sumac are too soft to be practical for voracious chewers but are well suited to smaller birds such as budgies, conures, quakers, *Poicephalus,* and African greys.

Behavioral Applications

Most companion parrots in the United States today, except for the quaker parrot, are cavity-breeding creatures who feel sexual motivation to chew wood. Unless a particular bird is suffering from failure of curiosity or is tremendously over-stimulated, most companion parrots respond favorably to the addition of branches with peelable bark. Older parrots are usually more voracious chewers, as motivation to chew wood develops as the bird matures and is especially apparent during the nest-search phase of breeding cycles.

Appropriate branches with interesting fresh bark can be instrumental in the prevention of feather chewing, screaming, and other attention-demanding behaviors. Most branches can be presented with or without leaves. Some birds prefer to chew the leaves off branches, and some react fearfully to leaves.

An enterprising bird will methodically eliminate all leaves, twigs, and loose bark, eventually remodeling the indoor "bird tree" to resemble those smooth perches I like to avoid. And then, it is time to replace them, for while this beak-modeled shape is not inappropriate, I believe it is just

this remodeling process that helps to save our parrot companions from the mind-numbing boredom that can contribute to screaming, fearfulness, lethargy, feather chewing, and other common parrot behavior problems.

Low-stress Grooming: A Behavioral Perspective

Grooming can be traumatic to an unprepared bird. Some veterinarians occasionally even recommend anesthesia for grooming very reactive or uncooperative birds. However, with a little socialization and sensitive grooming techniques, anesthesia should be unnecessary for almost all companion birds. Some forms of low-stress grooming are even possible on poorly socialized or otherwise unconditioned birds.

The following techniques are intended to be minimally invasive, both in the process of the grooming and in the effect of the grooming on the bird's future confidence, and on its ability to comfortably regrow feathers. Even low-stress grooming can be scary the first time, however, and conditioning to tolerate grooming is an important part of being a responsible parrot owner.

The Least Invasive Procedure

Most companion birds I groom, including regular clients and "tame" incidental grooming clients, will endure having their wing feathers trimmed without toweling. Trimming can often be accomplished even with a bird that has not been conditioned to tolerate this procedure. Therefore, I consider trimming only wing feathers without toweling to be the least invasive form of companion bird grooming. This ultra-modest grooming technique is especially appropriate for a baby parrot's first grooming, and subsequent groomings of usually cautious birds such as African greys and *Poicephalus* parrots. Feathers are minimally trimmed to allow wings to retain a little wind resistance so that the bird is able to fall or dive safely. On the other hand, this is not the type of wing feather trim that can ever be trusted outdoors. This is an indoor trim for maximum comfort for indoor birds. Birds trimmed as suggested here should be unable to lift off indoors, but not outdoors.

Because it's easy for poor balance, falls, and other effects of improper grooming to contribute to behavioral problems, companion birds should be trimmed absolutely symmetrically for the bird's maximum comfort and confidence. Baby birds, especially heavy-bodied baby birds, need very little trimming to effectively ground them indoors. No wing trim should be trusted outdoors where a strong gust of wind can blow even a severely trimmed bird away. We will trim only four to seven of the outer primary flight feathers (four feathers in younger birds, and up to seven feathers in hearty older birds). We will gauge our cuts based on how much of the feather extends out of the shorter covering feathers or coverts. For baby birds, we'll trim away about half of the part of the feathers showing beyond the coverts, but older birds and better flyers may require trimming up to two thirds of the visible part of the primary feathers extending past the coverts (when the wing is viewed from above or behind).

If the wing is gripped carefully at the shoulder and is gently stretched out, up, and away from the bird, the bird can't reach the groomer's fingers with its beak. It might take a little practice, conditioning, and loving reinforcement to acclimate the bird to allow its wings to be extended. Be sure not to hold or extend the wing only by the feathers, as this can be painful to the bird.

This balanced minimal wing trim also works well for most mature African greys. The remaining feather length provides good support for new feather growth and adequate balance for the bird to enjoy holding onto the top of the cage for energetic flapping.

Trimming for Safety

The bird's safety is the primary goal of wing feather trimming. The bird's comfort is the secondary goal. That's why we no longer use trims developed for the poultry industry, such as uneven trimming (cutting all primaries on one wing close or under the coverts and leaving the other wing full) for companion birds. This leaves the bird uncomfortably unbalanced.

Trimming Wings Without Toweling

With the bird sitting on a comfortable waist-high perch, facing in the same direction as the groomer, looking down from behind the bird, using the left hand, the groomer grasps the bird's left wing by the bone closest to the body, the humerous, as grasping the end bones could damage the wing. Carefully spread the wing out and up. First examine the wing feathers to ensure that none of them still contain a blood supply (if the blue-white casing of a blood feather is cut, the bird will bleed). Then with scissors in the right hand, reaching up from below and behind the bird, and with the scissors pointing away from the bird's body, trim one half the visible portion of the outer four to seven longest wing feathers extending past the coverts. Trim in a curving shape that roughly mimics the shape of the covering coverts.

Then, again with the left hand, the groomer grasps the right wing by the bone closest to the body. Extending the wing out and up, and, reaching up from below with scissors in the right hand, one half the visible portion of the outer four to seven longest wing feathers is trimmed.

Be sure the scissors point up or out and away from the bird's body to avoid accidentally cutting a toe. (If both the bird's feet are comfortably gripping the perch, this can't happen.) Scissors should be nice and sharp so that they leave smooth edges on the trimmed feathers (this prevents potential feather chewing intended to "fix" jagged feather edges).

Even something as simple as holding onto the top of the cage and flapping is complicated by the huge amount of lift and wind resistance provided by the one full wing as opposed to virtually no wind resistance to flapping the cut wing. This leaves the bird's tail held radically to one side, with the spine curved to that side. This can't be comfortable, and, indeed, young birds, especially, trimmed in this manner tend to fall more than symmetrically trimmed birds. Older birds who have been trimmed in this manner for a long time tend to be inactive, a condition that can contribute to all sorts of other physical and behavioral problems.

Safety is also why we don't leave those two or three outside primary feathers long, as it's not unusual for those long unprotected feathers sticking out to get caught in cage bars or accessories. In addition, if there are only two feathers sticking out there, and one is molted, then the other mature feather is more vulnerable to being knocked out, leaving a new blood feather coming in completely unprotected. Cockatiels, especially, respond better to having half to two thirds of the extending pri-

Potentially harmful trim leaves no support for blood feathers (top). The least invasive trim offers protection for regrowing blood feathers (bottom).

mary flight feathers trimmed rather than leaving the end flights long, because the exposed long feathers can be easily knocked out during their famous "night frights." Leaving the end feathers long can also contribute to special problems in phobic, extremely shy, or untamed parrots.

Low-stress grooming also includes protecting the bird's ability to regrow feathers easily. While some birds seem to tolerate and recover from short trims, other birds encounter disastrous results. Wing feathers that are trimmed up to or under the coverts are especially vulnerable to being knocked out as they molt and regrow one at a time. Each individual blood feather is exposed as it grows past the coverts. Without the protection and support of (partial) feathers on each side, each primary blood feather can be repeatedly broken or knocked out when it grows past the coverts. This can be painful for the bird and not only can result in feather cysts and the inability to regrow these feathers, but also can produce a sedentary bird that prefers not to use its wings, a bird that chews feathers, or a bird with a phobic or aggressive personality. Inappropriate cage, perches, and overgroomed nails can also contribute to this painful condition.

Maintaining the Low-stress Trims

The bird's wing feathers should fall out (molt) in a symmetrical pattern along the feather trails (paths of circulation), regrowing two feathers at a time, in mirror image, one on each side. That's the way it's supposed to work, so that the feathers molt and regrow symmetrically and the bird retains maximum flight ability.

Of course, with a minimally invasive wing trim like this, some birds can regain flight with only one feather regrown on each wing, and, therefore, this noninvasive trim must be maintained more meticulously than some more severe trims. This can be accomplished in the home during towel play or other socialization processes. That is, once the new feather regrows completely, it can be trimmed along the same line as the adjacent feathers. We must wait for the protective cuticle encasing the feather (when it contains blood supply) to flake away, revealing the completely formed new feather. If we trim the feather before it is completely regrown, we risk cutting the blood supply (then the feather would have to be pulled) or having the cut end of the feather continue growing outside the line of the trim (this can be easily remedied by trimming again once the feather has reached full length).

Toweling with Conditioning to the Towel Game

While most companion parrots will tolerate having the wing feathers groomed without toweling, it may become necessary to wrap the bird in a towel for medical examination or for grooming toenails or beak. If a companion bird has been well conditioned to playing peek-a-boo in the towel, then necessary toweling is tremendously easy. In this way, the

Leaving the end feathers long can be dangerous and can contribute to problems in phobic, shy, or untamed birds. (Quaker parrot.)

towel game can actually save a sensitive bird's life.

Toweling Without Conditioning to the Towel Game

Even if the bird is not conditioned to accept the towel, good technique can usually ensure a successful low-stress grooming experience (see p. 121). First put the bird on the floor,

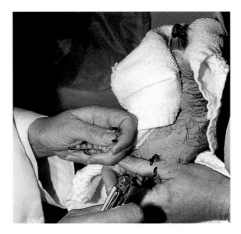

This parrot is so docile that it will lie on its back and allow nail filing.

allowing it to be sort of herded into a corner. At this point, just before the towel would be thrown, dropped, or quickly placed over the bird, turn the light out in the room so that the bird doesn't see the "predator" coming. Once the bird is safely contained in the towel, turn the light on, and spend some time on sweet words and pet-

Toweling a Bird for Examination or Grooming

Begin as you would for the towel game (see p. 153). Place the bird on a waist-high perch and approach from below rather than from above as an avian predator would. First, restrict the bird's movement inside the towel. Then, placing it approximately in the center of the towel, grasp the bird around the neck with one hand, carefully joining the thumb and opposing finger (outside the towel) just under the lower beak. Even if there is a little space in the circle formed by the fingers, if the fingertips meet directly beneath the beak, the bird is restrained, and cannot bite. Hold the bird's feet with the other hand, being careful not to restrict the in-and-out movement of the breast (a bird has no diaphragm and cannot breathe if the chest cannot expand).

Once the bird is safely restrained in the towel, a second person can examine the bird, groom wing feathers, toenails, or beak, or perform whatever other procedure is necessary.

ting to calm the bird. Practiced and documented successful petting techniques, including those discussed in *Guide to a Well-Behaved Parrot,* are especially beneficial here. A terrified bird can also sometimes be calmed by making comforting humming sounds. Be sure not to "shush" or hiss at a screaming, terrified bird, as this is what a reptilian predator might do, which could further terrify the bird.

Grooming Toenails

While we usually allow baby birds to have sharp toenails (so that they won't fall often and develop related problems), we want to maintain our adult parrots' grooming so that the ball under the end of the toe is not displaced off a flat surface by the length of the nail. Some birds may be socialized to allow a favorite person to file the tips off the toenails with an emery board. Most birds will probably have to be toweled to have toenails groomed, even by a professional groomer or avian veterinarian.

I prefer grooming the toenails of birds smaller than a cockatiel with tiny little human nail clippers. For birds the size of a quaker or larger, I prefer to grind toenails with a cordless Dremmel. The cordless tool minimizes the risk that a large bird could chomp through the power supply cord during grooming.

The heat produced by the spinning of the grinding stone can cauterize the blood supply in the toenail as the nail is being groomed, thereby minimizing the risk of bleeding. Occasionally, however, a little blood is encountered, and care must be taken to ensure that the bleeding is stopped. I prefer Qwik-Stop coagulating powder rather than a styptic pencil because it is more versatile and less painful.

Grooming the Beak

Grooming the beak is probably the most stressful part of grooming for most birds. An active, interested parrot with sufficient wood of appropriate hardnesses seldom requires beak grooming.

Birds that are well acclimated to the towel game often enjoy having their beaks gently filed by favorite humans. This can seem to the bird like an allo-preening interaction. The beaks of unsocialized or uncooperative birds may require professional grooming.

A few species, red-lored Amazons for one, have occasional tendencies to beaks that become malformed with growth. Often a beak malformation of this type involves a maxilla (upper beak) growing to one side and a mandible (lower beak) growing to the other side rather than maxilla and mandible being centered over each other. This condition would require beak reshaping, which must be done gradually and by a professional.

A professional groomer or veterinarian should know that a Dremmel must not be used on the beaks of birds smaller than the Timneh African grey, because the vibration of the tool could injure or kill the bird. The beaks of small birds such as quakers, *Brotegeris*, cockatiels, and budgies can usually be maintained easily with an

Beak grooming should be done by professionals unless the bird is well-socialized and enjoys the process. (Quaker parrot.)

emery board. Done sensitively, lightly filing the tip of the beak with a fine emery board can seem like mutual bird-to-bird grooming (allogrooming) to a well-socialized bird.

Application of This Technique

Low-stress wing feather trims are used primarily for companion birds, as wing feathers are maintained in more specific and more varied ways for breeding and show situations. This technique is intended, especially, to ensure the bird's comfort when feathers are regrowing, as the single most common error I see in wing feather trims involves cutting the feathers too short to be able to regrow easily. Unfortunately, as I travel around the country for educational events, I often see young birds, especially African greys and cockatoos, enduring painful situations including acquired tendency to wing feather cysts and a breast that is repeatedly split open by falls because flight feathers were trimmed up to or under the coverts.

Chapter Seven
Behavioral Development

Making the Most of the "Baby Days"

When a sweet, perfect, newly weaned handfed baby parrot moves to its first home, a predictable behavior cycle usually follows. There is a "honeymoon" period followed by a developmental period in which the

Training should begin even before the baby bird goes to its first home. (Hyacinth macaw.)

rapidly learning creature tests the limits of the social environment. If everything is in the right place at the right time, good socialization is easy. After all, how could a well-meaning human start with a perfect baby bird and wind up with a biting, screaming, or feather-chewing bundle of neuroses?

As with humans, early socialization appears to influence lifetime behavior patterns. If the bird is trained to expect to be held all the time, and if it is then reinforced to get its way by screaming or nipping, in less than two years the baby bird may be looking for a new home. If, on the other hand, the bird is taught to respond dependably to step-up commands; if it is reinforced to entertain itself; if it is shown limits of acceptable behavior; if it is guided to make successful decisions; if it is not allowed to become territorial regarding a cage or human, the adult bird will be a pleasure to be around for generations in its very first family.

The goal in socializing a baby parrot is to produce an adult bird that is neither fearful nor aggressive, noisy nor quiet; a bird that is eager for attention when the time is right, but can readily entertain itself when we have other things to do. Without proper socialization during the post-weaning honeymoon period, negative behaviors usually begin appearing during the developmental period (sometimes called the terrible two's). If these behaviors are reinforced intentionally or unintentionally, they can become permanent patterns enduring for the bird's life. Careful training and environmental design during the honeymoon period is necessary to ensure a smooth transition through the developmental period without the acquisition of problems like screaming, biting, eating disorders, fearfulness, or feather chewing. Liz Wilson reminds us that parrot owners have a responsibility to socialize their parrots appropriately so that they can be placed in a new home if the bird outlives the owner.

During the honeymoon period, begin encouraging the bird to make choices. Offering more than one type, shape, size, or color of food is such an opportunity. Selecting from various alternatives provides intellectual stimulation and confidence-building experience that enables the bird to overcome fear of new people and new things in the future. The bird should have opportunities to choose from various toys or other solitary play activities. It should have access *only* to appropriate choices so that undesirable behavior patterns cannot be inadvertently reinforced.

Many baby birds love human contact so much that any attention can easily be interpreted by the bird as a reward for the previous behavior. Every effort should be made to reinforce only positive behaviors in the baby bird. Intermittent rewards for quietly playing alone are important. It is also important not to reinforce negative behaviors—such as jumping on the dinner table and walking through plates or stealing food—no matter how cute they seem the first time we see them.

Effective socialization begins with love, but too much handling during the honeymoon period can be behaviorally damaging. I often encounter written or verbal advice to "take time off to hold the new baby bird a great deal during its first few weeks in the new home." While this is not bad advice for a wild-caught imported parrot, it can harm the disposition of a handfed domestic bird.

Depending upon how the baby was previously socialized, it may require more or less handling for effective transition to the new environment and to reinforce a sense of security. If the bird was rushed during the weaning process or was removed from clutch mates to go to the new home, it may need more hours of direct attention to develop healthy behavioral habits. The bird must learn several important skills such as eating, climbing, flapping, chewing, and playing independently, in addition to cuddling. But there will be a need for at least a little cuddling every evening to develop the rapport necessary to bind in the new home.

Holding a newly weaned baby bird sets a pattern for the bird's expectations. If the baby is cuddled 8 to 10 hours today and 8 to 10 hours tomorrow and 8 to 10 hours the day after, then suddenly two weeks later when we have to go back to work, the bird may feel abandoned. Numerous negative behaviors can result. The bird must learn independent exploration and play habits rather than just cuddling.

This is not to say, don't hold the baby. A baby parrot needs more cuddling at first, but it also needs a variety of other interactions. In the grand scheme of things, playing and step-ups are probably more important than cuddling, but you must give careful attention to all these things during this period.

Toys and Playing

A parrot in the wild is never at a loss for how to occupy its time. The tasks that are essential for the bird's continued existence allow for little spare time. A captive parrot never has to learn all things it was designed to do in the wild. In captivity it must learn replacement activities that will help it cope with captive life and how to avoid the behavior problems associated with the frustration of not knowing what to do with its time. We call this problem boredom, though it probably bears little resemblance to our own description of boredom.

Toys are the objects we give a parrot to help it occupy its time. We would like to do the same with the bird as we would do with a child, that

is, hand the toy to the bird and say, "Here, play with this."

Unfortunately, birds will often ignore or be fearful of toys if they have not learned the benefits of chewing, banging, and shredding the objects hanging in the cage. Parrots are best encouraged to be playful and curious at a young age. Given a rich, stimulating, ever-changing environment, a young bird usually takes to this naturally, quickly, and with gusto.

However, a parrot can miss out on this learning experience. An individual like this will need special encouragement from its owner. Teaching a bird to play can be complicated, but the following two suggestions are usually all that is necessary to generate play behaviors in a young, healthy bird.

1. The owner can become a bird toy. The bird's favorite person attaches toys to an old sweatshirt and wears it while holding the bird. Just as birds are often drawn to chew on buttons and jewelry, the bird will probably start chewing on the toys. Invite your friends, neighbors, and spouse also to play with the toys. Delighted coo's and praises from the favorite human will encourage the parrot to play with the toys. The same toys can be put into the cage before the bird is returned to it. Again, praise the bird when it explores a toy in order to encourage it to continue playing independently.

2. "Keep away" is an excellent game for piquing a parrot's interest in a new toy or new food. This game is played by showing the bird the toy or food only very briefly. The bird is not allowed to see the toy long enough to become frightened of it.

Then the favorite human can show excitement over having the toy and begin playing with it. If the toy can be shredded, the person should shred it a bit. If it can be eaten, the person should eat some, all while the bird can watch what is happening. Show the object to the bird again. Give it to a rival that will enjoy it. Show it to the bird again. Play with it again. Eventually the bird will start leaning closer and closer to try to find out what it is. By the time it is given the object, the bird will be very excited to have it. Most birds will succumb to curiosity within a few minutes. Some birds may take several sessions.

Some birds may prefer objects that are not bright and colorful. Shredded paper, twigs, natural rope, or leather may be more interesting to some birds. Pompoms made from newspaper or some other paper that is not shiny can be irresistible to some birds. Weaving paper, leather, or bias-cut cloth in and out of the cage bars near the bird's favorite perch can draw a bird into chewing. Or bundles of twigs can be attached to the sides of the cage. Branches where the bark is already starting to peel can replace plain perches.

Birds that are simply afraid of new toys can get used to them while they are lying near the cage. The toys can be gradually moved closer and even hung on the outside of the cage before being placed inside. "Keep away" also helps these birds over-come their fears. Once a bird has seen many new toys, it will usually start to welcome new additions. Then comes the challenge of finding a toy that survives more than a few minutes before being destroyed.

Step-ups

The step-up drill is considered the primary behavior necessary for good social adjustment. Emphatic rein-forcement of the step-up command during the honeymoon period not only establishes the handler's imme-diate authority, it lays the ground-work for future control. The bird should step up immediately to any properly offered hand or perch (the prompt location is where the legs join the belly, not in front of the beak).

It is easy to neglect daily step-up exercises during the honeymoon period because the bird is so sweet, it doesn't really seem to matter whether it responds instantly to the command or not. While it is tempting to coddle or overnurture the juvenile bird, behavioral patterns set during this important period can make or break a healthy disposition. The step-up response must be so well entrenched that the bird will automatically per-form the behavior, even if it is in an out-of-control hormonal rage, sitting in a treetop, or being rescued from a fire. The step-up command should be so well reinforced that when you say "step up" the bird will immediately dis-continue whatever it is doing and lift that foot!

During this period, it is easy to accidentally reinforce the bird to bite.

Most of the "beak on skin" activity during the honeymoon period can be described as "teething" behavior in which the baby parrot tries jaw muscles for their effect. The baby parrot must learn just how much pressure to exert on any given object to obtain the desired result. Much interest and devotion is given to this delightful educational process. When the bird exerts too much pressure on skin, care must be taken that the response is neither enjoyable nor provocative to the baby parrot. Drama is fun; and if the response to the bite is fun, the biting may become permanent. If the response excites the bird, it could provoke increased or continued aggression.

The best response to baby nibbles is no response at all. If this is unsuccessful, try to distract the bird by gently wobbling the hand the bird is perched on, blowing swiftly into the baby's face, pushing the beak away, or giving the baby something else to chew on.

Bonding

Toward the end of the honeymoon period you will see the beginnings of the development of a protective attitude toward territory, both actual and human. It is important at this time to move the bird's cage occasionally, to rearrange and change toys periodically, and to require the bird to maintain balanced relationships with at least two people.

Step-up conditioning also helps the bird to overcome territorialism as you train the bird to be "transportation dependent" in a well-planned environment. The bird should have at least two regular areas in which to spend time: a roost (cage) in which to sleep, and one or more foraging areas. The bird should be dependent upon humans to get from one area to another by stepping onto the hand to get from the cage to the perch or shower every day. This transportation dependence helps the bird to understand that successful interactions with humans are rewarded with interesting, exciting things to do. Transportation dependency can also help to overcome the flock-like instinct to pick on everyone other than the favorite person.

Although the bird will often, but not always, demonstrate an obvious preference for one person over another, this tendency should be discouraged. A young bird that expresses aggression against a less-favored person during the honeymoon period might change loyalties during the terrible two's and begin attacking the previously favored person. I have seen periodically changing loyalties frequently in African greys, cockatoos, Amazons, and conures; but I believe there is probably potential for this behavior in any psittiforme-type bird that is allowed to attack all but the favorite person.

The bird should interact with numerous "regulars" and "strangers." It is a very good thing for the bappy to attend as many human gatherings as possible in a safe and structured way. If the young bird expresses dislike of one person, and it can be determined that the bird's responses are not related to the signals or body language of that person, then efforts must be made to improve the relationship with that person. This is not usually true dislike of a person, but rather expression of a flocking instinct that stimulates the bird to try to drive all but its favorites away.

The person who is being picked on should be the one upon whom the bird must depend for daily transportation to the foraging areas. The person and the bird should share showers and outings. Other household members should use the two creatures' names in tandem such as "Barney's Paco" and "Paco's Barney."

Other Things to Watch Out For

A particularly problematic form of aggression can develop if the bird is allowed to establish dominance of the human shoulder. A bird that will not immediately and peacefully comply with the step-up command will often develop aggressive behavior if allowed access to the shoulder. The baby parrot needs to know that you are a loving benefactor, not a "place" to be defended.

An unweaned or under-six-month-old bird that is already threatening and biting people or inanimate objects must be given sound behavioral back-up immediately, as this can be a sign of serious problems developing. Aggression in an unweaned or newly weaned bird can be easily reinforced as the bird's personality is being formed. That aggression will,

Any bird that treats its human like territory cannot safely be allowed time on the shoulder. (Yellow-headed Amazon and greenwing macaw.)

most likely, escalate. Don't be shy about needing professional assistance. A successful, long-term avian professional knows when to enlist outside help.

Extreme repeated fearfulness developing during the honeymoon period may also indicate severe problems to come. Most any avian behavior consultant will verify that feather chewing is more common in handfed domestic parrots—particularly African greys and cockatoos—than in like-species imports. I believe this statistic is an indictment of socialization and environmental practices used (or, more frequently, neglected) on those birds. Timely implementation of the techniques described above—a little training, a monitored environment, and lots of love during the first months in the first home after weaning—will produce an eager parrot pupil that will respond favorably through the next, very exciting developmental period.

The Developmental Period

As previously discussed, a handfed baby parrot usually begins life in its new home with an idyllic honeymoon period including much cuddling and snuggling. During this time, when the bird seems to need discipline and limits the least, a caring owner takes great pains to ensure loving authority over the bird

Large hookbills are naturally curious about human eating utensils. (Scarlet macaw.)

by reinforcing the bird to respond immediately, happily, and unquestioningly to the step-up command.

While practicing the step-up command may seem unnecessary and redundant during the honeymoon period, these daily exercises are preparation for the months and years to come, for this phase often ends abruptly and confusingly when the bird begins to realize its own (sexual) agenda. The behaviors arising can seem a little like the terrible two's or adolescence in humans.

If a satisfactory understanding has not been reached between owner and bird before this behavioral period arises, various problems such as biting, overbonding, phobias, territorialism, and attention-demanding behaviors can develop into long-term habits. These changes can appear with startling swiftness, seemingly overnight. If an effective authority-based relationship has not been previously established or is not established at this time, the bird might never know its place in the family social structure (pecking order) and may seem to be going through painfully intense status struggles for the rest of its life.

This developmental period can be especially striking in juvenile Amazons (particularly in some yellow-napes), conures, and macaws (particularly in some severes and in some scarlets), but it can become conspicuous in any companion parrot's behavior. It is not unusual for me to receive a call from a tearful owner reporting that their nine-month-old bird has "turned" on them, biting everyone (often including the previously most-favored person). Attempts at discipline may have been met with aggressive and hostile resistance. The owner's heart and ego have suffered damage; and the owner is considering giving away a bird that was the light of his life just a few months ago.

Various techniques may be employed to modify the negative behaviors that arise. Certainly all efforts should be made to ensure that the biting, fearfulness, territorial or attention-demanding behaviors not be reinforced. Ideally, an unwanted behavior should be anticipated and prevented—perhaps by wobbling a nipping bird (see p. 157) or by diverting a bird screaming to active play—so that only appropriate behaviors are reinforced.

Teach the Bird that All Its Needs Will Be Met

While developing behavior problems should be addressed specifically as they arise, the real key to solving both new and long-term behavior problems is providing adequately for the bird, and also teaching the bird to know that it will always be provided for. That is, the bird's life (and lifestyle) must be secure, and the bird must know that its life is secure. Diet, appropriate space, light, temperature, and moisture are necessary. Quality social interaction, balanced bonding, outings to prevent phobias and territorialism, opportunities to make decisions and express

energy, frequent drenching showers, a constant array of interesting things to do, and an understanding of the passage of time are equally important to satisfactory long-term adjustment.

Provide Quality Social Interactions

Quality social time with a companion parrot means sharing activities such as eating, bathing, talking, singing, exercising, and expressing affection with other humans in the presence of the bird. Even if it doesn't enjoy being handled, a parrot has a compelling need to spend time with its social group. I have seen many difficult-to-correct behavioral problems develop in birds that are not allowed to see the human flock eat, and in birds that cannot, because of their location, see what humans are watching (usually the television).

Provide Challenging Activities for the Bird

Possibly the most significant need the juvenile parrot has at this time is to learn independent activities. This is your ticket to freedom in the future, for if the bird does not learn independent activities, attention-demanding behaviors are just around the corner.

Just as teenagers and healthy, developing baby parrots go through periods of requiring large amounts of food—devouring everything within reach and demanding more—young children and birds go through periods of extreme intellectual gluttony (compulsive curiosity). Any youngster being frustrated in the quest to see

Stimulating Activities for Young Parrots (Jobs for Junior Birds)

Climbing. It takes a special kind of coordination for a bipedal creature to climb flexible branches emerging at odd angles from one another (a tree) or to climb a knotted level, vertical, or diagonal rope (vine). Provide stimulating transportation and learning opportunities by joining play areas with branches or rope suspended from the ceiling. The bird must learn to climb a rope across the ceiling to go from one approved play area to another. Try always to provide several different types of materials in various ways so that the bird has an opportunity to make decisions about how it spends its time.

Chewing. Just as the attraction for catnip develops as a kitten becomes a cat, the instinct to chew becomes more prominent as a young parrot matures. The majority of these birds are cavity breeders, and the appearance of chewing behaviors is tied to the stirrings of instinctual sexual needs. If the bird has no destructible chewables, including branches with bark, soft and harder wooden toys, appropriately prepared fabric (see sidebar p. 201), and paper towel "bows" (see sidebar p. 187), then it can easily begin damaging the only destructible thing it can reach with its beak: its own feathers.

Toys. A parrot in the developmental period has a much-greater-than-normal need for an assortment of interesting, interactive toys. They love bells and climbing toys as well as destructible and take-apart toys (be sure that these toys are designed for birds and that the sizes of pieces of take-apart toys are too large for your bird to swallow). I love the new bird-activated music boxes. Avoid allowing the bird access on demand to anything resembling a mirror.

Pulling up a bucket for a treat. With the exception of some cockatiels, most parrots love to hold things in one of their feet. An easy,

all, hear all, do all, and know all can exhibit behavior that can, in turn, frustrate his elders.

The bird's need to learn is just as great during this important period as its need to eat. If the juvenile bird's intellectual needs are not met at this time, the adult bird may be just as handicapped in future life as a bird suffering nutritional deficiency during a growth period.

In the wild the bird would be learning to fly in the wind and the rain, learning to land on rigid branches and bouncy twigs, learning to avoid predators, and to rejoin companions when separated. A wild bird would learn to spend more than 90 percent of its waking hours finding and consuming food. Merely providing food creates an enormous need for stimulating activities in a companion par-

but challenging activity that can be readily learned by most medium and larger hookbills and even some small hookbills is pulling a bucket up—with a combination of beak and foot movements—for a treat. Start with an extremely short rope or chain and gradually lengthen the distance the bird has to lift the bucket for the treat. Of course the size and weight of rope and bucket container must be appropriate to the bird. Many smaller ropes carry the potential of tangling, so don't leave a bird unattended with a dangerous length of flexible cord.

Eating with a spoon. Many larger hookbills, particularly large cockatoos and full-sized macaws, are naturally curious about eating utensils and may learn to eat and drink with a spoon with little or no assistance other than naturally occurring modeling (eating with a spoon in sight of the bird). You might start by providing a spoon that can be hung beside or attached to the food or water dish. (This saves having to repeatedly pick up the spoon and give it back to the bird, an activity that can degenerate into a favorite parrot interactive game—"I'll drop it and you can pick it up.") Start with sticky foods like peanut butter or baby parrot handfeeding formula and gradually add seeds by dipping the sticky food into seed.

Pass the bird. It is extremely important that a juvenile bird not be allowed to become overly bonded to its owner. A well-socialized bird will peacefully go to most anyone who uses neither threatening nor provocative handling mannerisms. A good exercise for a juvenile bird is to go to and accept food from every human in a group. One macaw breeder I know has group meetings often in his home, and baby macaws are given their favorite treats only from the hands of unfamiliar humans. It makes for some very friendly macaws!

rot's environment. Juvenile parrots must be provided with many opportunities to learn new physical and intellectual skills, or they will improvise sometimes undesirable activities to fill their time.

The period between fledging and sexual maturity is the time of life during which the parrot is most able to learn, and the time during which the bird's desire to learn is the greatest. After that, the bird will be distracted by reproductive urges. In the wild, the young bird would be learning to differentiate between hundreds, maybe thousands of plants and plant parts to learn what is dangerous and what is beneficial. Limiting choices and experiences during this time limits the bird's intellectual and behavioral development. It is not unusual for baby companion parrots to learn

Opportunities to make successful decisions between multiple bird-approved toys contribute to confident behavior in young parrots. (Timneh African greys.)

walk, it is suddenly punished for touching and examining everything it can reach.

With both parrots and humans, this desire to investigate everything isn't limited to a desire to investigate every physical thing. During the terrible two's youngsters also study the social environment by examining their position or status in the family pecking order. Healthy, intelligent parrots go through several such periods in which they test their social rank like an athlete challenging the next player up the tournament ladder. But if effective authority-based relationships have been established, these contests are transitional and pass quickly.

Provide Opportunities to Make Successful Decisions

In order to avoid the formation of phobias or fearfulness that may lead to feather mutilation, young parrots must also have opportunities to make successful decisions. In an inadequately designed environment, it is possible for a young parrot to find lots of unacceptable things to do, and Mom or Dad can wind up yelling "Don't!" or "Stop it!" all the time. Constant corrections can be damaging to a young parrot's behavior just as even well-intentioned criticism can damage children.

It is important, therefore, for a bird to have appropriate options about how and where it spends its time and to have numerous toys with which to play. Even if a bird chooses not to play on a small second perch joined

multiple new words or phrases very quickly during this exciting time. They also learn or improvise many new behaviors.

The onset of this period is directly linked to physical development, as the arrival of physical coordination facilitates exploration. The bird has an almost-compulsive desire to examine every detail of every aspect of life.

If the bird has not already learned some behavioral and environmental limits, then this period may be very difficult. There may be an enormous clash between the owner's wish to teach the bird to "be good" and the bird's desire to "be everything." A human baby that has been encouraged to touch and examine everything within its grasp may be frustrated when, upon learning to

to its main play area by a rope or if it decides not to play with a particular toy, the presence of the second toy or play area has provided an opportunity for successful decision making.

Stimulate Good Behavior with Suggestive Praise

During this period it is valuable to learn to stimulate acceptable behavior with the use of praise. For example, sometimes when McPaco MacAwe, Jr., a 13-month-old juvenile macaw, is sitting on the hand, if the human companion looks away, the demanding baby might respond with a nip. Obviously you can't maintain eye contact every moment you hold your bird, and the bird should be trustworthy enough to not bite if you discontinue eye contact.

If you suspect that Junior will nip for attention when you look away, try telling him to "be a good bird" before you look away. Making your positive expectations known can help the bird to develop some reasoning ability. The smart baby macaw will soon learn that if it isn't a "good bird" by your definition after being told to be so, it will receive a "wobble correction" (see p. 157), be put away, or be required to do step-up (see p. 5) or flapping exercises (see p. 190). Not only does the bird quickly learn what good behavior is ("Shall I chew on my toy or take off that tasty-looking button?"), but it learns how to choose whether or not to be good. This can also be an exercise in willpower and understanding, for if the bird enjoys what the owner considers to be pun-ishment, then the behavior is being reinforced and will continue or recur. If the bird continues to nip when eye contact is discontinued, remember to put it down before discontinuing eye contact so that a pattern of nipping is not reinforced.

Promote an Understanding of Time

A bird inhabiting a controlled environment never sees the shadows grow long, then short, then long or hears the frogs start croaking exactly 30 minutes before sundown. An indoor bird never knows the heat of the noonday sun followed by cooling afternoon rain showers. During my in-home evaluations, I am often entertained with stories of birds that stare at the clock for 10 or 20 minutes before Mom or Dad gets home from work or start screaming 30 seconds before the car turns up the block for home in the evening. I believe a bird that has an opportunity to easily perceive the passage of time is not as likely to self-mutilate or demand attention because it knows that there will be time for its needs to be met.

The juvenile parrot must understand that there is time for every-thing—time to play, eat, and shower with the flock, and time to play, eat, sleep, and bathe alone. To accomplish this, you can design environmental elements that demonstrate the passage of time—a chiming or coo-coo clock, a full-spectrum light that comes on and goes off every day at the same time, or a television on a timer that comes on at the same time with the same program a few hours before you get home from work. My own birds love the clock that features a different song bird every hour—they know exactly what hour it is every daylight hour.

Of course, one bird might need more careful patterning, and another might need more stimulating activities, while still another bird might absolutely have to have a bath every day. Be ever alert to averting behavioral problems by anticipating your bird's physical and emotional needs, for negative behaviors evolving during the developmental period can be enduring and life-threatening.

What to Expect as the Bird Matures

As in other creatures, the instinct to reproduce is the parrot's strongest instinct. Unlike companion dogs and cats who are spayed or neutered for behavioral reasons, companion parrots are allowed the full influence of their reproductive urges. A parrot expressing the influence of this very real natural instinct might chew Grandpa's rocker to toothpicks; decide to allow no one near the end cabinet near the cappuccino machine; sing lengthy, lusty, loud parrot songs at sunrise; regurgitate in strangers' hair; or masturbate on the dog.

As with humans, instead of surgically altering the animal, you must learn to alter its behavior. The tech-niques described here are intended to enhance favorable behaviors in companion parrots and to suppress or minimize most behaviors related to breeding.

It's tremendously important to continue handling the maturing companion parrot on a daily basis in order to maintain tameness. Some birds will be easily kept tame; some will be difficult. Expect every bird to be a little different, with vast differences between species and between successfully socialized birds and unsocialized birds of the same species. The more consistent you are in all interactions, the more predictable the bird will be.

As the time to breed approaches, you will see heightened exploration and physical and emotional experimentation. The bird might even change emotional or territorial loyalties, becoming aggressive around a newly selected territory or a new favorite human (mate substitute). If a parrot has been allowed to overbond to one human in the past, at this time, the formerly favorite human might be dumped for a more easily dominated companion. We must be ever vigilant at this time to ensure that the bird is not excessively defensive of the territory around any human so that previous and predictable loyalties will not be abandoned. It might be necessary to take an arrogant young bird out of its familiar territory for at least a few days each year in order to repattern the bird and to require interactions with unfamiliar humans. Vacations and indoor outings (visits to unfamiliar territory) are very helpful at this time. Even a simple car ride with the bird in a carrier can make a wonderful difference in a parrot's disposition. Careful transporting and meticulous wing feather trims will ensure safety on these outings.

At home the maturing parrot will become increasingly concerned with control issues, especially immediate environmental control. The bird might start attacking tissues, or people sneezing, or blowing into tissues. A maturing parrot might also attack someone cleaning with quick motions with paper towels. The bird might suddenly decide it loves (or hates) a particular dog or cat or stuffed animal.

A maturing parrot allowed a great deal of liberty in the home might become hypervigilant or aggressive around a suddenly and mysteriously selected territory. The bird will be seeking both companions and interlopers in its reflections. Expect heightened reactions to mirrors, shiny objects, and small appliances. The bird might attack the vacuum cleaner or hair dryer. At this time the bird might fixate strongly on an inanimate object, treating it either as a potential mate or an enemy to be attacked.

There must be at least one enemy who can be regularly thwarted. To a very real extent, the bird must select or identify this enemy independently. Most parrots will do this. Of course, it's very important for this enemy not to be a living creature or a treasured human possession, so several potential approved "surrogate enemies" must be provided. Safe, unbreakable toys such as the "Little Birdy Man" or loud, safe bells are excellent candidates for this parrot-selected enemy. If a companion parrot has no opportunity to release natural aggressive energy against an approved surrogate enemy at this time, the bird is likely to begin to express that excess energy against whatever or whoever is closest.

If the bird is enjoying attacking a toy, leave them both alone. There will continue to be many times when the bird will solicit human attention. Those are the times when even a mature bird can be successfully patterned to cooperate with the use of praise, rewards, and patterning. The more successful behavioral experiences you have at this time, the more the bird is patterned and reinforced to cooperate, the more likely the bird is to cooperate when it becomes fully mature.

Chewing and Other Developing Behaviors

By two to three years of age, most parrots will be exhibiting chewing behaviors. You will see a transition from a time when toys were hardly scratched, through a time when they are dismantled into parts, to a time when they are completely demolished into splinters. As these behaviors develop, it's necessary to increase the number and frequency of chewables in the restricted environment of either the cage or the play area.

As with human children, new behaviors will seem to appear out of nowhere. For months, the bird will leave the picture frame behind the cage alone. Then one day, the picture frame is splintered on two sides. For years, the bird might put nothing into the water, then one day it will begin filling the water bowl with debris. A maturing parrot might suddenly begin pulling newspaper up through the bottom grate. These behaviors are probably part of the parrot's instinctive need to attract a mate. An industrious mate is highly prized in the wild. The bird is doing what it was programmed to do. We must provide other appropriate things to chew and reinforce the bird for chewing appropriately.

Transitional Stages

As parrots mature, they will become increasingly obsessed with control of their immediate environment. Different birds will react differently to these phases; some will go through nippy phases and some will go through fearful stages. Consistent handling is the key to bringing a maturing bird through any suddenly appearing episodes of unwanted behavior. To ensure that these phases are transitional, to ensure that they will pass, do not reinforce unwanted behaviors. That means, especially, don't laugh when the bird does something you don't want to see again. This is a place where having a good disposition can be detrimental. It's hard not to laugh when the bird decides that no one is

allowed to touch the chrome sculpture on the coffee table, but repeated battles over just such turf can lead to bloodletting.

In some parrots, especially some African parrots, if they are repeatedly confronted in ways that stimulate and reinforce panic, they will become increasingly shy. At this point, shy, cautious, or fearful birds must be permitted to hide whenever they choose. You must carefully discontinue eye contact (see p. 20) and do everything you can to avoid stimulating the bird's instinct to fight or flee.

If you see a trend of developing fearfulness, take action to improve the bird's confidence, perhaps allowing it to live higher (or lower depending upon the bird), allowing it to choose whether to leave the cage on its own, or providing a place to hide. A little fabric tent, or just a towel over one end of the cage, can provide a sense of security for a cautious companion parrot. While you might see an increase in territorial aggression, in such a case, this is exactly what you want to see in this bird. You can seldom treat fearfulness without seeing at least a small increase in aggression.

It's probably more likely, however, that a companion parrot will go through at least one nippy period. These phases will appear and disappear, sometimes with great regularity throughout the bird's lifetime as breeding seasons come and go and pressure to breed asserts itself. As when dealing with aggression appearing for any other reason, enhanced step-up practice, the towel game, and use of hand-held perches will easily compensate for these transitional behaviors. It's important to remember not to completely discontinue interactions during these periods, as many unwanted behaviors can be reinforced by neglect.

Sexual Maturity

There will come a time when threats might be accompanied by aggression; a bite might actually break the skin. A sexually mature companion parrot is usually more difficult to handle than a strutting little adolescent whose challenges might be mere practice for the future. At this time, new programs, people, and changes might be met with strong resistance. If, however, the bird has been patterned to accept newness and change, the bird's behavior might be maintained merely by manipulating the environment.

If a parrot has not been appropriately patterned to cooperate until this time, attempts to socialize or resocialize might be met with resistance from the bird. During this time it is not unusual for both predictable and unpredictable bites to occur, especially in the bird's perceived territory. Usually there will be plenty of warning: hypervigilance, eye movement, wing or tail display, charging with beak open, or any other body language that usually accompanies aggression in a particular individual.

The best way to deal with aggression at this time is to give the bird space to be obnoxious. That is not to say, reinforce obnoxious behavior. Never allow the bird to chase or harass. Merely remind the bird to "be a good bird" then return it to the cage in the calmest possible way. A bird nipping during a step-up might be sensitively wobbled by the hand it is sitting on (see p. 157). A bird being prompted to step up might be distracted with a toy or other inanimate object when being given the prompt for step-up. We call this distraction technique "good hand/bad hand" (see p. 158). The distraction object must be neither too large (which might scare the bird off the perch), too small (which might be ineffective), nor toxic (soap or a piece of lead or solder).

You might also choose to handle an otherwise-well-adapted bird either with the towel or with hand-held perches during nippy stages. Don't discontinue handling now because the bird's interactive behavior might be lost. It's more difficult to regain lost interactive behavior in some parrots than others, but it's usually easier to keep a bird tame than to retame it later. You also don't want to reinforce biting. Careful techniques can help to maintain tameness here, for if the bird has no chance to bite, biting can't be reinforced.

Environmental Manipulations

Raising or lowering the bird's usual relative height, combined with increasing access to (shower) rainfall, destructible chewables, and

Saucey's Choice

When Lolita the blue-crowned Amazon came to live with us, it was obvious that she had been through something awful, something like a prison camp where some individuals were injured and died (see story on pp. 209–212). She had survived, like some humans have survived such nightmarish settings, by finding the only kind of pleasure she could access, self-gratification. When Lolita arrived in my home, she was habitually masturbating several times per hour in the noisy Amazon way called "winking."

You could hear her from anyplace in the house, and within a few months, Saucey, my male bird was doing the same. The sounds they each made during their amazing displays were not typical of any other sounds they customarily made. These characteristic Amazon sounds inspired some of my on-line Amazon friends to call this behavior the "cluck dance." Sometimes the birds would do the cluck dance at the same time. Sometimes they would do it at different times.

One afternoon, hearing much honking and clucking from the other room, my friend Vera and I peeked around the corner to see what was going on. There was Saucey noisily flaring eyes and tail in full masturbation display. Lolita was situated directly in front of him with her tail straight up in the air in front of his face. Looking over her left shoulder, she repeatedly said, "Step up! Step up! Step up!"

Saucey, alas, was more interested in his own silly dance than in mating with Lolita. We saw this same interaction about twice after that and never saw it again. Like any other unreinforced behavior, this one was not repeated.

exercise will help to compensate for pent-up energy that might otherwise be expressed as aggression. A bird that suddenly becomes excessively territorial must have its territory manipulated either by moving the cage or redesigning the cage interior.

Mature companion parrots occasionally decide that a particular chrome appliance is either a mate or a rival, leading to many courtships with toasters and wars with hair dryers. A sexually mature companion parrot might decide that no one is allowed in the kitchen. A bird that has fixated on a human-owned object or territory must be denied access to them. An attacking bird might be picked up using a hand-held perch, a towel, or "good hand/bad hand" (see p. 158) and placed with the approved "surrogate enemy" toy. Again, encourage the bird to express hostility against an "approved enemy" toy. This is usually a self-rewarding behavior. Hostile energy will be expressed somehow; it is best expressed against a toy.

Sexual Behaviors

Parrots are very sexual creatures. We can expect to see masturbation behaviors in almost all healthy, solitary male birds and in a high percentage of female birds. Although many companion parrots will limit sexual behaviors to courtship behaviors, including chewing, eating, and feeding, many birds will more overtly seek to gratify their natural instincts. A companion parrot might solicit copulation from a favorite human or engage in masturbation, a masturbation display, or anxiety behaviors that sometimes include sexual gestures.

Actually, masturbation behaviors are an occasionally dependable way to determine gender, as male and female birds tend to masturbate in positions approximating mating postures. In most species, the male bird stands on the female bird's back, she elevates her tail and everts her cloaca. The male bird lowers his tail and after rubbing his cloaca against hers deposits semen onto her everted cloaca. The semen is then retrieved when the hen's cloaca pulls back into her body. A male bird, therefore, often masturbates with tail down on perch or toy or human hand. A female bird does so with tail straight up in the air behind her by backing into something like the corner of the cage or a favorite person's ear.

Each different bird's masturbation process is usually accompanied by that species' characteristic sexual sounds. An astute owner can tell what's going on by hearing that particular sound, which is made only at that time. My own hen cockatiel, Pearl, who neither talks nor whistles at other times, whistles a typical male cockatiel song as she backs into the corner of her cage.

It's probably not a good idea to encourage these behaviors as they can be accompanied by aggression or feather picking. In addition, a companion bird that habitually engages in masturbation behaviors may later chose those behaviors over mating even if a mate is offered. Just ignore these behaviors; don't reinforce them. If the behaviors don't get attention, they're less likely to appear frequently. However, because self-gratification is the very definition of self-rewarding behaviors, masturbation behaviors may continue regardless of whether they are reinforced by humans or not.

Exaggerated chewing, allofeeding, and regurgitation are also commonly seen sexual behaviors. If the bird is regurgitating on humans, just put it down. This is neither to be rewarded nor discouraged, with this exception: if the bird has a problem with excessive vocalization. Reinforcement or provision for occasional sexual-related behaviors such as chewing and beating up toys can replace some unnecessary vocalizing if other distraction techniques and frequent drenching showers prove ineffective.

Chapter Eight

Occasional Behavioral Issues

When the New Baby Won't Eat Independently

Harriet, a four-month-old Hahn's macaw, was immediately snugly at the bird show where her new family fell in love with her. And she was quiet. As they left the show, she began making something like baby sounds when she would throw back her head and lift up her wings. It was cute at first, but within a few days, she was doing it constantly except when she was asleep. What was this "Ack" noise and why was she constantly making it?

Also, she would not sit up very well on her perch or on the hand, but usually rested on her breastbone. Her legs seem fine, and she frequently climbed all over the cage and even tried to escape; but then she would hunker down whenever they had her out of the cage, and she continuously made that awful noise.

Was she hungry? She seemed to eat well, and the new family had been assured that she was fully weaned. She made the noise when they played music and danced. She made it when they talked to her. She made it when they held her; she made it when they didn't hold her. She made that awful noise constantly.

What was going on? Obviously, this situation is not normal, but it is also not uncommon in parrots nurtured by humans. It's sort of the parrot equivalent of a colicky baby (similar behavior, different cause). This condition can be seen in most species of parrots, but it is very common in cockatoos, especially cockatoos that were first weaned by that handfeeder. The crying and begging postures may indicate that the bird either wasn't fully weaned or that the bird regressed to an unweaned state.

Our first concern is physical health. A baby bird is a tiny creature that can succumb to illness quickly. A sudden physical decline, which might take only hours, is called "crashing." A bird that was fully weaned, then suddenly discontinues eating could be demonstrating a physical or a behavioral response. If the baby bird has not already seen an avian veterinarian by the time the crying problem appears, it should be taken as quickly as possible to the veterinarian. Because the baby bird's immune system is not fully developed, try to schedule the veterinarian's first appointment in the morning so that the baby won't be exposed to dust from other birds. If possible, take the baby in its own cage and cover the bottom of the cage or carrier with a plastic garbage bag so that it won't leave or pick up germs when it is set down in the veterinarian's facility.

Some species simply take longer to wean than others. A breeder with experience with conures, quakers, or lories might have weaned the bird a little early. However, experienced breeders know the signs of weaning no matter what the type of bird, and even thoroughly weaned babies sometimes regress, especially young cockatiels, macaws, greys, and cockatoos. Many breeders mention it in their instructions to new owners and suggest bringing the bird back for a few days for resocialization. Many breeders with closed aviaries won't allow the bird's return, but will suggest phone support. A breeder with a connection to a behaviorist would probably suggest that you consult the behaviorist, for the problem is not that the bird is weaned or unweaned, but

that it's having an adverse reaction to whatever is going on.

To complicate matters further, things are not always what they seem. Parrots are wild animals, not pets or human babies. Dave Flom, a breeder of trick-trained and flying show macaws as well as curator for the Rainforest Cafe's 20-plus international locations, suggests that anthropomorphic snuggling may be a contributing factor here. Dave says that mother birds snuggle, cuddle, and feed their babies when they are small, but once the babies are expected to learn to eat independently, their mother ignores their pleas for feeding and actually pushes them away when they beg. When the baby bird is adopted by humans (who are accustomed to holding, snuggling, and cuddling babies for years rather than weeks) the return to snuggling seems like a signal to the baby bird that things have returned to the way they were. The baby bird thinks, "Ah, all I have to do is beg more and louder, and they will feed me."

Sometimes the begging is a trick. The baby bird might be eating sufficiently when humans aren't there. Evaluate this possibility by weighing the bird the first thing every morning before it has a chance to eat. An electronic scale that measures weight in grams is invaluable for this process. They can be purchased for around $60 and up, and will be an invaluable tool during the bird's entire life. Sunbeam scales modified with perches are available from Love on the Wing at 612-898-3878. However, if you do not wish to purchase a scale, some astute and caring breeders will provide a scale on loan during the new bird's first six months in the new home. If the breeder or dealer has scales to loan for this purpose, expect to be asked for a deposit to ensure return of the scale in good condition.

A baby bird will drop some weight just before the time of fledging. This enhances the bird's chances of successful first flight. If it has been determined that a healthy baby is dropping weight other than that expected at fledging, then you can presume that it is not getting sufficient nutrition. If the bird is being offered a healthy balanced diet, then you must also presume that this bird is simply unwilling to eat independently. The baby bird is trying to convince humans that it will die if it is not better cared for (sometimes this can be true). Most of the time, however, the bird's perception that it will die if it isn't fed is merely a misconception based on the bird's own limited experience with life. Now it's time for the baby bird to learn how to be an adult bird, but this particular baby bird is not convinced that it must eat independently.

What to Do

If a true handfeeding process is necessary, do not heat the baby's food in a microwave oven. The unexpected effectiveness of this very popular product has inadvertently injured many baby parrots in both skilled and unskilled hands. When used to heat baby formula, microwaves create hot spots that are easily missed unless a thermometer or the handfeeder's finger is run completely through all areas of the baby food. Even then, a calloused finger can cause a sleepy or tired human to miss a formula hot spot large enough to fatally injure a baby parrot. Even professional handfeeders are best advised not to use microwave ovens for the heating of baby formula.

Begin this process by feeding what the handfeeder was feeding and mix it fresh every feeding. The bird needs warm food immediately, first thing (after being weighed) every morning. Offer warm baby formula, occasionally warm oatmeal, warm nutritious whole grain toast, or chunky warm food like cooked pasta or sweet potatoes every morning before the "Ack Ack" starts. The bird needs to see you and other birds sharing food also. The bird should more willingly accept warm food than room temperature or cold food any time of day. Jean Pattison suggests that giving the bird only a few bites of warm food from the hand can stimulate the bird to be interested in food in the bowl. Some birds will also want or may prefer a warm meal before bedtime.

The baby will probably accept warm chunky foods from the hand. Try to find some Harrison's Bird Diet (available through a veterinarian) or other balanced and respected avian formula. Rinse the Harrison's cubes with warm water and offer them moist (one at a time) from the hand. When offering vegetables, such as fresh or thawed frozen mixed veg-

Toys made from food are especially beneficial for newly weaned birds. (Severe macaw.)

etables, to the baby parrot, try sprinkling the moist vegetable mixture with a little Earth's Best Instant Mixed Grain Baby Cereal. The cereal increases the protein and other important nutrients missing in the vegetables, and the gloppy nature of the mixture served warm probably resembles chunky masticated food from the parents.

In the wild, young birds have fewer distractions during weaning. Even something so well-intentioned as toys can be distracting during this time. Dave Flom suggests that the weaning process can be easier and evolve more naturally if all the bird's toys during this time are made of food. Additionally, Dave suggests that no matter where the bird is perched, it should be able to reach interesting nutritious food at every moment. That means either providing multiple sources of food, or providing access to perching only beside the food. Dave also advises using exactly the same food that the handfeeder was using and not offering a variety so that the bird will not be confused about what to eat. Some other experts suggest offering an interesting selection of nutritious foods in a variety of sizes, shapes, colors, and textures for the bird to explore and play with. As the bird plays with the food, it will gradually begin actually consuming it. There's plenty of time for the bird to learn to play with nonfood toys. Now is the time for it to learn to be a bird by eating like a bird. It also helps to demonstrate the concept that "eating is fun" by eating with enthusiasm and gusto and by sharing food with the baby bird.

Other Possibilities and Pitfalls

Each incidence of crying or fussy begging must be averted before it starts. The bird must be distracted to exciting food or other acceptable activities before the begging begins. If the bird has eaten and continues to beg, consider the possibility that the behavior is related to something other than refusal to eat independently.

Some babies exhibiting this fussy begging may be suffering from a nutritional problem, for baby birds fed incomplete nutrition also sometimes retain or relapse into this behavior. This retained begging problem was much more widespread when handfeeders were trying to make their own formulas. Since the advent of quality pelleted and handfeeding diets, I see far fewer of these cases. Because every bite is balanced nutrition, try warm, moist Harrison's cubes or other good quality diet offered from the hand.

Be sure not to supplement vitamins without the supervision of an experienced avian veterinarian. Especially with mini macaws, *Brotegeris*, and some other parrots, including birds with weakened liver or kidneys, excess vitamin D_3 can hurt or even sometimes kill the bird.

Some birds that are begging for cuddling can be distracted to bathing. This can help the young bird to express in a more productive way the nervous energy that is coming out as fussy begging. Other forms of exercise such as step-ups, climbing, and flapping can also replace the retained baby behaviors. But the real key to success here is to guide the bird to become interested in the real work of a companion bird: destroying things, starting with food, and progressing to other items in its cage.

Consider the possibility that the bird is reacting to the room's temperature. It is a baby bird, and its tolerance for temperature changes is poor. If the bird has regressed to handfeeding, be sure to keep the room temperature at least 75 to 80°F (23.9–26.7°C). Or consider the possibility that the bird may be reacting to being kept too warm and try lowering the temperature a few degrees.

Unintentional Reinforcement

This problem can be from a true behavioral source, for the cuddling interaction might be rewarding and reinforcing the crying behavior. Humans are notoriously accommodating of darling baby animals, and a darling baby parrot is fully capable of wrapping a human around its little toe. The young bird wants to be treated more like a baby just at the time when it needs to be developing independent behavior. As with other types of behavior problems, improved daily practice of the step-up drill can provide the bird with a sense of what is expected and build confidence rather than the emotional dependency provided if snuggling is the primary way humans interact.

Be careful not to cuddle and comfort a begging bird; instead, demonstrate independent eating by eating in front of the bird and offering to share food. Play with the bird with food toys when it's hungry. Save those cuddles for the times when the bird is engaging in behaviors you wish to see continue or for the evening when even adult birds may naturally snuggle up together.

In the more intelligent species, such as the umbrella cockatoo, it is possible for the bird to get the upper hand in the entire interaction, sometimes rendering humans unable to discontinue handfeeding. This is emotionally and behaviorally difficult for both the bird and for the humans involved. Ultimately, both the humans and the bird can develop severe emotional and behavioral reactions that may take years to overcome. Professional help from a bird behavior consultant may be necessary.

Weaning a cockatoo, a macaw, an African grey, or, indeed, most any large hookbill takes an experienced hand, a special talent for convincing baby birds that they don't know what's best for them, and sometimes other birds to lead the way. The consequences of trying to successfully wean a parrot are so dire that weaning should be left only to experienced professionals with all the resources necessary to produce a sweet, interactive companion parrot that is also confident and independent. The bird will form a parent/offspring bond with the handfeeder and mate/flock member bonds in the new home. The types of interactions needed to help the bird develop independent behaviors, including independent eating, are the interactions youngsters would normally have with other youngsters, as well as the types of interactions adult birds would have with other adults. Birds mature quickly. Take cues from wild parent birds and treat that baby more like a participating member of the flock. The bird will soon learn that "big birds don't cry."

Beyond Biting: Patterning Techniques for Maintaining Peaceful Behavior

One of the most potentially troubling aspects of living with an undomesticated exotic bird is that this animal will sometimes bite humans. Whether the bird is biting because it is afraid, because it is defending its perceived territory, or because it simply wants to get its way, most humans are unaccustomed to tolerating such behavior. Many people who were, themselves, socialized with punishments, are naturally inclined to want to punish biting birds; however, there are several important reasons why this is not a good idea.

As a child of my parents' generation, when I first began writing about socializing birds, I was not immune to the punishment-to-deter-behavior school of thought. Although I knew better than to advocate hitting or squirting a bird as punishment, I was not above the use of time-outs as a response to aggressive biting behavior. And although I've seen time-outs work many times and never cause harm in 20 years of observations, I'm aware that a bird might have a bad

reaction to this technique. I've also learned that there are better and faster ways to modify bird behavior.

Punishment and Bird Behavior Modification

Things have changed in all areas of behavior modification. We now know that adults who were hit as children are more likely to hit others. We now potty train puppies by keeping them in den-like crates until it's time to go to the potty-approved area. It's easier. It works more quickly. We now know that any punishments are inappropriate as tools for the modification of behavior in companion birds.

Although punishments may sometimes appear, initially, to work (or may not), the dangers of punishments used against birds far outweigh possible benefits. The physical dangers of squirting a bird with a stream of water include potential complications from water forced into sinuses or aspirated into air sacks and injuries from falling, flying, or thrashing. There are also behavioral dangers. A bird that is punished with a squirt of water is in danger of developing behavioral complications such as fear or resentment toward the human administering the squirt, overall nervousness, feather chewing, and an aversion to bathing (one of the only ways a companion bird has of burning off excess energy). These behavioral complications can be observed as direct responses to squirting or they may be reflected in more subtle reactions that don't show themselves until later.

Birds that are dropped or thumped on the beak are in danger of physical injuries as well as adverse behavioral reactions. A sensitive bird that is punished with time-outs might develop phobic or self-mutilating behaviors. Additionally, when a bird is punished with painful or frightening techniques, it is not learning peaceful, cooperative behavior. Like human children, a bird that is punished with punitive methods is probably more likely to return aggression or to express anger or annoyance later. Therefore, rather than punishing birds, we guide them to cooperate by stimulating them to replace unwanted behaviors including biting with practiced behavioral patterns.

Patterning

Each time we do anything, it becomes easier and easier to do. When we do something for the first time, assemble a bicycle or operate a computer program, it is often terribly difficult and time-consuming. Each time we go through the motions of a task, that activity becomes both easier and faster until, after a time, the patterned activity is not only easier to do, but it actually becomes difficult to do something different. This can be defined as habitual behavior. If a parrot or a human is habitually cantankerous and uncooperative, then we must expect that individual to repeat the same or similar behaviors. Any time a bird bites a human, it's easier for that bird to bite that human next time.

Maintaining peaceful behavior in a parrot is dependent upon the regular practice and performance of redundant, interactive exercises. If a parrot is habitually cooperative, we can expect cooperative behavior throughout all areas of the bird's behavior. Each time a bird peacefully interacts with humans, it's easier for the bird to react peacefully the next time.

Patterning exercises are, therefore, interactive routines performed by birds and humans together that establish favored patterns that can be stimulated by the will of the humans. Additionally, the act of stimulating the pattern establishes the human as dominant in this status-oriented relationship. The patterning exercises I use most frequently are step-ups, the towel game, and interactive submissive postures.

Step-up Practice

Step-up practice (see p. 5) is the most significant tool for maintaining cooperative behavior throughout the companion bird's lifetime. Any parrot will exhibit mood changes. They can be little feathered dragons, and sometimes they must be allowed to breathe a little fire. But daily step-up practice combined with weekly towel games can usually return peaceful, cooperative behavior in a young, well-socialized bird.

The Towel Game

This might also be called "peeking out" patterning. It's an easy way to access a sense of safety for both birds and humans (towel-covered hands are more difficult to bite). The towel game really isn't like restraining

(top)
Begin the towel game by joining the bird in the towel.

(bottom)
A happy bird playing "the towel game" will become progressively more docile.

a bird in a towel for physical examination; it's more like playing peek-a-boo under the covers, only you use a towel instead of a blanket (the bigger the towel the better, so that at first one or more humans can get under there, too). Just try to make the bird feel happy and secure and let it peek out (cavity breeders spend a lot of time in small spaces peeking out) and sometimes hide the bird's head or eyes and then expose them and say, "peek-a-bird."

Begin by modeling the towel game with another human or pet. Sit low, across the room from the bird and hide your face with the towel, then lower the towel, peek around it, and blink, giggle, or say "peek-a-bird."

If this interaction is fun for everybody, including the bird, in a very short time, it will be a useful tool for gaining the bird's attention. Soon, you'll be able to put the bird on its regular step-up practice perch, maybe a chair back, in unfamiliar territory, and, approaching with the towel draped over both hands from below, gently surround the bird with the towel. At first, you don't even have to pick the bird up, but the approach from below is extremely important. If the bird is approached from above, the towel can stimulate a feeling of being attacked by a predator. Later, you can step the bird up onto a towel-covered hand or scoop up the bird enfolded in the towel and snuggle it like an infant.

Eventually, you will be able to cover only the bird's head with the towel, and the bird will think it's inside the towel. Then you can pet any known-to-be-enjoyable place that the bird can't see. (The neck is a good place to start, of course.)

Another way to start is with the towel laid over your lap with the long ends hanging down on each side. Put the bird on your lap and put one hand under each end of the towel. Lift the ends of the towel up to the sides of your face, making a sort of canyon or cavern with the bird and your face inside. At first you don't have to put your hands together; but you can eventually, and you can drape each end of the towel over the bird and then start looking for the bird and playing "peek-a-bird."

Another fun type of towel play is with two humans and one bird under the towel together. Put one end of the towel over each person's head, and sit facing each other (knee to knee) or stand a foot or so apart, and bring the bird up into the cave formed between your faces and the towel, then flirt, pet, and play with the bird. Actually, there's no wrong way to play peek-a-bird; any form of towel play is probably beneficial if the bird is interacting and enjoying the process!

It's usually easier to teach a baby bird to enjoy the towel game than to teach an older bird. However, older birds often naturally enjoy spending time in restricting enclosures such as a nest box. It is not unusual for even a retired breeding bird to be easily conditioned to absolutely adore the towel game. One cock umbrella cockatoo who was removed from active breeding because of his murderous advances on his mate was turned into a total pussycat with the towel game. It took him only a few weeks from being a devoted slasher and bringer of blood (he even broke a roommate's finger) to a creature that would dive breast-first into a snuggly towel and commence cuddling with amazing enthusiasm.

If a particular bird resists or fears a towel, try going to something that looks less towel-like, such as a nice,

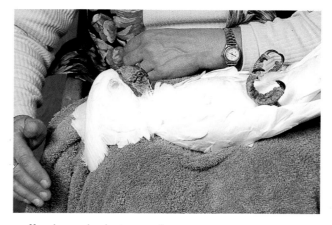

puffy down jacket or a large comforter. I see some benefit to using a towel about the color of the bird's body or under wings.

Extreme towel stress appearing at the wrong time can harm a bird physically or emotionally. Towel stress, as any experienced groomer or veterinarian can tell you, can kill a bird. A good professional avian behavioral evaluation should include an evaluation of the bird's responses to toweling. A bird that is extremely afraid of towels is existing in a life-threatening state and should receive behavioral intervention, possibly professional behavioral intervention, as quickly as possible.

Interactive Submissive Postures

This set of patterning techniques has been used for years by all kinds of successful bird owners. It involves putting the bird in a submissive position, possibly including only voice, or direct, intense, or severe eye contact; lowering the bird, or restraining

This umbrella cockatoo is completely mesmerized by the towel game.

the bird or some part of the bird; and suggesting appropriate behavior. This gets the bird's attention, reinforces the authority-based relationship, and suggests what you expect of the bird.

The most common interactive submissive posture is probably what some people call "the evil eye." This might also be called a "termination stimulus." It's a way of reminding the bird to terminate an unwanted behavior or the threat of an unwanted behavior. This process seems to work well in some birds, works not at all in other birds, and is too frightening for some birds. The evil eye probably stimulates a fear response in sensitive parrots because it's similar to the straight-on, even-eyed gaze of a predator. Parrots are prey species, not predators, as can be demonstrated by the eyes on the sides of their heads. This enables them to see danger approaching from beside or behind so that they can escape being someone's meal. When a bird is examining something with great inter-

est, it looks first with one eye and then with the other eye. When approaching a shy or unfamiliar bird, use less threatening eye contact, with one eye closer, and nose pointed to the side of the bird.

Straight-on eye contact in the manner of a predator can freeze a knowing bird into stillness. Once the bird's actions have been stopped by the gaze, humans can then suggest an appropriate behavior to replace the unwanted activity. Be careful when using new or unpatterned submission devices, as even a straight-on gaze can be too frightening for some birds, while flipping another bird over on its back might just barely get its attention.

Although some owners report success by merely looking in a particular way at their birds, others must revert to more direct interactive submissive postures. The second most common interactive submissive posture probably involves holding the bird still, possibly loosely restraining the beak by holding the maxilla (upper beak) gently with the thumb and first knuckle of the index finger on each side. Some birds enjoy being cuddled this way, and the owner should encourage this.

Preferred behavior is then suggested, with the patterned phrases, *"Be a good bird"* or *"Be careful."* Be sure not to shake the bird's head, as this can provoke anger or annoyance in the bird. Be sure not to hold the bird in the submissive posture too long, as this can stimulate other unwanted reactions. A bird that doesn't voluntarily and peacefully submit to the submissive interaction should be released within a couple of seconds. Then you must start over and gradually introduce and desensitize the bird to the interaction.

Temporary Distractions

If cooperative patterns have not yet been established, a biting bird may be temporarily distracted in order to begin patterning. This, too, will require some special planning and focus, because we know that it is difficult for most humans to ignore pain.

Part of the charm of companion parrots is their tendency to interact differently with different people. That is, a companion parrot might be nice as pie to some of the people in the home and might routinely nip or bite others who try to handle it with different techniques. Ideally, all humans interacting with the bird should be trained in the use of the same techniques, as companion parrots will respond to the same stimuli with the same behavior and to different stimuli with different behaviors. The primary distraction devices I usually recommend for biting during step-up interactions are the *wobble correction* and *good hand/bad hand.*

The Wobble Correction

This is a distraction device commonly used when the nipping or biting bird is sitting on a hand or on a hand-held perch. It is best employed just before the bird nips or bites; it may also be used just as the nip

occurs. The hand or perch that the bird is sitting on (not necessarily the one being nipped) is gently and quickly wobbled so that the bird must momentarily pay attention in order to regain balance. This is usually best accomplished by quickly tipping the outside end of the hand or hand-held perch first down and then back up. The bird will have to discontinue whatever it was doing to retain grip and balance. Be sure to maintain eye contact and remind the bird either to *"Be a good bird"* or to *"Be careful."*

A behavior that is not reinforced does not become a permanent fixture. As the bird tests the use of the beak on flesh, it might become necessary to respond a little more directly to test nips occurring during step-up practice. First be sure that the hand is being offered properly, coming from below and just over the feet near the place where the leg joins the belly. Then, if the bird nips the hand being offered, quickly dip the fingers of the hand the bird is sitting on (not the hand being offered and nipped), then return the hand to its former position. This must be accomplished carefully with a shy parrot so that the bird does not fall or become fearful during the process.

The bird will have to discontinue a nip in order to regain balance. It will soon understand that nips during step-ups cause "earthquakes." This correction must be done quickly, gently, and sensitively so that the bird is not overly affected either physically or emotionally.

"Good Hand/Bad Hand"

A bird might begin to bite even a well-placed hand prompt for the step-up command. The most common time for a nip or bite of a hand offered for step-ups is when the bird is being removed from a familiar perch, the inside, or top of the cage. This behavior can usually be defeated with improved technique and more frequent step-up practice in unfamiliar territory.

Maintain eye contact and offer the hand to be stepped on, approaching from below, as usual. Just as the prompt hand begins its approach to the bird, present an unfamiliar object just out of reach of the bird's beak (with one hand) and give the "step up" command (with the other hand) followed by *"Be a good bird."*

That is, if a bird is threatening to bite the hand I want it to step on, I can pick up a small object (a spoon, a telephone, or piece of junk mail) and hold it about an inch below and in front of the bird's beak, give the step-up command, and suggest good behavior. Usually the surprised bird, responding to the familiar behavioral pattern, and knowing what "good bird" means, responds also by being what it is expected to be (a good bird).

Eye contact is especially important here. A bird will often maintain eye contact rather than bite. If the bird's eye is distracted by the introduced object, it will seek to regain eye contact immediately rather than take the time to bite after being distracted.

Even if the bird bites, that unfamiliar object, rather than the hand being offered, will probably be bitten. Care must be taken to ensure that the distraction device is not frightening to a shy parrot. The distraction object must be neither too large (which might scare the bird off the perch), too small (which might be ineffective), nor toxic (a lead or painted object).

Rainfall

Even rainfall might be used as a distraction device. A bird that has been sitting around storing up energy might have a powerful urge to release that energy by first attracting, then biting, a human. If you know that a particular bird engages in this behavior, the bird might first be distracted from the biting behavior and helped to release unused energy by the exercise provided by a shower bath.

A bird that has been patterned with redundant practice to enjoy, or at least endure, frequent showers can be distracted from aggression, roaming, screaming, or other unwanted behaviors with a sensitively administered spray bath. This differs from squirting as punishment in that it is administered carefully in a manner resembling rainfall *before* unwanted behavior occurs. The source of the spray, usually a spray bottle, is held lower than the bird's head and far enough away from the bird that the bird is not focused on the tool providing the spray mist. The spray mist is aimed over the bird's head so that it falls down on the bird like rainfall rather than being directed at any part of the bird's anatomy. A bird that is

What Do You Do if the Bird Is Biting You?

Of course, the best way to deal with biting is to prevent it (see Beyond Biting, p. 152), but if all efforts have failed and you are looking down at a tiny cockatoo lacerating your flesh and unwilling to quit lacerating your flesh, what do you do?

Dianalee Deter suggests that if the bird is sitting on your hand or on a perch, it's pretty easy to get the bird to release by pushing the hand being bitten toward the bird. Of course, this is absolutely counterintuitive. Anyone who knows how human reflexes work probably knows that most humans experiencing a painful bite want to pull their hand away. A human who pulls away runs the risk of ripping flesh, injuring the bird, or actually teaching the bird to bite by a response that will reinforce the behavior.

In addition to the wobble correction (p. 157), some relief may be seen by putting the bird quickly, gently, and unceremoniously on the floor. Some birds will release if light-blocking fabric is placed over their heads. If the bird is hanging on and grinding, you might try forcing something else into the beak, deflecting the bird to bite down on a magazine or a handy pair of glasses.

Eye contact is really important here, for often, if you can catch the bird's eye, it will usually release the bite. A manufactured distraction may be necessary to change the determined bird's focus on the bite. That could mean slapping a magazine loudly against a table with the other hand, popping a balloon, or suddenly turning the television volume way up with the remote.

responding to rainfall, either by cheerfully bathing or merely tolerating the water, will not be engaging in other unwanted behavior.

The Appropriate Response

The very best response to a baby bird testing beak on flesh—especially if it is merely testing or using the beak for balance—is no response at all. A behavior that is not reinforced is less likely to become a habit, and very interactive birds might perceive almost any response to be reinforce-

ment. While humans not reacting to a nip might seem counterintuitive or unlike the way humans would naturally react, this course of action eliminates the possibility of accidental reinforcement of the behavior, for sometimes any reaction may be perceived by the bird as reinforcement of the behavior.

You must absolutely avoid the possibility of accidentally reinforcing a nip, for a behavior that is reinforced stands a chance of becoming a habit. A practiced and accomplished nipping habit can easily be expanded (accidentally, of course) into a biting habit.

Accidental Reinforcement

The laughter of the favorite human is probably the most powerful reinforcer of companion parrot behavior. The one companion bird behavior principle that is, in my opinion, "cast in stone" is "Never, never laugh when your bird bites your spouse." This would be the ultimate cruelty—reinforcing a naturally self-rewarding behavior (a bird biting a rival) into an irresistibly patterned habitual urge.

A biting bird is often looking for any kind of attention. Even the drama generated by a cry of pain from a nipped human can be all a creative young parrot needs to decide that beak-on-flesh thing is really fun! Just put the bird down. This is probably the opposite of the attention the bird is seeking. Better still, try preventing a bite by maintaining eye contact when interacting with the bird. Often, this one simple manipulation is all that is necessary to prevent a curious, attention-seeking young parrot from biting.

Put the bird down if you wish to discontinue eye contact. This is where that safe, interesting portable perch comes in. A greater frequency of side-by-side interactions rather than constant face-to-face interactions leads to healthier, more independent relationships with companion parrots.

On the other hand (if you'll pardon the pun) you can also reinforce any appropriate use of beak on flesh. A parrot that learns that it will get all the attention it needs with sweet, sweet kisses will be most likely to use that beak sweetly and sensitively each time it touches human skin.

Reinforcing Introduced Behavioral Changes

A parrot behavior consultant seldom encounters birds that completely resist behavioral change. The vast majority of birds usually respond to predictable environmental or handling manipulations: rewards, bathing, eye games, step-up training, petting, exercises, and so on.

Often the behavior consultant is asked to modify what is described as a behavioral nightmare. The bird may be called "Freddie Kruger" or "The Evil One." The bird may be said to be so skittish that the owners fear it will thrash about and injure itself.

What I usually find is a normal, perhaps stubborn, animal that is simply giving off incomprehensible behavioral messages. The bird may be poorly socialized or slightly socialized—possibly in an inappropriate or understimulating environment. In the presence of professional sensitivity and behavioral techniques that have been around for years, most of the birds I see behave like little angels. Because the behavioral professional seldom sees the bird's worst behavior, the success of the intervention depends upon a successful partnership with the owners (who are well aware of how the bird usually acts) serving as the primary mechanism for observing and reporting the bird's true behavior.

A behavior modification session, conducted in a calm but festive manner in the presence of shared food, verbal caresses, mists of water, silliness, and snuggly towel cuddling, usually reveals—within a very short time—a responsive, cooperative animal. The owners are often stunned, moved to tears, and comment that they "don't recognize" or "don't know" that creature responding so compliantly to tried and proven methods.

Are the Changes Permanent?

Possibly. Even step-ups are just a quick fix if they are done only by the behavior consultant. You probably have a window of opportunity of two to four days to reinforce the changes. If the bird returns to exactly the same physical and behavioral environment, the behavior will return to what it was before.

Actually, few behavioral changes can be described as permanent, for behavior evolves with time, changing—sometimes subtly, sometimes dramatically—over the years. Even behavioral changes in humans aren't usually permanent and most changes that become permanent start out temporary.

Any human behavioral counselor, especially an addictions counselor, can tell you that the hardest change to bring about is the first one. A

human counselor will also readily admit that just because someone discontinues a well-entrenched habit for one day or one week doesn't mean that person's behavior is permanently changed. Ongoing support and reinforcement are considered necessary to bring about real, long-term behavioral change.

Bird behavior isn't always immediately and permanently changed by behavioral intervention either; however, the benefit of immediate changes being demonstrated can be the turning point in the attitudes of

Even teenage Amazons seldom resist introduced behavioral changes. (Blue-crowned Amazon.)

161

humans who create the bird's environment. Because it is difficult to change human behavior, quick fixes used to demonstrate what a companion bird is capable of may be the best way to convince humans that if they change their ways, the bird's behavior will also change. That's a bigger *if* than it sounds. It's a real temptation to train the bird and stop; but if humans are not adequately trained, the intervention may be unsuccessful even though the bird responded perfectly.

Verbal Rewards: Molding a Parrot's Behavior with Praise

A few summers ago, a tall, shy man brought his baby cockatiel to me for taming. The bird was a parent-raised pearl hen of exceptionally charming demeanor. The owner was unsuccessfully trying to teach her to enjoy interactions with his hands. She would not step up or allow petting. Seeking to scratch the little bird's neck, the tall man would quietly, stiffly reach out to touch her; and she would bite him.

I said, "Talk to her the way you talk to your wife. Tell her that she's pretty and that you love her and want her to be happy."

He gave me a strange look, then practiced whispering sweet nothings to the little bird, who just seemed to melt in his hands, learning not only to step up, but also to be petted in somewhat less than half an hour.

A few weeks later, bird and owner returned for a grooming lesson. The little cockatiel was sweet, tame, and affectionate. The man looked even taller than before. When I commented on the changes—the well-reinforced step-up response, etc.—the happy cockatiel owner grinned and said, "If you think that's something, you should see the change in my wife!"

This astute client had learned that verbal reinforcement (praise) in anticipation of good behavior (cooperation) is one of the strongest tools available in the modification of behavior in any creature. He had used this tool to initiate and reinforce quickly generated behaviors in his cockatiel. He had also successfully applied this technique to improve a human relationship.

While spouses, lovers, and baby hen cockatiels obviously respond well to verbal praise, even the wickedest, wildest parrot (or human) can respond to conscientious application of this technique. Actually, it's quite common to accidentally reinforce behavior, especially in a creature that is looking for any kind of attention (reward). A normal, creative parrot trained to anticipate praise (reward) for good behavior usually becomes more willing to seek new ways to generate rewards. The bird will also gradually abandon behaviors that do not bring at least occasional reinforcement.

Training with verbal rewards may sound subtle, but the results can be spectacular. This is absolutely the easiest way to train a bird. It is often successfully employed even though humans may be unaware of what they are doing. A "verbal praise" style of training might be more commonly used naturally or as a matter of conditioning by females and may contribute to the large number of companion parrots that favor females.

What About Food Rewards?

Food is more important to some birds than to others. I like to spend the first half hour of the in-home evaluation watching what the bird and humans do while sharing pizza. Many socially bonded birds will begin either begging or eating before the pizza box is opened or placed on the table. This is expected behavior in established companion Amazons, macaws, and conures—birds with a reputation for being easily enticed and reinforced with food.

Some birds will do anything for food rewards and respond to them like they read somebody's book on the subject. But food rewards might not be in the bird's best interest. Some of the popular types of parrots have a tendency to become overweight and develop related health problems if food, especially high fat human junk food, is given often. Food rewards must be carefully monitored to ensure that they contribute to good physical, as well as emotional, well being.

Many birds don't appear to be motivated by food at all. Some stubborn individuals might have to be half starved before they will take food from the human hand and eat it. While a few of these birds are demonstrating alienation, the overwhelming majority, especially cockatoos and many domestic handfeds, are simply so crazy about people that they would rather play or cuddle than eat when humans are present.

Cockatoos have a frequent tendency to this play-rather-than-eat behavior. Many cockatoos would rather have face-to-face interaction such as being held or talked to than side-by-side interaction such as eating together. Training or correcting problem behaviors in these birds sometimes proves more difficult for new parrot owners because there is so little instruction available in the use of nonfood rewards as a behavior modification tool. I suspect this situation exists not because food rewards are more effective, but rather because nonfood rewards are so difficult to explain.

The Set Up

The first step to molding a bird's behavior with verbal rewards is to teach the bird the meaning of "good bird." Most birds respond emotionally to melodious voices in soothing tones. Teaching a bird the meaning of the words "good bird" usually comes very naturally, as a soothing, cooing intonation conveys the meaning quite effectively. The bird may pinpoint or display in response to this type of verbal caress. Then the "good bird" verbal reward can be used any time the bird is engaging in appropriate behavior or any time the bird is not engaging in inappropriate behavior.

Be careful not to overdo verbal praise, for too much adoration can come to seem like a courtship song to a sex-starved companion parrot. If strutting, pinpointing, tail-fanning sexual displays are frequently reinforced, we might wind up with a beautiful little "fire breathing dragon" who often bites, regurgitates, and masturbates.

Anticipation

In the past few years, I have come to believe that it is undesirable to use negative terms such as "bad bird," especially when you are prompting to step up. If we want the bird to do something, it's very confusing to be saying both "step up" and "no" or "bad bird" at the same time. I prefer to use the words "good bird" to both reinforce appropriate behavior and to prevent inappropriate behavior. A sensitive owner can see a bite or a screaming fit coming, but no amount of yelling *"Bad bird!"* will stop a bird from screaming (actually, it might reinforce the screaming). On the other hand, a calm, authoritative demeanor combined with a stern verbal reminder, *"You'd better be a good bird!"* will remind the feathered companion not only that you are the boss, but also that good things come to good birds!

A Sense of Cooperation and Loving Authority

It is not unusual for a bird to abuse a human who talks sweetly but fails to effectively pattern a cooperative relationship. If the bird doesn't see a particular human as dominant, then that human might be treated as territory, a possession, or a rival.

I believe that a successful relationship between human and companion bird casts the human in the role of loving parent. Because parrots have a strong instinct to understand what is expected, a lovingly patterned authority-based relationship is probably the best way to maintain a long-term cooperative relationship between human and parrot. This is easily accomplished with the frequent (most days) practice of the step-up command, which functions in the bird's emotional and behavioral environment much like prayer or meditation to a human.

Just as parrots who favor females may be responding to a particular style of reinforcement, parrots who favor males may be expressing an attraction to stolid body language and successful use of authority. The bird's behavior is changed by coaching the human client either to improve nurturing or effective authority interactions.

While one bird might respond better to more snuggles and praise, another bird might respond to more patterning to cooperate with loving authority. In most cases, however, both behavioral tools must be balanced in order for the companion parrot to effectively maintain acceptable-to-humans behavior throughout its long life. Without loving reinforcement, the use of authority is inappropriate and usually ineffective. Without authority, the loving reinforcement might not be enough.

Forgetting Foul Language and Other Nuisance Sounds

An old preacher I used to spend time with loved to say:

"Live so that you could sell the family parrot."

This means, of course, to be careful what you say in front of the bird, because the bird will repeat in its next home what it heard in this one.

Of course, caring, modern parrot owners know better than to intentionally teach their birds profanity. Sometimes, however, in spite of the best intentions and carefully edited adult language, even the most well-meaning parrot owners wind up with a bird that screams profanities at battered toys, whistles shrill electronic signals at ear-splitting decibels, or turns belching into avian opera.

While the screaming parrot may present a problem for neighbors, frequent or untimely nuisance sounds or profanity can adversely affect the quality of a bird's life by annoying humans in its own home. A foul-mouthed bird may be increasingly isolated and left to gradually lose interest in interactions with humans. Often, foul-mouthed birds are banned from exciting, mind-expanding outings as well as social interactions with honored guests.

Preventing Profanity

Probably the most common nuisance word or phrase for a companion parrot to acquire is an occasional obscenity, "hot damn" or "darn," or more colorful expressions that most of us would not repeat in front of parents, children, or priests. A parrot doesn't exactly spontaneously invent words (although it can happen); the bird is usually copying some sound it relates to. So how did those particular words or sounds wind up coming out of this bird? The bird is mimicking what it heard. It's amazing how many humans seem truly unaware that they are, obviously, saying the words that their birds are repeating.

But something else has to happen in order for the new words to become a part of the bird's behavior. There are three components to the establishment of habitual behavior: modeling (being shown what to do), enactment (doing the behavior), and reinforcement (being rewarded for enacting the behavior). Even if a bird has learned to speak a human word, the word will not be repeated frequently if the bird is not rewarded, usually with attention, for saying the word.

Distracting to Different Behavior

The easiest way to get a bird to discontinue saying something is by getting it to say or do something else. This usually involves an initial inventory or evaluation of the problem followed by diverting the bird to different words or behavior before the unwanted words or sounds are made. This may or may not be necessary in dealing with a new word

Kenya Sue

When my baby Jardine's parrot, Kenya Sue, started exuberantly screaming a popular but unacceptable phrase (and I don't mean Felix Unger) at her favorite toy, I was shocked and certain that my mouth was not the source of such words. I called the store where Kenya Sue was raised and asked the owner if my baby bird could have heard those words there.

"Well," Dianalee reluctantly admitted, "she wouldn't hear that here from a human, but I took in a couple of macaws that say it. They get really 'wound up' in the evenings, using lots of profanity after the store closes."

But why would Kenya Sue suddenly develop this behavior? Examining the environment further, I realized that she might have heard those words during a remodeling project in the room adjacent to hers. Kenya Sue heard those words first at Paradise Found, then later when she heard them again, it was only natural that she would then repeat them.

As soon as I was able to identify the source of that most obnoxious phrase, I could discontinue it, Kenya Sue no longer heard it, and she was less likely to repeat it. I was careful not to laugh or to reward her with attention at any time when the behavior was repeated. I spent a few minutes every day providing appropriate distractions to other fun new behaviors.

Thankfully, those awful words disappeared within a few days. I really don't expect to hear them again (unless Kenya Sue hears them again). This occasional behavior was not reinforced and, therefore, did not become an established part of the bird's everyday behavior.

that has appeared only recently, for often, simply ignoring a newly appeared behavior will eliminate it.

Something I call "remodeling" is another valuable device that can be easily used to vanquish new nuisance words. If the bird is saying, for example, "damn it!," you can often "divert" the pronunciation of the newly acquired word to something like "can it!" This can be done either as a spontaneous response to the word or as a planned distraction used before use of the offensive word.

Remodeling can be combined with use of the model/rival method that is often described by Dr. Irene Pepperberg in her work with Alex, the African grey. This process involves setting up a competitive situation in which a human or other bird rival is rewarded for saying a more desirable word or pronunciation. If the bird says "damn it!" and is not rewarded, and the rival bird or human assistant says "can it" and is rewarded, then the bird, seeking to be rewarded, will learn to say "can it."

Habitual or Established Profanity

If a behavior has been repeated for about 21 days, there is a good chance that it has become habitual; that is, it has become an established part of the bird's routine behavior. A bird that has been habitually repeating a nuisance phrase or sound for a few months or a few years will be a more difficult challenge than a bird that has only recently started repeating a noxious expletive. Actually, the bird will never forget how to say a word that has become an established part of its vocabulary. Just as you can remember how to say a word that you may not have spoken in many years, and just as you can remember how to play Monopoly® and ride a bicycle (although you haven't done those things for quite some time), a parrot will remember things it said years ago. However, if there is sufficient reason not to say or do those old things from the past, humans and birds alike simply will not do them. How does this happen?

Behaviors that no longer serve a purpose become obsolete and are replaced by behaviors that have a purpose in the current environment. Superfluous old behaviors are replaced by useful new behaviors. But changing any habitual behavior usually isn't easy, and the first of the unwanted behaviors to be eliminated

is always the most difficult. (For example, for a habitual beer drinker, the next, first beer is the hardest beer not to drink.)

In helping a bird to discontinue an established, habitual use of profanity, begin by evaluating when the profanity appears. Is it during play or during the regular practice of the bird's vocabulary? Does it occur at a particular time of day or when events in the home stimulate it as a response? If you know when a sound is usually made, you are well on your way to replacing that sound with a different one.

A bird can often be enticed to play with a favorite toy rather than scream when humans leave the room. (Blue-fronted Amazon.)

Human Body Sounds

Although most parrots will probably manage to avoid the accidental acquisition of profanity in the vocabulary, many of them will acquire other nuisance sounds. African greys are especially fond of burps and belches and other gastronomic body expressions. Quakers and caiques just love to mimic human coughing and sneezing.

Guiding a companion bird away from human body sounds is usually more difficult than guiding it away from profanity, as few spoken words resemble these sounds. Again, we must anticipate the behavior before it occurs and distract the bird to different behavior. The bird must be distracted to sounds that are both more acceptable to humans and that are just as fun for the bird to make. Laughter is such a self-rewarding activity. It's usually easy to distract an interested, well-motivated bird to laughter before the gross body sounds begin. Again, if you've been unable to divert away from the rude sounds, be sure not to laugh after they begin.

Whistles and Beeps

Both greys and their cousins, *Poicephalus,* as well as caiques, *Pionus*, Amazons, and lories seem especially attracted to ear-piercing parrot versions of electronic devices: the alarm clock, the phone, the microwave, the smoke detector. These sounds often seem to resemble some of the more-or-less natural alarm calls that these birds use in the wild. Shrill whistles

and ersatz electronic beeps have the potential to be the most annoying of all nuisance sounds. They have the potential to be delivered at greater volume than annoying words, and they can be used more insistently as attention-demanding behavior as well as true expressions of alarm.

While the actual volume of these sounds might not carry even from one room to another, they can be outrageously painful to the sensitive human hearing mechanism (a bird's hearing mechanism can handle it). An agitated or excited bird might sit there and parrot the smoke alarm at outrageous volume for enough time to cause humans in the room to want to rip their eardrums out. And while time-outs or briefly covering the cage are ineffective at changing this behavior, if the bird is very wound up, briefly covering the bird might calm it enough that it can be distracted to a different behavior. Be sure to use a cover that is heavy enough to block vision and to block a significant amount of light. Be sure to set a timer so that the bird is not forgotten to sleep the day away. An alarm that goes off, maybe ten minutes later, can signal the beginning of step-up practice time or towel game time or some other pleasant but also beneficial activity. Showers may be especially helpful. A bird recovering from shower time is not usually motivated to attract attention by making annoying noises, and this behavior can be reinforced into a habit.

It's sometimes possible to replace or remodel these sounds to more appropriate whistles, sometimes whistles with responses. Occasionally, actual songs sung in human words can be interesting enough to distract a confirmed beeper. The phrase "peek-a-boo," enacted with or without the towel game, is often interesting enough to distract away from both annoying words and sounds.

Other Bird and Animal Sounds

Some of the most annoying and often treatment-resistant sounds acquired by parrots are the sounds made by other birds or animals. A few years ago, I worked with a Moluccan cockatoo that had somehow managed to acquire a lion's roar (at cockatoo volume!), and some of the most nervous grey parrot owners I have ever seen live with grey parrots who learned the monotonous call of the hen cockatiel (with grey parrot precision of tone and volume). While it's sometimes amusing to hear a lovebird's version of umbrella cockatoo screams, the Amazon version of "hen cockatiel" or the African grey version of "crow" can be exceptionally annoying.

Acquired animal sounds are, like human body sounds and electronic sounds, usually more difficult to modify than human words. They are, however, also sometimes more predictably enacted at a particular time of day. A companion grey parrot might do "hen cockatiel" at sunrise or a Jardine's parrot might do "blue-crowned Amazon" when it's time to eat. To divert from these behaviors,

the daily routine must be changed in some substantial way so that enactment of the behavior is avoided. The grey parrot that does hen cockatiel at sunrise might have to have a more-light-proof cover so that it doesn't know when the sun rises. Then the breakfast routine can be changed in some way to create an entirely different interactive ritual, maybe by removing the bird to a perch to eat breakfast rather than providing the morning meal in the cage.

Diverse Experiences

As with humans, a bird that finds joy in only a few things is likely to become obsessed with those few things. This is just one more example of how lack of stimulation creates bad behavior in companion birds. That famous old source of almost all bird behavior problems, boredom, also contributes to habitually redundant behaviors including the repeating of nuisance words and sounds. Here we can expand the bird's experiences so that it learns new ways to enjoy life. If the bird is encouraged to do many different, diverse behaviors, then statistically, the relative amount of time allocated to repeating nuisance sounds will naturally become smaller. The offensive words and sounds will gradually disappear.

Extreme Screaming

The neighbors are pounding on the door threatening to call the police, and McPaco McAwe, Jr. just keeps right on screaming. You're faced either with removing the bird from your home, or finding a new home for both of you.

Usually it doesn't get quite this far. Whether you're dealing with a full-blown screaming problem or simply trying to prevent one, the cure may be easier than you think. A conscientious program to reduce screaming can usually make a big difference from the very first day. With a little extra human attention and energy directed in a different way for only a few weeks, caring owners can recapture peace in the home.

You can't exactly erase screaming behaviors, but you can often replace most of them with quieter behaviors. You can also create locations in the home habitat where the bird will not scream.

Learning When to Scream and When Not to Scream

Redundant screaming develops like any other habitual behavior in companion parrots: it is improvised or copied from another source; it is reinforced; and it becomes a permanent part of the behavioral environment. Most screaming in human-identified companion parrots probably starts as attention-demanding behavior. That is, the behavior is used to obtain interactions with humans or the favorite human. But screaming has another component in parrots: it appears to be fun. Some birds appear to learn to scream simply because they enjoy screaming. A behavior that is fun to do just for the doing, like drinking whiskey and spending money, is called a self-rewarding behavior. Self-rewarding behaviors can usually be replaced only with other self-rewarding behaviors.

Older birds develop calls for mates and other types of screaming motivations, but these behaviors don't always become habitual screaming. Again, these screaming behaviors follow the usual path of development of any habitual behavior (see the section on the acquisition of nuisance sounds, pp. 165–169). Like other nuisance sounds and behaviors, screaming behavior is best modified sooner rather than later.

While it is probably unwise and unhealthy to completely train a parrot not to scream, it is probably more possible than most people believe. Having seen and heard many stories of surprisingly stealthful behavior, I know that wild parrots encounter situations and visit sites in the wild where they do not scream as a matter of safety. Obviously they have to learn this behavior from other parrots, for a wild baby parrot that attracts too much attention of the wrong kind will, by experience, soon be a dead baby parrot. That is, if people can be trained to function as well as wild parrots who teach (screaming or nonscreaming) behaviors to their young, then people can teach parrots to be quiet at certain times and in certain places.

Although my blue-crowned Amazon continues to occasionally scream in my living room, he doesn't scream on the balcony any more because he knows he will be removed immediately from the balcony. He likes his shady, lofty view of downtown Denver. Saucey is a teenager, a wild-caught *Farinosa* Amazon. He occasionally vocalizes a loud chirp, and he often pleasures himself at surprising volume when he is on the balcony. But Saucey has not screamed on the balcony in quite some time even though he had become habitually noisy before an assertive neighbor demanded silence. When Saucey is on the balcony, he no longer yells at all—not at the garbage trucks or ambulances or lawn mowers. He merely chirps loudly at marauding squirrels venturing within feet of his territory!

I don't know exactly how wild parrots teach their babies when and where to be quiet, but I can tell you how Saucey the blue-crowned Amazon learned to be quiet on the balcony and reduced his screaming by about 80 percent overall. Most companion parrots respond almost immediately to this simple three-step program. To correct excessive screaming:

1. Evaluate specific characteristics of the problem;

2. Anticipate screaming behaviors before they occur;

3. Provide irresistible self-rewarding distractions to replace the screaming behaviors.

1. Evaluate the Bird and the Environment. Carefully evaluate all elements of the bird's environment. Is the bird's cage large enough, short enough, and favorably located? Is the bird's foraging (play) area exciting? Does the bird have ready access to several interesting things to do: multiple branches to climb and peel, a variety of textures of destructible chewables, a selection of interactive toys, a choice of toys that make sounds? Does the bird have good quality lighting and at least 12 hours of sleep time per 24-hour period? Does the bird have constant access to fresh water? Is the bird's eating schedule regular? Is the diet interesting, nutritious, and diverse? Does the bird have adequate social time, with some face-to-face interactions (talking, step-ups, towel games, petting, etc.) and some side-by-side interactions (eating, showering, watching TV, etc.) with humans? Does the bird enjoy adequate exercise, access to bathing, and occasional excursions outside familiar territory? Does the bird have a television on a timer as a "passage-of-time marker" if alone during the day?

If its reasonable needs aren't being met, then the bird has cause to scream. Sometimes, something as simple as changing a fouled water bowl or providing new, bark-covered branches can create contentment and fulfillment in a bird that is otherwise both vocal and truculent.

In this process, you examine when, where, why, and how the bird is screaming. Usually either times of day or particular situations can be identified: *Mom is on the phone; Dad is reading the paper; isn't someone supposed to be holding me?*

Keep a log or journal to document the times of screaming. If the neighbor's complaints come in by phone, a caller ID unit that stores many numbers will have this information already recorded for you. Knowing the elements of a particular bird's screaming habits is crucial in order to anticipate and distract from the behavior.

Try to determine the cause of the problem, (e.g., a bird screams when you leave the room). Obviously, the true problem isn't that you leave the room, for you will sometimes have to leave the room. The solution to the problem is not doing what the bird demands (it is an unreasonable demand) but rather convincing McPaco that his needs are being met even though you are not in the room. This is a problem of poor socialization. McPaco has not yet learned to entertain himself.

If the bird, especially a cockatoo, macaw, or Amazon, is screaming with great volume, it might be wise to begin this program with ear protection for humans in the home. Hearing damage can result from a constant barrage of loud screaming. If the screaming behaviors are a response to a new infant in the home, you might have to send the bird away temporarily for behavior modification. This is probably unnecessary in most cases, especially if the home is large enough to offer shelter from the sound.

White noise—a TV, radio, fan, or soft music—or soundproofing between rooms may help to prevent the bird from yelling in response to baby or bird sounds from another part of the home. An acoustical consultant (listed in the yellow pages) can determine the decibel level of bird screams in various locations and advise whether these are dangerous or damaging levels. An acoustical consultant might also advise decorating elements or architectural modifications to improve sound absorption properties in the home.

It is usually especially helpful to know:

- the time, duration, and volume of screaming (McPaco screams at 5:25 P.M. for 20 minutes at a volume of about "5" or until we pick him up); and
- the behavioral stimuli for screaming (McPaco screams when he hears the baby cry, when we leave the room, or when the baby or the puppy plays with a rattle or squeaky toy).

2. Anticipate Incidents of Screaming Before They Occur. The process of solving a companion parrot's screaming problem is not unlike attending a murder mystery party where guests must confer with one another and examine individual clues in order to solve a "crime." The evaluation is a list of clues. Sometimes only one clue will be enough to break the case. Some of the clues may be relevant, some may not. You probably won't be able to tell the difference between the relevant clues and the irrelevant ones without investigating several different clues.

This written record is the most important tool in addressing any screaming problem. If there is no record of exactly how much the bird is screaming, how long, and how loud, then it's difficult to evaluate whether or not progress is being made. In particular, during the screaming modification program, expected to be about 21 days, every possible incident of screaming should be prevented before it begins.

Once you know when problem screaming occurs and what it is a response to, you can avert the behavior by removing the stimulus, if possible, or by offering distractions before the behaviors occur. Diet can often be manipulated to distract from morning and evening screaming. Give McPaco a new toy or make him mad at his bell (and model beating up the bell) by ringing it loudly in his face to stimulate a different behavior (attacking the bell) before you leave the room.

3. Provide Irresistible Self-rewarding Distractions. A parrot's screaming problem will best be resolved when the bird can reward its own good behavior. Therefore, built-in, environmental distractions (rewards McPaco can give himself) are the stuff that true emotional independence is made of. Intermittent reinforcement for spontaneous acceptable independent behavior may generate increasingly independent behavior. When the bird learns that it will be rewarded for playing alone, it will repeat the behaviors that generate rewards. The bird will also be more experimental in seeking new opportunities for rewards, fre-

quently innovating both active and passive forms of self rewards. That is, not only do birds frequently successfully learn to play alone, they often learn to provide their own rewards for doing so. I have seen and heard many stories of birds who often congratulate themselves on being "very good" or "very pretty" or "very smart"!

The Termination Stimulus

Covering or removing all sensory input by placing the bird in the dark is probably the fastest way to quiet a screaming bird. This will not usually change behavior. However, with some very intelligent birds, you can use an intermediate technique known as a "termination stimulus" to give the bird a chance to gain composure by giving clues about what is going to happen. This process can change screaming behavior. You know that you have to do something when an alarm goes off: if you don't get out of bed, you'll lose your job; if you don't take the cake out of the

Fresh twiggy branches can be irresistible to a companion Moluccan cockatoo.

173

Screaming is sometimes a true behavioral emergency wherein loss of home or living space is threatened. Sometimes, the only thing to do is first to find a way to immediately quiet the bird. Unless we can achieve quiet in the first place, we will have no acceptable behavior to reinforce.

If McPaco is screaming out of control, begin by finding a way to calm him without actually reinforcing his poor behavior. That might mean providing a spray bath (cold shower) or ringing a bell until he attacks the bell. Probably the only thing that will work more or less immediately is covering the entire cage with light-proof fabric or otherwise removing enough light from the room that the bird dozes off. Obviously, this is a quick fix, and long-term application of this technique without adequate controls and reinforcement can worsen the problem. It could even injure the bird's health.

oven, it will burn. The alarm clock is not a punishment. It's a warning that an unwanted consequence will occur unless an action is taken.

For screaming parrots, you can use a termination stimulus that I call "flagging." You signal the bird that if it does not stop screaming, it will be covered. Start the flagging or signaling process by placing the bird in the cage with one towel draped over the side of the cage from which the bird sees the most distraction. Advise McPaco that he must be a "good bird" or more decisive measures will follow.

If the bird continues screaming, a second reminder to be a "good bird" and a second towel applied to the second most distracting side of the cage further advise the bird that no screaming is allowed at this time. If the bird continues to scream, a light-proof cover is applied to the entire cage, and you set an alarm clock or timer for about ten minutes after the screaming subsides. This gives the bird time to cool off emotionally and, hopefully, to forget what was happening before the required "nap." Following the cooling-off period, direct social or indirect environmental distractions are provided, and the bird is reinforced for quiet behavior. Be sure to use a timer as a reminder to uncover the cage. It can be very hard on McPaco if he is forgotten and remains covered all day!

As the modification program proceeds, the first "flag" (or warning flag) may be all that is needed to quiet McPaco. If the bird stops screaming with only one towel in place, you have made real progress. The first time or two this happens, reinforce it immediately. As the program progresses, wait a minute or two to ensure that the bird has, in fact, stopped screaming, then reinforce the behavior. Wait a few more minutes, then remove the towel; if the bird remains quiet, reinforce.

Flagging contributes to the actual modification of screaming behaviors only if all the bird's needs are being met. If the bird has a legitimate gripe, if important elements are missing from the bird's environment, this kind of treatment may aggravate the situation. Influencing the bird to stop screaming is only a quick fix. True success in curing a screaming problem doesn't come when the bird stops screaming; it comes when the screaming behavior has been replaced with another (acceptable) self-rewarding behavior.

Exploiting the Environment

Never underestimate the influence of exercise, including bathing, on appropriate, well-measured behavior in companion parrots. Most of these creatures' ancestors evolved in rain forests and developed metabolisms that were capable of flying around, foraging for food, finding water and minerals, finding and defending nests sites, courtship, and raising offspring; and they had to be capable of doing so, sometimes in pouring rain, for more than 300 days a year. A bird that is not provided with adequate opportunities (or sometimes requirements) for exercise may be nervous, high strung. A bird that is neither flying around, foraging for food, and so on (see above) nor experiencing frequent drenching showers might have an abundance of unused energy. A bird with too much energy is a bundle of behavior problems waiting to happen, and screaming is only the first.

A bird going through a screaming phase during warm weather might be treated to several showers of different intensities during the day. This is not to say, squirt the bird in a "There! Take That!" kind of way, but rather provide nonthreatening misted "rainfall" falling from above in a "Where did those beautiful clouds come from?" kind of way. Recovering from being wet is often enough of a self-rewarding behavior that simply distracting to bathing before the screaming occurs will sometimes avert the screaming.

A regular feeding schedule can do much to minimize screaming behaviors; or if improperly planned or executed, a schedule might contribute to a screaming problem. If you note that the bird screams at a particular time, you can arrange to offer an interesting assortment of food a few minutes before the usual onset of screaming. If a behavior can be prevented even once and the replacement behavior can be immediately reinforced, you have a good chance to modify the original behavior. This quick fix might be the turning point to a long-term solution.

The bird might be stimulated to quiet down merely by being lowered or confined to the cage. The bird might be quieted by being briefly confined to a small cage on the floor or in a slightly darkened room, before being returned to its territory and rewarded for the quiet behaviors that have been stimulated. Other forms of direct distraction include daily and timely introduction of a new toy that makes noise. You might have half a dozen bells and rattles and music boxes that are routinely rotated (removed and reintroduced) every few days. The bird might be given an interesting destructible toy each day just before screaming would otherwise begin. I know a blue-and-gold macaw who receives a 2 inch × 4 inch × 10 inch (5 cm × 10 cm × 26 cm) piece of pine lumber each day and who daily reduces that lumber to splinters.

I consider fresh branches with peelable bark and a stimulating, ever-changing environment to be indispensable parts of the quiet parrot's habitat. A busy bird is not screaming. Branches are the easiest, least expensive way to quickly alter the environment and to keep a parrot busy. If the bird has indirect distractions such as interesting branches and textures to chew; if interesting direct distractions are provided before screaming behaviors occur; and if all appropriate, independent, and inoffensive behaviors are intermittently reinforced, the non-screaming behaviors will become a fixture in the bird's behavior. That is, you will have successfully replaced screaming with golden silence.

What if My Parrot Doesn't Talk?

Gina and Mark B. Dazzle dreamed of their own talking parrot. With books and magazines in hand, they carefully researched their choice to add a baby Congo (African) grey to their small family. Parrot fancy held great allure for the young couple.

Things being what they are, once it became known that Mark and Gina had a parrot, more parrots—almost immediately—seemed to come their way. They were given a pair of cockatiels that began blissfully laying eggs. They adopted Maizie, a Goffin's cockatoo, that would let no one near and turned her into a snuggle bunny virtually overnight. They inherited Zipper, a wild-caught quaker, when a neighbor moved to a state where quakers are forbidden.

Two years down the road, they shared their home with five birds, none of whom spoke more than one or two human words. Although they had tried audiotapes, videotapes, food and toy rewards, their dream of a good talking parrot had eluded them. They were very discouraged and also were depressed because their house was a mess. They were considering getting rid of all their birds. I was asked to help them decide what to do.

Why Does a Bird Acquire Human Speech?

While Mark and Gina had originally researched and acquired a type of bird known for talking ability, they had not studied the conditions under which such a bird acquires human speech. An examination of the environment revealed some pretty definitive reasons why their grey parrot wasn't talking. I believed a few easy manipulations would overcome their bird's reluctance to talk.

First we considered the reasons why a companion parrot vocalizes: to have its physical needs (food, housing, environment) and emotional needs (society, independence, confidence, reproductive urges) met. If any of these elements is missing, inadequate, or otherwise ill-suited to a particular bird's temperament, the bird may lack motivation to vocalize.

Feeling Connected

A parrot is a social creature. Parrots in a group communicate by using the same language. If a bird identifies with other birds, it is most likely to acquire the other birds' vocabulary, and it will be less likely to acquire human speech. A bird that identifies and relates to humans is more likely to want to mimic human sounds. A bird that is already using human words can stimulate a new bird to use human speech as a means of competing to attract attention. So the timing of the addition of subsequent birds is very important: *When* a second bird is added can determine whether or not the group (flock) acquires human speech.

Mark and Gina added their second through fifth birds, all nontalkers, before Johnny, the baby African grey, started talking. Maizie, the cockatoo, was extremely needy, so they handled her more than the baby grey. Apparently seeking to attract the attention given the cockatoo, Johnny picked up something resembling Goffin's cockatoo sounds, but not human speech.

I suggested that Mark and Gina embark on a program to play more

interactive games with all the birds, especially Johnny. They began playing more games like "peek-a-bird" around the corner: games that involved calling out to a hidden friend. They tried to entice Johnny to vocalize by mimicking the sounds he sometimes made. They were careful to handle the grey parrot at least as much as they handled any other bird in the house. All the birds did step-up practice at least once daily.

Appropriate Housing

Height and hierarchy in the pecking order can affect a bird's motivation to talk. It's not unusual for the first bird to believe itself to deserve the highest (most honored and powerful) position in the avian branch of the homebound flock. If subsequently added birds are housed higher than the first bird, you can expect behavioral reactions in the first bird. Discontinuance of talking or discontinuance of motivation to learn to talk are only a small part of the behavioral potential.

An African grey kept with a cockatoo may prefer to communicate with the cockatoo rather than with humans. (Umbrella cockatoo and African grey.)

The adopted Goffin's cockatoo had come with a larger and taller cage than Johnny's. This situation is not uncommon in cases where the added bird is larger than the first bird. Subsequently, the grey parrot's previously normal behavioral development as only (dominant) bird was thwarted, and the baby parrot had to reevaluate its lower status. Under many circumstances, birds in lower situations make no noise at all, possibly because of concerns about safety. It seemed that Johnny was reacting this way.

Gina and Mark agreed to purchase a cage like Maizie's for Johnny, situating his perches so that he was, if he wished to be, always looking down on Maizie and Zipper. His play perch was also situated higher than the other birds'. Because the cockatoo was new and had not established a rank in the family pecking order, and because she was enjoying snuggling for the first time, Maizie didn't seem to notice the relative height change. Zipper noticed the change and had to also be raised.

Aggression and Independence

Of course, raising a bird can contribute to increased aggression. In cases like this, that is exactly what you want to accomplish. When a good talking type of bird doesn't talk, you must examine other aspects of behavioral development. Did the bird exhibit the development of normal nippiness during the post-weaning stage? If the bird never expressed nippiness, it may not have achieved true emotional independence. In that case, the bird might not feel safe enough to vocalize. The development of a little aggression in a previously shy bird can signal the coming of confidence that can precede vocalization.

I had warned Mark and Gina that these height manipulations might lead to the expression of normal developmental aggression. That is, if Johnny was responding to the program, he might begin testing the humans with a little biting to express his desire for dominance. Appearance of this behavior signaled that Johnny's behavioral development was again following an expected path, and that vocalizations would follow. Meticulous step-up practice easily managed the temporary nippiness.

Sensitive Grooming

Most baby red-tailed grey parrots spend a great deal of time holding onto something and flapping. Johnny wasn't doing that. Again, he just didn't seem to feel safe. Since failure to vocalize can be statistically linked to shyness, anything to increase confidence can help to overcome the problem. We considered the possibility that Johnny needed more wing and sharper claws to improve confidence.

Mark and Gina decided to let Johnny's wings grow out. We wanted Johnny to enjoy more physical activity. Gina began including Johnny in her morning showers. We knew that increased bathing and flapping would stimulate Johnny's metabolism and hoped it would improve his motivation to vocalize.

A Perch Is More than Just a Place to Sit

I noticed that Johnny didn't grip the hand he was sitting on and also observed that his only two perches were too large for his feet to grip. The Dazzles removed his nail-grooming perch and replaced his large iron-hard perch with smaller, softer poplar branches. Johnny was encouraged to hold on and flap. The new branches had smooth, peelable bark that gave him true control over the shape and feel of his perches. Johnny first peeled the bark off the branch where he slept, then he went to work on other sites requiring remodeling. Within a very few days, Johnny's grip had improved and he was more active in the cage. Johnny was also spending more time on top of the cage, where he enjoyed many exciting moments in fantasy flight.

Lighting

I also suggested that the Dazzles' birds might all be a little inactive because they had insufficient lighting. All were housed indoors, and most of the home featured indirect lighting. We knew that other problems could develop over time if lighting levels remained low. The Dazzles added full-spectrum fluorescent light fixtures beside each bird cage. All the birds were immediately and noticeably more active and more vocal.

Diet

A bird on a boring or otherwise inadequate diet may not be motivated to talk. Mark and Gina were meticulous and organized and fed their birds exactly the same thing at the same time every day. We decided to play a little "peek-a-bird" along with feeding and tried to stimulate interest by offering different foods in different ways.

Mark learned that he could generate differing reactions by feeding the birds in a different sequence. Gina found that she could stimulate vocalizations by putting one piece of yummy fresh food in the cages, then waiting a little while to serve the rest of the meal. Of course, these techniques can generate screaming, but Gina and Mark combined this "wait-a-minute" feeding schedule with increased modeling (calling or talking softly to the birds and back and forth to each other) when out of sight.

Rituals, Modeling, and Delivery

A parrot must be excited by or attracted to the sound of a word or phrase, attracted to its meaning, or attracted to the emotions occurring with the sounds. For example, it is probably unusual for an Amazon or quaker to sit in a room where it can hear the sounds of people laughing and not pick up something resembling laughter. They also love ritual; in particular, many Amazons love to deliver a painful bite, scream with pain, then laugh. Some of them wait for the humans to fill in the painful scream, then they laugh. They are attracted to the drama associated with the sounds and the predictable sequence of the sounds.

You can stimulate interest in talking by manipulating the timing, presentation, and delivery of words you wish the bird to acquire. While an average parrot might never learn one word from a tape recording, it might pick up something from a tense television drama—especially something repeated often. An Amazon might be unwilling to mimic a male voice, but it might go nuts for a female or falsetto voice. A grey parrot might not like a high-pitched voice; it might even attack or run from a falsetto voice. Such a bird might pick up the first words a male human utters upon returning home.

Many parrots respond very favorably to the use of questions and answers or series that involve a response such as the Amazon biting sequence described earlier. I suggested that Gina and Mark begin a program involving ritual response. Each time they returned home, they would walk from cage to cage, starting and finishing with Johnny's cage, and say,

"Pretty bird."	(pause)
"Who's a pretty bird?"	(pause)
"Oh, Maizie's a pretty bird."	(pause)
"And Zipper's a pretty bird."	(pause)
"And who else is a pretty bird?"	(pause)
	(pause)
"Is Johnny a pretty bird?"	(pause)
	(pause)
"Johnny *is* a pretty bird!"	

The Dazzles were using the exciting moment of homecoming, coupled with the exciting sounds of "pretty bird," combined with the enjoyable element of ritual and a little rivalry to stimulate the motivation to talk. They also added "thank you" rituals at food time and "nite, nite" rituals at bedtime.

Self-rewarding Behavior

It is especially helpful if the words modeled are fun to say so that the bird learns them merely for the joy of saying them. Words that fall into this category include all the "itty" sounds, but the most exciting thing for most companion parrots to learn to say is probably "pretty bird."

Most companion parrots know and love what "pretty bird" means: owner attention, love, and admiration. A bird that understands the meaning of these words will not only use them to get attention, but also will use them as a self-rewarding behavior. A parrot loves to be told that it's a "pretty bird"; and since a healthy, happy parrot also loves hearing the sound of its own voice, most companion birds love to say "pretty bird." A healthy, happy companion parrot will incorporate these words into the courtship display. That means that the bird will look its prettiest when it is strutting around saying "pretty bird!"

Mark and Gina noticed that all the birds loved the new "pretty bird" ritual greeting. Especially, they could see more happiness behaviors: increased preening, puffing out, tail wags, soliciting, and foot lifting during the rituals. Within a few days, they were hearing increased muttering in the mornings before the cage covers were removed.

Occasionally Obstructed View

Birds that are occasionally covered are more likely to acquire human speech. If they are covered too often or isolated too severely, this technique can stimulate screaming and other behavior problems. On the other hand, if the bird never spends time in the cage or out of sight of humans, it may never develop necessary independence, and other, also serious, behavior problems could result.

Manipulating this element can be considered an artificial stimulation of barrier frustration, for it has long been observed that caged birds appear to talk more than birds housed on open perches. This is also a possible consequence of the feeling of safety that a cage provides. Manipulate barrier frustration very sensitively and in concert with other behavioral and environmental manipulations, for simply erecting barriers can lead to numerous complications.

Mark and Gina decided to cover their birds at night so that they could manipulate the visual barrier in connection with enticing feeding practices. Each morning they slipped a little grated low-fat cheese into each cage, then spent 15 or 20 minutes calling to the birds, asking if they were ready for the rest of their breakfast. Soon the birds were peeking out from under the covers and vocalizing for attention.

Health and Reproductive Urges

Vocalization is an important indicator of a bird's interest in breeding, and a bird's interest in breeding can be an indication of the bird's good health. Any program to stimulate talking in a nontalking individual of a good talking species should include a veterinary evaluation. There are many major and minor physical conditions that can sap a parrot's motivation to attract a companion, and therefore, to vocalize. Even a very minor health problem can easily affect motivation. Even a human can tell you that a sinus infection can be very uncomfortable; can a sinus infection be any less uncomfortable for a bird? The Dazzles had already eliminated health issues as a concern in this case.

Happiness Behaviors

When monitoring a failure-to-talk program, you know you are making progress when you see an increase in the number of expressions of happiness: preening, puff-outs, and tail

Look for interested, happy behavior when trying to stimulate human speech from a parrot. (Military macaw.)

wags. To stimulate these behaviors, always provide an interesting and diverse assortment of destructible and indestructible toys. Allow the bird to occasionally spend time in a very high place. Include a parrot on safe outings both inside and outside the home. (Parrots love to ride in the car and in elevators.) Include music and singing more often, especially in the car and in the elevator. Exciting music can work wonders in stimulating motivation to vocalize. Many companion parrots love Rossini's "Thieving Magpie" and The Artist's "When Doves Cry."

Gina and Mark, devoted videophiles, were amazed at their birds' response to music videos. They were surprised at how often Johnny and Zipper were wagging their tails. They could easily see that our program was working long before the birds actually learned new human words.

Attitude, Depression, and Family Planning

The number of birds in the home can easily affect the amount of attention each bird gets, the attitude of humans, and, therefore, the quality of life, connection with humans, and motivation to use human words. Humans can easily become depressed by the demands of maintaining the birds' environment. Improved equipment and accessories can make quite a difference in the amount of time and energy necessary to keep a parrot environment tidy, adding to the time available to provide for the birds' happiness.

The Dazzles repainted with water-proof paint, added mess catchers to all cages, and added (disposable) Astroturf under each cage. After much soul searching, they decided that flock size was an important part of "family planning," and that they were not cut out to be breeders. They learned to say "no" when they were offered free birds. They donated their cockatiel pair to a local bird club's "Aviculture for Youth" program and focused on the education of their grey parrot, Goffin's cockatoo, and quaker.

Acceptance and Expectations

Talking ability is only one of the many reasons humans enjoy life with companion parrots. Even a parrot that develops no human speech can wind up being the household favorite. It's not unusual for a bird to start talking after humans have discontinued their expectation of talking behavior. Maybe we all perform better when there's no pressure to perform. Sometimes lowered expectations bring surprising results.

Gina and Mark reassessed their expectations and decided they loved their birds whether they ever said one human word or not.

Within six months, Johnny had added a dozen words and phrases, including "step up" and "Johnny's a pretty bird" in Mark's voice, and gave kisses and called the dog in Gina's voice. Zipper had learned to say "thank you" for treats; and Maizie would say "night-night" repeatedly,

emotionally, only in the car (presumably, on the way to the veterinarian).

Recovering Confidence in a Fearful Parrot

A parrot is a prey species that survives in the wild with its unique ability to take to the air when danger threatens. This instinctual behavior is part of what scientists who study bird behavior call the "fight-or-flight" response.

While this instinct to flee danger serves the bird well in the wild, the same instinct can be difficult, even dangerous, in indoor situations. First of all, there is always the danger that a panicked bird could fly into danger (a mirror, a window, a ceiling fan) if wing feather trims have not been maintained. Additionally, fear reactions are stressful to the bird, and prolonged stress can affect the bird's immune system and its ability to fight off disease, ultimately weakening the bird physically. Prolonged or habitual fearfulness leads to the bird's isolation, as fearfulness is an undesirable social trait, which can make both humans and birds uncomfortable in each other's company.

Some species of parrots have a stronger tendency to flee fearful situations than others. Among the common companion parrots, African greys, *Poicephalus,* cockatoos, grass parakeets, and cockatiels are generally reported to more often

develop fearfulness as a part of the personality than their New World cousins. However, any type of common companion parrot, including large macaws, can develop fearful behaviors in response to pain, abuse, neglect, or other perceived threats occurring in its environment.

When Fearfulness Appears

Many birds have a natural tendency to be cautious, but when cautiousness turns to thrashing or falling off perches when humans enter the room, we can say that the behavior has crossed the line to fearfulness. Appearing in a young parrot between four and 24 months, this behavior could be a developmental phase that will pass as the bird gains a sense of strength and independence. Sudden-appearing fearfulness can be a response to inappropriate environ-

ment or to a sudden, surprising bad experience. If fearful behavioral responses are repeatedly stimulated, reenacted, and reinforced, they can become habitual fixtures in the bird's behavior.

Prevention: Patterning for Confidence

Early step-up patterning is especially helpful in the prevention and treatment of sudden-onset fearfulness. Try to provide an alternative to panic behaviors by daily practice of the step-up command and by early conditioning to the towel game. Even a bird that has no shyness in its personality might someday experience a tremendously fearful situation, and a sense of security can be returned to the bird with the practice of the towel game (see p. 153). If step-ups have been well reinforced, then usually at least one person in the family can continue step-up drills even during a fearful phase.

Early towel game patterning (see p. 153) is also extremely beneficial in the treatment and prevention of fearful behaviors. Towel game patterning is often even more helpful in treating fearfulness than step-up routines (although step-up routines should be improved unless the bird is too phobic to come out of the cage without injuring itself). Some birds that are terrified of hands can become absolute snuggle bunnies with appropriate use and maintenance of towel game patterning.

What to Do Next

If a bird has become fearful, humans can begin immediately to reestablish emotional connections with the bird with the use of the eyes, with the voice, and with body language (in this case posture). It is your goal at this time to convince the bird that you are not a threat. You will work first with your eyes.

The parrot's eyes are on the sides of its head to facilitate an almost 360 degree range of vision so that the bird may avoid predators approaching at any angle. Avoid every possibility of a straight-on stare, for unlike prey species with their eyes on the

Step Up, Step Up

Some trainers advise that each bird be patterned to respond to both a "step-up" and a "step-down" command, and some humans and birds are perfectly capable of maintaining both commands. However, some birds barely respond to one command. I believe one strongly reinforced pattern is more easily maintained than two. You will note that the system of companion parrot behavior management in this book advises the use and maintenance of only one command, "Step up."

Because the behavioral response to the command is actually the same response, stepping from one place to another, I feel that the same stimulus should always be used to obtain the same response.

Good technique during daily training involves holding the hand the bird is sitting on lower than the perch it is being prompted to step up on.

By using only one command for the expected behavior of stepping from one place to another, you are much more likely to achieve a dependable response from the bird. This habitual routine of prompting for a behavior, seeing the bird perform the behavior, and verbally reinforcing the behavior is the basis for all other cooperative interactions. If the bird is well patterned to cooperate with step-up commands, then it can be presumed to be motivated to please, to cooperate, and to interact with humans in other ways.

A well-patterned African grey parrot exuberantly welcomes new toys.

mal is submitting to or does not fear danger from the other animal. Demonstrate your trust of the bird by sleeping in its presence, discontinuing eye contact frequently, and stooping over to be always lower than the bird. A human who spent weeks or months looking at a baby bird but who suddenly discontinues making eye contact with the bird is sure to get the bird's attention. Combine this with stooping over to stay lower than the bird and you should see a bird that is almost overcome with curiosity. For you are at this time trying to stimulate the bird to choose to interact. Forcing interactions with a fearful bird will only worsen the fearfulness.

Continue with progressively more interactive passive eye games with the bird as suggested in the section called Passive Games Birds Like to Play in *Guide to a Well-Behaved Parrot* (p. 17). Gradually, you will go from making no eye contact to playing peek-a-boo around the corner, then to playing "blink" from across the room, to tapping back and forth with each other, and to playing tug of war through the bars of the cage with an interesting toy.

Environmental Manipulations

Once you have evaluated and adjusted the bird's responses to passive human interactions, you can begin examining the environment to determine if there are contributing factors there. Especially if a young bird is falling frequently in the cage,

sides of their heads, humans have eyes on the front of their heads like predators do. Many shy, cautious, or fearful birds will express fear when looked at by humans with a straight-on gaze. When a predator approaches, a bird sees two eyes of equal size staring. Compare that to the appearance of a parrot or other prey species bird examining food or other items with one eye at a time. Foster a sense of trust by looking at a shy bird with only one eye at a time, or with one eye closer than the other so that the eyes are not of equal size.

Additionally, because eye contact can be threatening to an animal, failure to maintain eye contact between two animals indicates that one ani-

you need to examine the sizes, types, and textures of the perches.

In some cases, nail-grooming perches will overgroom the nails if they are situated where the bird sleeps on them. Instead, try placing the nail-grooming perch—if one is needed at all—in front of the water bowl. Placed here, the nails will be groomed, but not overgroomed. Younger birds and clumsy birds should be allowed a little more toenail for gripping and should be provided with smaller branches of softer wood in order to prevent falls.

Larger birds and more voracious chewers will benefit from very hard woods such as manzanita and madrone (and humans like these woods, as well, because they're so easy to clean). Smaller birds need branches that they can both grip and destroy such as poplar, citrus, or Ailanthus. An assortment of branches of various sizes installed at diverse angles can provide interesting climbing opportunities that can build confidence in a bird that has been previously situated on inappropriate perches.

If the bird continues to fall, try raising the grate so the bird can't fall far if it falls. Some cages are designed to allow the grate to be moved up and down. Some cages may require that a special temporary grate be fashioned from welded wire, hardware cloth, or other material appropriate to the size of the bird.

The manipulation of height can be extremely helpful in countering the development of fearfulness. Some

If the Bird Is Afraid of New Toys

It's not unusual for a poorly socialized bird to fear the addition of new toys. A simple trick can often be employed to overcome this.

Start by rolling a clean, unscented paper towel from one corner diagonally as one might roll a bandanna handkerchief to go around a skier's neck. Tie the rolled paper towel around the bird's favorite toy. Most birds will immediately remove the paper towel bow by chewing it off. If the bird is reluctant, or if it takes more than a few hours to chew the paper towel bow off, try starting with tissue rather than a paper towel.

Once the bird has learned to remove the paper bow from the favorite toy so that it doesn't interfere with playing, you can begin introducing new toys with the bow already in place. If every toy is introduced with a paper bow around it and the bird has to remove the paper bow to get to the toy, then every toy will seem like an old familiar friend (or maybe surrogate enemy), and the bird will no longer fear new toys.

birds become more confident, territorial, and aggressive when they are higher. Some birds benefit from having a little wooden shelf up near the ceiling (as high as possible) with a branch or ladder up there to hold groovy toys and treats. Some birds, such as Patagonian conures and *Poicephalus,* dive down when frightened and can sometimes be calmed from fear reactions by housing lower, perhaps with a little visual shelter, such as behind a plant.

Location, also, can contribute to fearfulness by making the bird feel vulnerable to predators. A cage situated near a high-traffic location can increase fearfulness if the bird is repeatedly startled by noisy dogs rushing by or by quiet humans who seem to appear from nowhere as they rush through a doorway. You might be able to enhance a parrot's sense of security with the addition of hiding opportunities that might include a little tent (a hide box), a towel over one third of the cage, restricted sight of other birds, or moving the cage to a more sheltered location, perhaps across the room from traffic areas.

Provide the bird with opportunities to make successful decisions, such as deciding which of two toys to play with, which perch to sit on, and which of several foods to eat. Each time a bird makes a successful decision, you can presume that it is more confident to make another decision rather than merely respond to a situation with instinctual fear. Especially, don't force a fearful bird to come out of the cage, although it's easy to set up a situation in which the bird will almost always come out of the cage.

Some birds that aren't getting enough sleep may be irritable, but some birds that aren't getting enough sleep may be fearful and panicky. Be sure the bird has adequate opportunity for 10 to 12 hours of undisturbed sleep each night. Don't go in and out of the room at night, as some birds are absolutely terrified of nighttime disturbances. Most shy or cautious birds probably benefit from having at least half of the cage covered at night.

Loud sounds can easily destroy a bird's sense of security. For example, "Noisy species such as hyacinth macaws may upset shyer birds who perceive that the macaws' frequent vocalizations indicate the constant presence of danger."[17] Likewise, companion birds must be protected from loud construction noise and from the sounds of gunfire and fireworks. Obviously, the feeling of being in constant danger can harm a bird's disposition as well as its health.

Grooming and Confidence

The shy parrot's sensitive temperament is best served with very nonintrusive wing and nail grooming (see pp. 121–127). Consider the possibility that a bird outgrowing a fearful phase might regain self-assurance exactly as those old, cut wing feathers are replaced with full new ones. Consider the possibility that a parrot with a tendency to be overly cautious may require sharp toenails and full wing feathers or only very slightly trimmed wing feathers to retain confidence. Consult a professional, or carefully match the bird's confidence to the amount of trimmed feather. A snotty bird that's a great flyer would require a much shorter wing trim than a shy, pudgy bird that falls instead of flies.

Provocation and Other Messages from Humans

Sometimes, the stimulus for a bird's panic response comes from human caregivers. Of course, you must never allow humans or other pets to tease any bird, especially a shy or fearful bird. Some humans might even be provoking the bird's fear unintentionally. If a bird has developed a fear of fast moving hands or if hands it knows well change in appearance (read here, brightly manicured nails), the bird might be assisted by humans holding hands out of sight (in pockets or behind back) until calm behavior can be stimulated, patterned, and reinforced. Also expect reactions to changes in hair color, hair cut, or hats.

A parrot that has been previously panicked by severe eye contact might thrash, bite, or flee any human eye contact. This can be distressing when feeding or cleaning the cage. Try avoiding eye contact if you must service the cage with the bird inside. Remove the bird to a play area if this can be done without eliciting and, therefore reinforcing, fearful behavior. Start at the beginning of the Twelve Steps to Making Contact by Playing Games (p. 20).

The Human Connection

Sometimes a bird that is going through even an enduring fearful stage will meet a human to whom it is naturally, inexorably drawn. This can come like a thunderbolt, like love at first sight. Curiously, in some birds, this is not always a situation of overbonding wherein, after falling for a particular human, the bird remains fearful or aggressive with other humans. We have seen parrots who were previously panicked by contact, interest, or any interaction with any human learn to accept these things with other humans after meeting only one human it naturally connected with.

Sometimes a bird will encounter someone it considers a rival or a threat. Sometimes a parrot will suddenly decide that it is terrified of a person who has done nothing to deserve such treatment. The bird might be gently guided away from these feelings. Start with games and nonthreatening interactions (see pp. 20–21). Use the disfavored person's name in tandem with the bird: "Paco's Uncle Charlie" or "Uncle Charlie's Paco" when guiding the bird to include the person in its group of accepted associates. Progress to the towel game, step-ups, and outings.

Outings

Sometimes new and better bonds can be forged by outings into unfamiliar territory, especially outings with less favored humans. This might take the form of attitude changes generated by feelings of being the only safely familiar thing in scary, unfamiliar locations. Improved bonding can result, especially if there is an opportunity for a rescue scenario (see *Guide to a Well-Behaved Parrot,* p. 112).

Sometimes just taking the bird for a ride in the car will generate noticeable improvements. Many very shy birds cannot be easily removed from the carrier when they are out and about, but simply sitting in the carrier, in safe, protected places and enjoying the stimulation of excursions can enhance the bird's apparent sense of security.

Nervous Energy

As I have suggested previously, a wild parrot spends an amazing amount of energy flying around, foraging for food, finding and defending nest sites, and courting and raising young. And they have to do all of this sometimes in the pouring rain (it rains more than 300 days each year in most rain forests). There is always the possibility that the bird is high strung because it is not getting enough exercise.

In captivity, showers are among the most easily provided opportunities for exercise. The bird expends energy as its feathers go from wet to dry. Other opportunities for exercise for a shy bird might include round rope swings; long, hanging, swinging ropes; and provision of accessible places where the bird can hang on tight and flap its wings hard and fast in simulation of flying. This opportunity for flapping exercise is one of the most important reasons for symmetrically trimmed wings, for birds with only one wing trimmed will learn to avoid this exercise and will ultimately suffer behavioral consequences, possibly including fearfulness.

Feather Chewing, Snapping, and Plucking

Few behavioral problems are more troubling to owners of companion birds than the self-destruction of feathers by the bird. And while a small amount of feather chewing is probably not harmful to a companion bird, its development is usually considered to be a reaction to stress, an indication of something gone awry. Feather chewing can appear suddenly over a period of minutes or hours, or can develop gradually, taking months or even years to be noticeable.

Because self-induced feather damage is generally considered to be a reaction to some form of stress, the first place to look when this syndrome appears is for illness or physical problems. Make an immediate appointment with the avian veterinarian at the first sign of unexplainable feather damage. Don't wait; go quickly, before the behavior becomes habitual. It's all right to ask about potential illness, zinc and calcium levels, yeast and giardia. New challenges appear in this rapidly changing field every day, so be prepared to hear your local veterinarian's experience with contributing health-related issues in your specific geographic area. Sometimes the veterinarian will find no health-related issues and will suggest diet or habitat manipulation or behavioral counseling.

When treatment is necessary, often merely treating the health issue will resolve a feather-damaging incident immediately. Sometimes, however, even though the primary factor stimulating the initial stress reaction is identified and eliminated, ongoing feather destruction can remain. At this point, you must consider the possibility that you are now dealing with a behavioral issue, for habitual behaviors can remain even after an initial physical cause is removed.

Some veterinarians may wish to treat self-induced feather damage with drugs like Valium, Haldoperidol, or Prozac. While I am well aware that medical treatment is absolutely necessary when illness or other uncomfortable health conditions exist, I have not seen particular benefit from the use of tranquilizers or other mood enhancers. I would consider these treatments to be a temporary, last resort sort of thing after all efforts have been made to resolve the problem with behavioral or environmental techniques.

Molting and Other Explainable Feather Loss

A surprising number of new bird owners are convinced that their baby birds are "secretly plucking tail feathers" because feathers are found on the bottom of the cage. I am usually unconcerned if these are individual feathers or feathers in pairs and if this event occurs during the spring, summer, or fall, as this is part of the warm-weather occupation of molting. During this time, the bird will lose and regrow all feathers in a symmetrical configuration along the lines of circulation known as the feather tracts. This is the facility by which wing feathers are molted out and regrown in a mirror image that would not, in the wild, inhibit flight ability. If, for example, a bird is taken in for wing trimming and the flight feathers are not regrowing symmetrically, this could be an indication of damage to the feather follicles on one wing or an indication of feather cysts. This would be a good time for the veterinarian to take a look at those wings.

Certain other forms of feather loss or removal are explainable or appropriate and not usually ongoing. These include feather loss or damage caused by other birds or by occasional seasonal or other transitional behavior. New owners are sometimes concerned when they go to pick up parent-raised baby birds and notice bare spots, or chewed or irregular feathers on the back of the head or neck. This is not uncommon in parent-raised birds and is evidence of the vigor with which parents sometimes seek to quickly wean and fledge chicks. The appearance of feather chewing on places where the bird cannot reach, such as the cheeks, head, or nape, is an indication that the bird is being chewed by another bird. It is a clarion call to separate the birds.

Happy, exuberant juveniles are also well known to damage feathers during active play. Baby African parrots, macaws, and cockatoos commonly have bent, dirty, or completely broken off tail feathers. This situation usually resolves itself by age two, when you can expect to see a clean whole tail. If the situation persists after age two, it might be time to consult a veterinarian (nutritional deficiency?) or a behaviorist (suspect a housing problem). Baby birds who have not experienced their first molt are also known to occasionally chew off dirty or damaged feathers. This is not usually cause for concern and will probably not be ongoing.

If all of a companion bird's wing or tail feathers suddenly wind up on the floor of the cage, you must consider the possibility of a pretty traumatic incident. Although tail feathers can be extremely loose, especially in hot weather, the wing feathers are connected to the cuticle of the bone and are intended to stay in place and function even under the most arduous of circumstances. Night frights in cockatiels (see p. 95) and some grass parakeets result in the loss of all tail feathers, and occasionally result in the loss of wing feathers. If the bird is not a cockatiel, then the event is more uncommon, and you must consider the possibility of a nighttime disturbance that was truly terrifying to the bird. Efforts must be made to protect the bird from being frightened into self-injury, but this is probably not an indication of the development of feather chewing.

Feather Chewing, Shredding, or Fringing

Feather chewing or shredding is the most common form of self-inflicted feather damage. It begins with damage to the edge of the barbs of the contour feathers. Both mild and progressive feather shredding behaviors can sometimes exist for years before anyone notices them. The first sign of this type of feather damage is often visible as individual floating "fibers" or remnants of the barbs observed in the air or as dust in the room. These filaments may be seen floating on the surface of the water dish or on the papers in the bottom of the cage. This form of feather damage might be related to soiled feathers, boredom, anxiety, feelings of abandonment, poor diet, or inadequate lighting, but it can also often be related to slow molt or inappropriate preening.

Inappropriate preening is a behavioral issue probably related to the bird's inability to enjoy independent play. If the bird thinks that the owner is the one and only fun toy, then it will not play with toys and will not develop independent play behaviors. It will instead usually sit around preening and preening in anticipation of that treasured interaction with the favorite human. The more the bird preens, the more likely it is to overpreen, accidentally or purposely damaging feathers. I sometimes call this overpreening behavior in emotionally dependent birds "beauty school syndrome." Those new beauty school students don't really intend to wreck their hair. They are simply trying to learn to look as beautiful as possible and to learn their trade as groomers as quickly as possible.

On the other hand, feather fringing can also result from slow molt or brittle feathers. If this behavior is ongoing, especially in older overweight Amazons or budgies, you must improve nutrition, exercise, lighting, and showers, and consult an avian veterinarian about adequate nutrition for the thyroid gland. Sometimes improving access to calcium and iodine-rich foods, as well as eliminating or manipulating fat content in the diet, especially from peanuts, will help here.

Feather Snapping

Feather snapping is a more acute, quickly progressing form of feather damage. This involves the breaking of the feather shaft. This can begin in a small way when a bird snaps off the rachis or central feather shaft near the outer end of the feather, resulting in feathers ending in a "V" shape. In its more acute phase, this behavior might involve snapping the feather off at the base, leaving no contour feather visible outside the down.

This is the form most sudden-appearing feather damage takes when a bird is apparently in full feather one minute and there's a naked bird with a pile of feathers under the perch a half an hour later. I saw this behavior twice, most recently in a Goffin's cockatoo (Cacatua goffini) who was very offended by the arrival of a noisy Patagonian conure who was housed a couple of rooms away in a very large house. The owner went to take a shower, and 20 minutes later

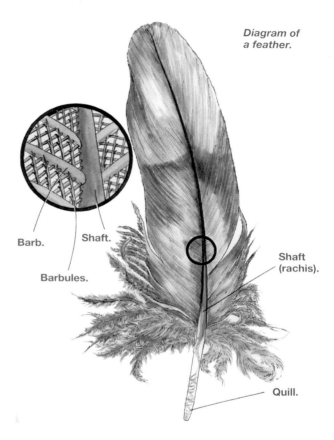

Diagram of a feather.

Barb.

Shaft.

Barbules.

Shaft (rachis).

Quill.

returned to find a Goffin's cockatoo covered only by down, with all contour feathers including the tail on the floor under the perch. This bird had a history of feather-damaging behaviors from the past and had merely reverted to this behavior when presented with what he considered to be a stressful situation.

Feather Plucking or Pulling

This involves the bird pulling the feather out, sometimes making the bird version of an "ouch" sound in the process. This might be ongoing or it might be a simple temporary response to dirty or damaged feathers. Feather pulling is especially common around the vent or around the uropygial (preening) gland as well as around the neck where dirty feathers might be especially annoying to a bird. Pulling or chewing off dirty feathers is common behavior in baby parrots that have not yet experienced their first molt. Some birds have been reported to pull cut feathers from the wing, apparently to facilitate faster wing-feather regrowth. I suspect that these cases are generally feathers that have already molted out, but have not yet fallen from the tightly held feathers of the wing.

If there are no health-related issues, occasional feather pulling, especially by juveniles, often resolves itself spontaneously with the first molt and is not something to be overly concerned about. However, a juvenile pulling, snapping, or chewing off dirty or damaged feathers should be bathed more often, exercised more often, monitored carefully, and not reinforced. More frequent bathing is absolutely necessary both to provide a way to express excess energy (exercise) and to prevent the bird from perceiving that this feather-pulling behavior is necessary. Additionally, interesting and entertaining environmental elements must be available to distract from the behavior.

Feather pulling, more than any other form of self-inflicted feather damage, is suspected to have an organic origin. You might suspect food, fumes, or allergies when this

behavior appears. This is a time when you begin trying to determine food sensitivities by manipulating the diet. Sometimes eliminating salt or oil from the diet and improving calcium rich foods will help. Occasionally, radical evaluation of the diet must be made, possibly removing all but one food from the diet and then gradually adding foods to observe their effect on the bird.

The Necklace

Sometimes a ring of damaged feathers appears around the neck. This might be fringed feathers or it might be pulled out feathers. The gradual or sudden appearance of a "necklace" is a good reason to go, again, to the veterinarian, as I believe this can be an indication of either of two of the most common sources of feather chewing in the United Sates: yeast or giardia. Either of these conditions is probably uncomfortable, as the sudden appearance of a necklace is sometimes accompanied by increased vocalizations of apparent frustration.

If a particular veterinarian doesn't find something, then it might be a good idea to go to a different veterinarian, as each doctor has different experience and will test for and look for different things. Sometimes just a slightly different perspective can be all that is necessary to find and eliminate the primary source of stress in a feather-damaging incident. Rely on the veterinarian's experience and testing mechanisms. Avoid treating a problem "in case" it exists. This could make things drastically worse by increasing the bird's stress and setting its body off balance.

Feather Chewing and the Environment

It's neither common nor unusual for a young parrot (under three years old) to develop a feather shredding problem. A majority of these are probably African grey parrots, although this problem is not unusual in juvenile cockatoos, *Eclectus,* quakers, conures, *Poicephalus,* macaws, and Amazons. Many of these cases present us with some surprising environmental similarities. Not infrequently, the cage is centered in front of a window, toys hang under rather than beside the bird, and all cage elements including toys are indestructible. Many birds are provided with exclusively horizontal perches made of smooth hardwood dowel, PVC, or, sometimes, manzanita. Any or all of these environmental elements can be stressful to a bird and can stimulate feather chewing, snapping, or plucking for the following reasons:

1. A cage in front of a window is too exposed. A companion bird exhibiting a stress reaction needs at least one side of the cage against a wall, preferably two sides, such as in a corner.

2. Toys should be easily accessible to the bird, preferably hanging beside rather than under the bird. At least a couple of toys should be so obtrusive that the bird must occasionally put beak to toy in order to pass by the toy.

3. Safe, nontoxic branches with chewable bark should be provided at various angles in various sizes and textures.

Exercise and Rainfall

Encouraging daily flapping exercises until the bird is just slightly winded activates the cardiovascular system, stimulating the bird's metabolism and improving circulation.

Bathing also functions as exercise in companion birds. Allowing the bird to dry naturally, even though it might shiver just a bit, provides similar metabolic and vascular benefits to flapping and climbing exercises. Additionally, frequent showers assist in the completion of molting, remove particle contaminants that might prevent the parts of the feather from locking together, and help the bird to express energy that must be expressed.

Water from the faucet might be too forceful for some birds, but not for this green-cheeked Amazon.

Babe: A Case History

The little gray down-covered Mexican red-head *(Amazona viridigenalis)* was not on public display. She was perched quietly in a private area of a friendly, dependable bird store. At the age of seven months, she had seen the veterinarian several times. He had pronounced her healthy and chewing feathers for behavioral reasons. Her head was held high, in spite of two plastic Elizabethan collars stapled in place to prevent her from further damaging her feathers.

Not one to miss an opportunity to work on a behavior problem, I said, "Give me that bird!"

With a twinkle in her eye, the store's owner handed the bird and the cage to me.

That December 9, Babe was my special Christmas project. I was determined to help her, and on the way home, while I stopped to visit a friend, the plastic collars were removed. Babe responded by immediately, frantically pulling out several beakfuls of down. We misted her gently with warm water, and to our amazement, she stopped pulling down, held out her little fuzzy gray down-covered wings and, in true Amazon fashion, reveled in what might have been her first adult shower. I tucked the moist bird inside my long wool coat and continued on my way.

Arriving at my office, I set up her cage, knowing that she needed a cage both here and at home. Within half an hour, the little bird was dry and pulling feathers again.

"Well," I thought, "if she doesn't chew feathers when she's damp, I guess she'll just have to stay damp until she grows feathers."

That December was not especially cold in Denver, Colorado, but it was chilly enough that wherever I went, I wore my long wool coat with the unusual "accessory" of a damp juvenile Amazon under the coat with me. I found that if she was not left alone and was misted slightly with warm water when her feathers became dry, she did not chew feathers, and she was willing to

December 9, Babe's first day in my office.

investigate the various textures of destructible chewables we provided in her cage. Her cage at home was outfitted with branches with soft, peelable bark, attached to the sides of the cage in a manner that would allow her great height.

A couple of weeks later, observing that we had made progress in guiding Babe away from feather damage, her veterinarian suggested an unusual operation. Because she had chewed the flight feathers off her wings, and because it would be another six to nine months before she could molt, her avian veterinarian decided to give her a "head start" at regrowing these feathers by pulling every other chewed off flight feather so that new wing feathers could regrow immediately and the emerging blood feathers would provide mutual support as they grew out. Of course, this procedure is performed only in certain unusual circumstances by a qualified avian veterinarian, and because it is extremely painful, it must be done only under anesthesia. Babe had endured a great deal of bad luck for a bird so young, and the veterinarian wanted her to have every opportunity to recover. On December 18, he anesthetized her and performed her feather-pulling surgery. All went very well, and within another few weeks, there were tiny bright green tips emerging from the even rows of blood feathers on her wings. We

By January 18, Babe had regrown all down and two contour feathers.

were careful at that time not to provide hanging toys, and to pad the bottom of the cage to prevent injury from rowdy play.

But there wasn't much playing in the beginning. In addition to daily showers, as soon as the blood feathers on her wings had opened,

By April 24, Babe was almost fully feathered.

Babe: A Case History (continued)

Babe was required to do daily flapping exercises in order to stimulate circulation and metabolism. Gradually, she learned first to chew and then to interact with the various toys and accessories I had provided her. It took weeks for her to get the notion of attacking a surrogate enemy toy, but by January 18, one month after her surgery, she was regularly beating up her Little Birdy Man. She was destroying rope, twine, fabric, straw, and cardboard. She not only had wing feathers, but two tiny contour feathers on her lower left breast. By the end of April, Babe was almost fully feathered and ready to go to her new home.

Collars, Body Stockings, and Other Devices

Plastic collars called Elizabethan collars are sometimes necessary to halt active, acute self-inflicted feather or skin damage. These devices, including the new tube-types, are not to be considered cures for feather damage, but rather, are temporary means of preventing the inappropriate habit. They are especially helpful when there is an obvious health-related issue such as a staph infection of the skin that is undeniably stimulating the bird to self-damage. These devices, combined with improved behavioral practice upon removal, are necessary and often quite beneficial.

In more behaviorally difficult cases, body stockings or "teaser" bandanna handkerchief devices designed to encourage the bird to chew on the device rather than to prevent chewing may also be of great value. These devices are sometimes needed long term rather than simply as a transition. One Moluccan cockatoo I know never recovered from chewing a hole in its breast when its owner died and it had no access to food for a couple of weeks before the death was discovered. That bird has, however, adjusted very well to wearing a bandanna handkerchief worn (in the manner of a cowboy) over the breast. This induces the bird to chew the fabric rather than its own breast. The bird looks nice when people are present and chews skin only when alone, usually only during sleep times. Because of the danger that these fabric devices might get caught on something, they must be used only with careful supervision.

The Development of Coordination and Confidence

Of course, behavioral feather chewing is a complex problem, and many factors are involved. Appropriate patterning for cooperation, a cage that is neither too large nor too small, careful positioning of cage, gentle handling, full spectrum lighting, and appropriate diet are only a few of the elements needed to raise a happy, independent feathered companion. The bird must have balanced bonding between multiple humans or locations. It must have an understanding of time, of limits of acceptable behavior, and of appropriate authority-based relationships. The bird must be encouraged to develop self-rewarding or independent habits to prevent the development of feather chewing, attention-demanding, and other problematic behaviors. The bird must learn that it will never be abandoned, that when people go away, they always come back.

Good emotional health starts with confidence, and confidence in parrots develops first with physical coordination. Like all infants, baby parrots are at least occasionally clumsy. A baby bird with an inappropriate wing feather trim, too closely trimmed toenails, and inappropriate perches may be very clumsy. This is especially true of heavy bodied birds such as baby African greys. In the wild, where a fallen baby parrot would be somebody's dinner, baby greys develop extremely sharp toenails as a survival mechanism. In the companion environment, sharp toenails can lead to anxiety by irritating the tender skin of the handler. Failure to allow those sharp toenails, however, combined with the use of smooth, hard perches, can contribute to frequent falls resulting in damaged or broken feathers. This can, in turn, lead to the development of feather shredding as the bird learns to overpreen, first by removing tiny single filaments from damaged feathers, then progressing to removing larger parts of feathers and eventually chewing off whole feathers. Add a little unintentional reinforcement or a little bad luck, and we can easily see the development of a behavioral feather-chewing pattern.

Confidence can also be enhanced by manipulating height. In some birds that means raising the bird, and in some cases it means lowering the bird. Some families such as *Poicephalus* and some species such as the Patagonian conure dive down when frightened and may appear calmer and less threatened when they are housed low, possibly behind a plant or other obstacle designed to improve the bird's sense of safety.

Expect the bird's behavior to change as a result of the height manipulations. Hope to see a little aggression appear. While this is not behavior you want to keep, it's a good transitional behavior because it shows that the bird is confident enough to defend territory, and a more confident bird is less likely to damage feathers. Unless you see the bird express a little territorial behavior, you can assume that this is a part of behavioral development that this bird has not yet experienced, and this might be part of where the feather damage is coming from.

Some cautious, phobic, or merely shy birds benefit from having places to hide. Often this is provided by covering a part of the top of the cage in a manner that allows the bird to go sit out of sight. Some birds actually need a hide box or a small dark enclosure to sit in. Some birds are too motivated to sexual behaviors by an actual hide box, but might respond well to one of the little brightly colored fabric tents.

Of course, failure of confidence resulting in damaged feathers is not always present at the onset of self-inflicted feather damage nor is this the only component in its development. A complex set of situations—illness, inadequate diet or light, inactivity, low thyroid, slow molt, perceived abandonment, fearfulness, failure to learn to play, sexual motivation, failure of curiosity, failure in the authority-based relationship, and failure to develop natural preening and chewing behaviors—are also often present in the development of feather-chewing behaviors.

Toys, Enemies, and Environmental Enrichment

While the role of toys might seem frivolous to some humans, they provide companion birds with opportunities for decision making, manipulating parts, chewing, snuggling, talking, masturbating, and dominating. Multiple interesting toys with movable parts, with chewable parts, and with sound-producing parts will help to keep the bird occupied in ways other than grooming, overgrooming, chewing, snapping, or pulling feathers.

The development of a surrogate enemy toy is especially important, for that toy represents a flock member of lower status, and beating up the toy represents the maintenance of position in the pecking order to this highly status-conscious animal. A companion bird that does not have a surrogate enemy toy or a surrogate enemy among household members may be suffering from developmental failure that will lead to feather chewing.

A companion parrot that is not motivated to chew things other than feathers must be inspired to turn that beak to other elements of the environment. New, unpainted baskets, grapevine wreaths from the hobby store, clean new little brooms, cardboard, paper, or fabric elements may be introduced to stimulate destructive chewing of external elements rather than feathers. Little plastic whisk brooms can be run through the dishwasher and raw edge fabric must be specially prepared.

Diet

Correcting the diet is also usually essential to the resolution of feather chewing. Be sure that the bird is eating a premium quality diet that has been well-tested on this particular type of bird. You can ensure this by calling the food manufacturer. Be sure that the bird is not being given so many treats as to throw the food's nutritional balance off. Some quality food formulas are designed to allow up to 30 percent supplementation with vegetable-source, but not animal-source, foods.

Salt and fat are often identified as factors contributing to feather damage. There is more salt in processed foods than most people realize, and elimination of any processed human foods such as bread or seasoned pasta may be necessary to resolve feather chewing. In warm climates, it's even sometimes necessary to advise loving owners to wash sweaty skin before handling their birds because some of the birds will lick salt (or other contaminants) right off human skin.

Consult the veterinarian about fat requirements for the particular bird. Most birds benefit from the reduction or elimination of fat from the diet; however, a few birds, probably only the large macaws, may benefit from increasing oil sources in the diet. Peanuts do seem to be problematic and, like french fries, should be eliminated from the diet of birds engaging in self-inflicted damage to feathers or skin.

Some birds such as caiques and *Eclectus* appear to benefit from enhanced access to sources of fructose such as fruit, or even lory nectar. Some birds, such as lories, may benefit from reducing levels or changing the source of fructose in the diet.

The presence or lack of hemp seed in the diet has been observed as an influence in feather chewing. If there is no hemp in the bird's diet, try adding up to 5 percent hemp seed. If there is this much hemp or more in the diet and the bird starts damaging feathers, try eliminating the hemp.

Don't forget the importance of constant access to clean, fresh water, as the stress of dirty water has caused more than one bird to chew feathers or to pick up illness or other health-related problems that cause feather chewing. In many places it may be necessary to use pre-boiled or bottled water in order to be absolutely certain that the source of the stress causing the feather chewing is not arriving in contaminated water. Vitamins and other additives to the water can be considered contaminants to feather-chewing birds who bathe in the water.

Shredable Fabric

Pure cotton fabric can be provided in configurations intended to replicate the filaments of shredded feathers, but special care must be taken to ensure that the threads peeling off the raw edge of the fabric are not so long that they can wrap around little toes, restricting circulation, and causing the loss of the toe. Woven goods about the weight of quilt or bandanna handkerchief fabric can be cut into strips along the grain of the fabric. Then about every inch, the fabric can be clipped along the edge so that the fibers peeling off the edge are only about an inch long. Tie these fabric streamers on toys, perches, or cage bars in places beside where the bird spends time. You want to distract the bird to shredding the fabric rather than shredding its own feathers. Paper pompoms and paper woven into cage bars or hung from treat holders will work, too.

Lighting

Because of the importance of calcium in the development of healthy skin and feathers, and because of the role of vitamin D in the assimilation of calcium, it's absolutely necessary for a bird to have access to full spectrum lighting. I have seen many birds regrow feathers after the addition of this one additional environmental element.

Chewing Skin or Feet

While feather damage is often mild and not an outright threat to the bird's health, self-inflicted damage to skin requires immediate professional intervention. The self-destruction of skin, the skin on the feet, or even toes can be related to poor diet; to inhaled environmental toxins, including nicotine; or to perch size. Cigarettes, especially, must be absolutely eliminated to avoid the danger of progressive damage.

Grooming Wings and Nails

Inappropriate wing and nail grooming can contribute to self-inflicted feather damage just as correcting grooming can assist in recovery. We have previously discussed how too-short toenails can contribute to falls and to failure of confidence. However, too-long nails can be just as harmful since they might get caught in fabric or in cage parts causing stress as the bird moves around the cage. Sometimes merely grooming the nails can precipitate a recovery from feather chewing. A ragged or too-short wing feather trim can contribute to falls and

to preening disorders. Sometimes a ragged trim can be corrected with very sharp scissors. Many birds recover from an incident of self-inflicted feather damage when wing feathers are allowed to grow out completely, then are trimmed only slightly after the bird learns to fly.

Examination, Distraction, Reinforcement, and Judgmentalism

Examine the environment for newly added elements that might be stressful to the bird, such as new art, light fixtures, carpeting, sound-producing clocks, other animals, or provocative humans. Consider the possibility that human or other creatures in the home may be secretly provoking the bird.

Keep a journal to determine exactly when the bird is chewing feathers and exactly what is happening when the feather chewing occurs, including the favorite human's reaction. Once you know when the behavior is occurring, then the bird can be distracted to other behaviors, such as showering or exercise, before the feather-chewing behavior begins.

Of course, at no time should a companion bird be reinforced for engaging in feather-damaging behavior. Humans must provide for, stimulate, and reinforce other appropriate behaviors. Too much attention paid to a feather-chewing bird can cause the continuation of the unwanted behaviors.

That is not to say that owners and caretakers should be judged or criticized for owning a parrot with chewed feathers. Many caring humans have spent hundreds of dollars and thousands of hours working to help their birds recover from self-inflicted feather damage. Owning a feather-chewing parrot is not unlike having a teenager with a habit of nail biting or a fascination with tattoos or piercings. We can't withhold love from a beloved human or bird merely because we don't approve of that individual's personal grooming or ornamentation tastes.

What to Do: The Feather-chewing Checklist

- Go to an experienced avian veterinarian for a feather workup.
- Examine the environment for elements that might cause stress for the bird.
- Manipulate the environment to enhance curiosity and confidence (adjust height, cage, location of cage, hiding places, perches, and toys).
- Spend time assuring the bird that it will never be abandoned; establish a pattern of going away and coming back.
- Increase regular play time with humans.
- Increase access to rainfall (frequent drenching showers).
- Increase access to exercise, including daily flapping exercises, until the bird is slightly winded.
- Improve diet, eliminate salt, monitor fat.
- Provide full spectrum lighting at least eight hours daily.
- Work to ensure that the bird has a full 12 hours of sleep each night.

Feather chewing must sometimes be treated with distraction devices actually attached to the bird. (African grey.)

- Consider a better water source and change water more frequently.
- Keep a journal of the bird's behavior so that it can be distracted to appropriate behaviors before a feather-chewing incident would begin.
- If you've seen little or no improvement by mid-summer, go to the veterinarian again, perhaps to a different veterinarian. There's only a little more of molting season available to help the bird overcome this problem this year.

Professional Behavioral Intervention: When to Look for It, and What to Expect

The bird has decided not to allow your significant other into the house, and he or she is only too willing to accommodate. The bird won't let you out of its sight without self-destructing and telling the whole neighborhood about it. You've read every book you can find, and the bird still has you wrapped around a slightly overgrown toenail.

It's not unusual for mere humans to be very anxious about asking someone into their homes to help with their bird's behavior. Could this sort of thing be a painful and intimate experience like psychoanalysis? Where do humans get help with bird behavior problems, and what can they expect when they do?

The word *behaviorist* is key here, for an effective behavioral counselor probably works more like a golf or tennis coach than a psychiatrist. A behavioral consultant should be more focused on how to change the bird's behavior than on judging how the bird's behavior came to be that way. A good behaviorist will deal compassionately with the bird and with the owner.

Of course, in order to change the bird's behavior, one must have an understanding of the forces that stimulated and reinforced the behavior into patterns. In this way distractions and more pleasing patterns can be planned for, stimulated, and reinforced. Most behaviorists will prefer to do an in-home consultation and will probably take a history in order to quickly determine possible factors contributing to the bird's current behavior.

Your favorite breeder, bird store, or avian veterinarian should be able to refer you to an avian behavior consultant in your area. If they are unfamiliar with a local working in the field, they might recommend telephone counseling. Try looking at the behavior consultant ads in the back of your favorite bird magazine. There are quite a few behavioral alternatives on the Internet. Some are wonderful; some are awful. Look for places where kindness and open minds prevail. Ask for references from others who have actually consulted with this particular behaviorist about a similar problem in a similar type of bird. Watch out for someone who seems to know everything, but who offers that advice at no charge. Don't be offended if a professional expects to be paid for his time. Sometimes you get a bargain; sometimes you get what you pay for.

Expect an initial screening consultation by telephone. Before making an appointment, a companion bird behavior consultant will, typically, spend a few minutes on the phone asking the age, source, type of bird, nature, and duration of the problem. You may then expect a description of what kind of expenditure of time and money might be expected in order to determine how to correct the problem. A professional will also be evaluating your responses and trying to determine whether or not the two of you have a rapport. Expect to be referred to a different consultant if either of you doesn't feel a good emotional connection.

For example, consider a best-case scenario (the majority of my business would probably fall into this category), something like a nine-month-old blue-and-gold macaw nipping a particular family member. If all family members are cooperative, only one in-home visit or a couple of hours of phone time may be required to determine how to alleviate the behavior problem and train the owners to change and reinforce the bird's new behaviors.

In a worst-case scenario, say, established self-mutilation in an African grey, it might take multiple visits to identify the solutions, especially if some family members fail to participate in a consistent plan. A great investment in counseling time, improved diet, and compensating accessories might be necessary if success is to be achieved.

The consultant might offer group, telephone, or in-home counseling depending upon the location and nature of the problem. Group work must be done very carefully for reasons of health. Telephone counseling is attractive for simple problems of short duration, but in-home evaluations remain the most dependable way to solve long-term, enduring problems.

While an in-home visit might appear more expensive at the outset, it probably offers greater opportunity for success, for sometimes only direct observation by an outsider can reveal what is happening to perpetuate a behavior. In the long run, one-on-one, in-home counseling is usually the most cost-effective option for correcting established behavior problems in companion parrots.

The bird behavior consultant will be looking for things such as diet, housing, and handling elements that might be contributing to the bird's behavior. The consultant will be looking for indications of typical interactions between the bird and other family members as well as making observations about how the bird is responding with this unfamiliar person in the home. The bird is often perfectly behaved during the in-home visit (see Reinforcing Introduced Behavioral Changes, p. 160). This gives the humans in the home a good idea of how much control the bird has over its own behavior.

Most behaviorists will probably groom or towel the bird in order to observe the bird's responses to being toweled. This can ultimately save the bird's life, for a bird that responds poorly to being toweled is existing in a life-threatening state.

Parrot behavior training can often be accessed through seminars and conferences as well as through private in-home consultations.

The behaviorist may make recommendations regarding the bird's responses to the towel.

The behaviorist may make recommendations about the strength of the bird's step-up response with particular members of the family. The counselor may offer suggestions as to form and technique in order to build better responses between humans and bird.

If the behaviorist is there to see a shy bird, the bird might never be touched, because too-invasive handling can worsen such conditions. Especially in cases involving shyness or fearfulness, expect the behaviorist to offer suggestions regarding adjusting the bird's behavior through making changes in the environment. This response to the bird's behavioral needs is often the easiest, most obvious, and most effective way to change bird behavior. Some environmental manipulations might worsen or reinforce the unwanted behaviors, so sometimes the environmental elements are manipulated in various ways to study the ways the bird responds to the changes.

Expect some basic information on the role of diet in the bird's behavior. Missing, unnecessary, or empty, unfulfilling nutrition can easily affect a bird's behavior, and changing diet can change behavior (see *Feeding Your Pet Bird* by Petra Burgmann, Barron's Educational Series, 1993).

The behavioral consultant might want to observe feather condition and the bird's responses to showering. The easiest way to do this, of course, is to give the bird a bath as a part of the behavioral evaluation. It's not unusual for the consultation to wind up in a waterproof room such as the bathroom. You might want to tidy up a bit if you are shy about strangers in the bathroom, although a real pro won't care whether the bathroom is sparkling clean, and certainly would protect this confidence, anyway.

Expect confidentiality. Expect the behaviorist to talk about your case, but an ethical behaviorist will not reveal your identity or connection to the case without your permission (except to another professional working on the case who should also respect your confidentiality).

Expect the possibility of a veterinarian referral. Expect a responsible companion bird behavior consultant to refer you to an appropriate avian veterinarian if there is suspicion that health issues may be factors in the case.

Expect to enjoy the interaction and to have your life touched in a significant way. It's not unusual for family members to weep with joy when they make a major breakthrough in the rehabilitation of a troubling parrot behavior problem. It is important to like and to trust the professionals who work with your bird, for your life and your bird's life may be changed from this day on.

[17]Harrison, Greg J., DVM, and Harrison, Linda R., BS, *Clinical Avian Medicine and Surgery,* Lake Worth, FL: W. B. Saunders Company, 1986, p. 601.

Chapter Nine

Stories About Companion Parrots

Dolley Madison and Uncle Willy: The First Lady and Her Macaw

If you've heard the overture, you know there must have been some scary war in 1812. Actually, there were several wars in 1812; and to make matters even scarier, one of them was not fought on foreign soil (unless you happened to be British). It was a "civilized" war in which our presidential parrot—between bouts of entertaining at parties and traipsing through valuable state documents—received diplomatic immunity. Uncle Willy, the First Lady's blue-and-gold macaw, resided safely in the home of the French consulate when the Presidential Mansion and much of Washington, DC, was burned to the ground during the War of 1812.

Uncle Willy's owner—the socially astute, usually turbaned—Dolley Madison enjoyed numerous loyal friendships with persons of diverse political persuasions, races, and genders. As a close friend of the "Bachelor President" Thomas Jefferson, she served as surrogate First Lady for social functions in the sparsely furnished (but paid-for) Presidential Mansion in which she resided. By the age of 40, during her husband's (James Madison) presidency, Dolley Madison was called the "Queen of Washington." Not unlike first ladies today, in addition to being extremely popular, she was also insulted on the streets, defamed, and ridiculed in the newspapers.

According to Rita Mae Brown's meticulously researched novel, *Dolley, A Novel of Dolley Madison in Love and War,* we know that during the Madison presidency, Uncle Willy slept in a cage in the presidential bedroom, that he was covered at night, and that he engaged in occasional scuffles with King George, the presidential cat. We know that Uncle Willy ate sunflower seeds and stayed up late for parties, that he could be noisy, and that he sometimes ran to his mistress with wings outstretched for a hug. Uncle Willy was also hawk wary, exhibiting great noise and excitement when observing hawks in the fields of Montpelier, the Madison family's country home.

During the war, Uncle Willy's survival depended upon Jean Souioussant, who served as Dolley Madison's major domo and lifetime friend, for "French John" often provided assistance with Dolley's animals. This "cosmopolitan Frenchman," well remembered for his many tattoos, also later saved Mrs. Madison's cow. In those days, there were no pensions for widowed first ladies. The financially challenged widow Madison once had to decide whether to give up her carriage or her cow. True to her reputation as a lover of dairy products, there was little question that Dolley would keep the cow even though it was difficult to find accommodations for a cow in the city.

Mrs. Madison doted on her intelligent, talking bird. Uncle Willy was often the center of attention and was ". . . as colorful and entertaining as the First Lady." It is also reported that the President and First Lady, in spite of strict religious backgrounds, would laugh when the bird used "bad language."

In August 1814 when U.S. troops were defeated at Bladensburg, Maryland, President Madison sent word to his wife to leave Washington quickly. She received his message at about 1:15 P.M. as she sat down to a lunch of cold cuts. With the smell of smoke in the air, Uncle Willy screeching at approaching artillery fire, and British soldiers within sight of the Presidential Mansion, our devoted First Lady worked quickly to remove the important papers of state. In one hour and fifteen minutes, Dolley Madison would save the letters of President George Washington, the Constitution, and the Declaration of Independence from the fires that soon engulfed the Presidential Mansion. One particularly problematic rescue was the full-length portrait of George Washington that was screwed to the wall. Mrs. Madison borrowed a knife and cut the canvas from the stretcher, departing in her carriage less than 30 minutes before British soldiers ate her lunch. The Presidential Mansion was burned at 3:00 P.M.

There was no way to take her precious macaw in the carriage. Mrs. Madison asked French John to take Uncle Willy three blocks away to the Quadrangle, temporary home of the French Minister, Serurier, where the bird resided for the duration of the British occupation of Washington.

By September 1814, the Madisons had moved back to Washington and into the Quadrangle for a time before moving "for political reasons" into a row house—the end dwelling on the "Corner of the Seven Buildings at Pennsylvania Avenue and Nineteenth Street." Here, it is said that the President and First Lady lived happily with plain rugs and second-hand furniture in a house whose windows opened directly onto the street. The tiny house was frequently so packed with Washington society that the parties were called "Squeezes." When there were so many people at the parties that there was no room for lighting, Dolley Madison arranged for servants to hold torches outside the windows for light. This social tradition of "Night Parades" of lighted torches—carried south by another presidential parrot owner (Andrew Jackson)—survives today in New Orleans as Mardi Gras and in San Antonio as the Parade of Lights.

At this time in her life Dolley took great delight in her parrot. School children gathered daily to look into those street-level windows to watch Mrs. Madison and her bird. She would feed Uncle Willy, enticing him to talk for the children. One Washington resident, remembering his childhood, said, "She, as well as her pet, was very engaging. I can clearly recall her as she appeared in her inevitable turban."

Mrs. Madison's macaw is known to have outlived President James Madison, who died in 1836. On Dolley's 70th birthday, it is recorded that Uncle Willy was still entertaining his remarkable mistress.

This story was written from the following resources:

Dolley, A Novel of Dolley Madison in Love and War, by R. M. Brown, NY: Bantam Books, 1994.

Dolly Madison, Her Life and Times, by K. Anthony, NY: Doubleday & Company, Inc., 1949.

Bird Talk, February 1991, T. S. Shank, "All the Presidents' Birds," pp. 101–107.

Lolita Lowers the Volume

Lolita spent the winter in a trendy ski resort. She lived with her mate and over 30 large macaws in an unheated dog run. Most of the birds survived through March on a diet of seed and water in unwashed bowls. The kennel owner, who had no previous aviculture experience and incomplete care information, eventually realized there was trouble. By that time four birds were dead, and several had lost toes to frostbite or to animal bites. Twenty-four birds required extensive veterinary treatment and 14 were adopted by a group of individuals paying into a pool to reimburse their medical expenses.

It's a dismal tale, but not the one I want to tell here. Lolita was one of the lucky ones, the only surviving Amazon. I'm told that her mate bled to death after having his leg torn off by a wolf/dog hybrid. Lolita was there, watching and screaming, no doubt. I wonder how much of that she remembers.

She's one of those odd, probably wild-caught members of the *Farinosa* group, probably *Amazona farinosa guatemalae*. In California, she might be called a lilac-crowned mealy. In Colorado, she's usually called a blue-crowned Amazon, with the speaker then making a distinction between this subspecies and the one with the totally blue head. They are unusual birds in captivity. They are also unusually large. My living room companion, Saucey, weighed 740 grams the last time he went to the vet, and I'm sure he's put on weight since Lolita moved in just a month ago.

She arrived on a Thursday night. Lolita quietly ate most of my Good Times hamburger on the way home, but she was immediately vocal when she saw the handsome Saucey sitting there in perfect feather.

In a bleating, Amazon wail, she began calling out, "Elllll Greckkkkkkko, Elll Greckkkkkko, Elll Greckkkkkko," and would not be silenced until the light was turned off.

Since Lolita had already been quarantined, the next day, both birds were allowed to sit in the bathroom while I bathed. Lolita looked squarely at Saucey and said in a sweet, sincere voice that tore my heart out, "El Greco, El Greco, how are you?"

Looking up, I corrected her, "No, Lolita that isn't El Greco; that's Saucey."

Regarding me with an odd expression that seemed to be a mixture of puzzlement and concern, Lolita first paused, then replied, "Bummer!"

Saucey was even less happy with her than she was with him. He was especially offended by her behavior. While I'm not suggesting that he would have been any more receptive if she had been prettier, I feel that Lolita's appearance and condition must be mentioned here. Her feet remain always cold to the touch. All of the toes were still attached, but each had multiple cracks and erosions in the peeling skin as a result of vitamin A deficiency and having been repeatedly frozen. Her feathers showed obvious effects of the severe Alpine winter the birds endured.

Lolita looked a little like something to be used to mop the floor. Instead of "flour" covered pale apple green feathers with iridescent undercolors, her contour feathers were dull, broken, chewed, and tattered, with multiple patches of gray down poking through. She had only one whole tail feather, with all other remaining tail quills being less than an inch long.

I kept telling Saucey that she should be beautiful in only six months. This feather problem would take care of itself with time, good diet, and a stimulating environment.

One thing that had remained quite thoroughly intact was Lolita's libido. Saucey was *very* offended each time Lolita pleasured herself loudly in his presence—doing what one of my online buddies calls "the cluck dance." The first couple of days, this was a very frequent occurrence, and to make matters worse, she continued calling Saucey "El Greco" during those intense moments. He would lean as far over as possible trying to get around the barriers provided by his cage to get to her cage to bite her.

Another thing that remained intact was Lolita's big *farinosa* Amazon voice, which occasionally lapsed into a donkey-like bray (the infamous mealy bray). In Lolita's case, it also occasionally lapsed into something resembling the Madeline Kahn "note" (you know the one—the "happiness song" from Mel Brooks' movie *Young Frankenstein*).

From her very first day here, when Lolita was happy, she sang out in a loud soprano "Ahhhhhhhhhhhh!"

But most of the time Lolita talked or warbled a noisy Amazon call with all its clucks, honks, trills, yells, and downright screams. I had been working on a "noise problem" with my other Amazons and felt that my neighbors should be informed that the bird noise might escalate for a little while. I felt it was important to let these very understanding neighbors know right away that she was not an impulse purchase, that this new loud bird was an adoption born of necessity. Fortunately, everyone I spoke with was sympathetic about Lolita's recent emergence from concentration camp-like circumstances as well as Saucey's 15-year isolation from his own kind.

Most invasive was Lolita's tendency to express excitement on the balcony. My first efforts to soften her loud Amazon voice, as well as her learned barking and macaw calls, consisted largely of time-outs combined with modeling lower volume. Many times, I would say to her, "Say 'Hello,' Lolita. Talk don't squawk!"

This quick-fix effort was modestly successful, lowering her volume maybe 30 to 50 percent in the first couple of weeks. While time-outs did not alter frequency, the loudest screams were temporarily silenced, giving my neighbors a little relief. We also lined the wooden balcony (which seemed to amplify sounds) completely with Astroturf, instantly reducing noise levels.

We made further strides by manipulating environmental distractions before the onset of screaming, combined with verbal and food rewards for improved behavior. One month after her arrival, both volume and frequency seemed less than half of what they were the first week. And then one night we had what can only be described as a Helen Keller-and-teacher-at-the-pump moment in which Lolita finally figured out what I expect of her (quiet) when she's out on the balcony.

About an hour before dusk, Lolita was in a pattern of escalating volume, which usually prefaces yelling sessions. This evening, unlike previous times, my well-behaved Saucey was getting into the act, actually attaining loud volume well before Lolita did. Although silence had often been achieved by removing only Lolita from the balcony, this evening I was able to remove only Saucey—much to Lolita's surprise and delight. Walking away from the balcony with my male bird, I paused to model that operatic "Ahhh" at very modest volume.

Something must have clicked in that ratty-looking gray-green head, for Lolita stopped, eyes all awhirl, and broke into her own happiness note, "Ahhh"; over and over and over again, at very modest volume, "Ahhh"! She seemed to be trying to tell me that, well, of course she could do that if it meant she could stay outside!

Lolita has not yet figured out that she can also talk rather than scream, or chew or eat or play rather than scream, or practically anything else except scream; but she now knows that "Ahhh" is OK. It's a welcome insight and one that I hope will reward my neighbors with many peaceful afternoons.

But even if we can get Lolita's volume down to acceptable levels, there is no guarantee that she is a permanent addition to our home. My first loyalty in this matter is to Saucey; and if Saucey doesn't like her, she will not stay.

Things might be warming up between them, however. Sometimes I see him preening her head; and once, I caught him with a big, wet string of masticated food running from his beak to hers. (It was very romantic!)

He's waited 15 years for this first friend. She is looking prettier every day.

The Slightly Unsaintly Bernadette

I was contacted by a representative of the Catholic Church advising me that there was a large white bird, apparently a parrot, living wild on the grounds of the seminary near my home.

"It seems," he said, "that the bird has been living there all summer and is waking up the seminarians very early in the morning."

("Hmmm," I thought, "aren't seminarians supposed to get up early?")

"Besides," he continued, "They say that a hawk is stalking the white bird. They say that it caught the white bird once."

Taking Joey, a friend's umbrella cockatoo (Cacatua alba) as a lure bird, my assistant and I set out for the seminary. The grounds proved lavish that September, with fruit trees bearing apples, crabapples, plums, and peaches in surrounding neighborhoods and large locust tree bean pods present in great abundance on the seminary grounds. The spacious landscape was also rich in wildlife, including a large eastern fox with black legs, which we saw duck into a den under the sign at the main entrance.

Arriving on that first afternoon, we placed our lure bird (with well-trimmed wings) in a clearing on top of his traveling cage while we hid in a group of huge bushes and waited. Within minutes we noticed a change in Joey's behavior and heard the loud call of a cockatoo from a nearby rooftop.

The buildings were exquisite examples of Gothic style featuring lots of arches, larger-than-life-sized art nouveau statuary, ornate carvings, and red-tiled roofs. There on the wrought iron cross atop the library building was a lovely sulfur-crested cockatoo (Cacatua sulphurea): a hen. Her bright, terra cotta eyes were clearly visible from 50 yards or more.

She flew almost immediately to the cage top where Joey was bouncing, dancing, crest erect in the manner of

a bird who would fly to her if he could. We watched as she landed on the opposite side of the Preview Hendrix 125 cage. Her immediate posture indicated that she could be a bird of easy virtue. She was obviously soliciting Joey's sexual attentions. There was much crest flinging and hopping about, but what was it? There was something else. Something was awry.

Examining the bird through binoculars, we could see that one leg stuck out from her body at a right angle. She couldn't exactly walk, though she tried; it was the hopping gate of a biped with one limb half the length of the other.

Amazingly, it appeared that Joey (what a guy!) was mimicking her gate. He was responding to her as though the jerky, hobbled movements were part of her dance of solicitation. When she hopped, he hopped, bowing and throwing his crest in a mirror-image of her display. He was a most gracious suitor.

"Ahhh," my assistant whispered, "this should be easy. She looks tame."

"Wait here," I instructed.

Stepping into the clearing, I approached them, hands clasped behind my back.

"Hey, Joey, who's your friend?" I called in my softest, most soothing tones.

The birds regarded me for a nanosecond and then returned to their posturing. Approaching at a pace of no more than a few feet every 20 or 30 seconds, I was within an arm's length before she flew to a nearby locust tree.

Retreating to my shrubbery hideaway, I rejoined my assistant. After only a few minutes, the cockatoo with the red eyes swooped down toward the lure cage. But just as she was about to land on the cage, she executed a sharp turn to the west, landing in a different, more fully foliated tree. She was screaming frantically at Joey, and in truth, he looked worried. We waited for half an hour in ignorance of the danger. As the last rays of sunlight left the area, the hen cockatoo flew over the huge tile-roofed building to the east. Defeated for the day, we collected Joey and went home.

The Hunt Continues

For the next few days, we frequented the seminary for a few hours after sunrise and a few hours before sunset, usually enjoying the company of the red-eyed bird that we had christened "Bernadette, the Less-than-Saintly." We learned that she liked to spend her mornings in the area near the Grotto of the Virgin on the east of the library, and her afternoons in the locust bean trees west of the library. Sometimes we could find her; sometimes we could not.

On Saturday morning, Joey and I were working alone. Situating Joey on top of his cage in the clearing beside the grotto, I walked around the south end of the library to see if Bernadette was in her customary evening foraging area. Returning to the grotto, I rounded the library, maybe 50 or 60 yards from Joey's perch, to see the shadow of a bird circling over him. Drawing closer, I realized that a huge brown and white raptor was preparing to eat Joey for breakfast. The white cockatoo was sitting like a virgin sacrifice with trimmed wing feathers on top of his cage.

Running, waving my arms, and screaming like a banshee, I watched in horror as a Swainson's hawk in partial winter colors began the dive to grab Joey. While I was still at least 30 or 40 yards away, and the hawk was half way into the dive, I saw the bird slow, slow, braking with huge beats pushing forward the broad feathers on the bottom of the wing. The bird apparently realized that this was a larger bird, a different white bird, than the one he had hunted before. In mid dive, the hawk realized that Joey would be way too much work for a hawk with a field full of rabbits and prairie dogs only a stone's throw away.

Realizing my age and my mortality (and Joey's), we stepped into the grotto for a few moments of thankfulness. It was the last time Joey would function as a lure bird without the protection of a cage.

The Trap

I decided that Bernadette was not physically capable of stepping up, no matter how much time we spent with her. We began a new recapture strategy: we would establish a food dependency and trap her. I laid Joey's PH125 cage on its back and tied the grate inside the front of the cage, making a wire "bridge" or shelf across the opening formed by the open door. I attached one end of a long string to the door, threaded it through the cage bars so that it could be used to pull the door closed, and waited. Of course, I did not intend to pull the door closed since the grate was blocking the opening, but I wanted Bernadette to get used to the string being there before we needed to use it.

We put Joey into the cage through the bottom. That very first afternoon, Bernadette landed on the cage and shared a little bit of an ear of corn with Joey. But before she helped herself to the ripe fresh corn, Bernadette did something else. The first thing she did when she landed on the cage was chew the string off the door. On the next visit, we replaced the string with wire.

Leaving the corn and the cage in place, we did not return to the site until late the next day. By that time, the ear of corn was crumbles. We lowered the cage grate, wiring it about three or four inches below the opening of the door. At this point, Bernadette would have to stick her head into the cage to get to the corn. We hid in the car and watched as Bernadette immediately ate the refreshed supply of corn. Driving off into the sunset, we made plans for the next morning.

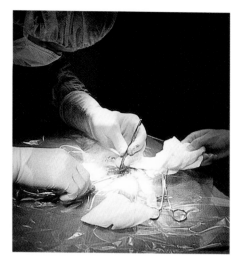

Bernadette's femoral resection surgery.

At sunrise the next day, I lowered the grate about a foot into the cage below the door opening. Placing both fresh corn and a few bright red slices of apple, I slipped back to my hiding place and waited with wire in hand. In only minutes, Bernadette was there, climbing confidently into the cage with one good leg and her beak used as a hand. I pulled the door shut behind her and took her immediately to the veterinarian.

Rehabilitation

The bird in the cage was sweet. She was obviously thrilled to have the option of fresh water from a bowl. As we drove to the veterinarian's office, she helped herself to a vitamin-enriched seed mix. She seemed oblivious to her injury.

Dr. LaBonde pronounced Bernadette fit and surgery was scheduled for two weeks hence. During that time, as well as her brief recovery

period, she lived in my living room on a free-standing tree perch, sleeping in the cage she was trapped in. She loved to fly across the room to whoever was sitting on the sofa. We didn't trim her wings because she couldn't really quite walk.

Her leg had been pulled so far out of the socket, that when it snapped back, it went inside her pelvis. The head of the femur had grown adhered to the inside of the pelvis. In a 45-minute surgical procedure, Dr. Jerry LaBonde scraped off the bone that had attached itself, amputated the damaged top end of the bone, pulled a flap of muscle over the hip joint, and sewed the end of the femur into a pocket in the muscle. Within hours, Bernadette was scratching herself with that newly functioning foot, holding food with it, and even doing just a little limping around.

At about that time, Bernadette was adopted into a home where the other pet birds also flew free. Bucy's dining room was an avian fantasy of trees in Christmas tree stands. The adjoining living room had been appropriately bird-proofed with a "halo" of 18-inch streamers encircling the ceiling fan. Bernadette could fly and would not have to depend on that damaged leg for lots of walking and climbing.

I visit Bernadette a couple of times a year to trim her toenails. She's a happy, well-adjusted, indoor bird who usually insists that all persons occupying the sofa must perform cockatoo petting duty every moment they're there.

Glossary

Please note that the following definitions set forth the meanings of these words as they are used specifically in this text. They are not intended to be full and complete definitions.

abandonment: the feeling of being left behind and out of the flock. To a parrot this can mean death.

adaptive behaviors: behaviors that increase the bird's chances of surviving (producing more offspring).

aggression: hostile nipping, biting, or chasing.

allofeeding: mutual feeding or simulated mutual feeding. One of several behaviors related to breeding.

allopreening: mutual preening or simulated mutual preening, as in a human scratching a parrot's neck.

alula: the triangular shape formed by the four feathers above the coverts at the shoulder of the wing.

anthropomorphic: ascribing human attributes to a non-human thing.

aviary birds: birds that live in captivity, but in a bird-identified setting in which they do not interact on a regular basis with humans.

baby days: a young parrot's first, impressionable weeks in the new home, an idyllic period before the baby bird's instincts for independence, dominance, and exploration develop. *See also:* honeymoon period.

baby tail: frayed or broken tail feathers typical of extremely playful baby parrots that are usually under two years old.

band: coded metal device placed around a bird's leg for identification purposes.

beaking: testing the feel of the beak on various substances, including skin, by a baby parrot.

behavioral environment: behavioral conditions, especially redundant behaviors including habits, present in the bird and in individuals around the bird.

bite: use of the parrot's beak in a manner intended to cause damage or injury.

bite zone: area in front of the bird's beak in which the hand can easily be bitten but not easily stepped on (*see* p. 152).

blood feather: unopened immature feather that is completely or partially covered by a bluish/white membrane indicating that the feather is currently supplied with blood.

bonding: the connection with another bird, a human, object, or location that a bird exhibits and defends.

breeding-related behaviors: behaviors with a source related to breeding habits in the wild such as chewing, emptying cavities, hiding in dark places, allopreening, allofeeding, masturbating, copulating, and aggression at the nest site (cage).

cage-bound: being so fixated on an unchanging environment that any change stimulates either aggression or fearfulness in a captive bird.

cage fray: damage done to feathers, usually of the tail, head, or wing, by frequent contact with the cage, toys, or other accessories.

cavity-breeding behaviors: breeding-related behaviors including chewing, emptying cavities, fondness for small spaces, peeking out, and aggression at the nest site.

chasing: to drive away by pursuing.

cloaca: also called the vent. Part of birds' anatomy where waste materials are collected for excretion. Also opening where sperm or eggs are deposited.

command: an order or instruction given by a dominant individual.

companion bird: a bird that lives compatibly with humans.

contact call: the word or sounds the bird greets all "flock members" with, such as, "hello."

contours: the layer of feathers on the breast and body that covers the down.

counterintuitive: going against intuition.

coverts: the layer of feathers protecting the base of the primary feathers of the wings.

crashing: succumbing quickly and obviously to illness.

crest: a set of feathers on the head used for expression of emotions in the cockatoo.

defensiveness: occasional, mild, or infrequent territorial aggression.

developmental period: a period of rapid behavioral development wherein

Poicephalus may demonstrate tendencies for dominance, independence, aggression, and panic. *See also:* terrible two's.

dominance: control; enforcing individual will over others.

down: the small fuzzy, unzipped feathers next to the body that are normally covered by contours.

drama: any activity that brings an exciting response, either positive or negative.

evert: sticking out, as in the hen everts her cloaca during copulation.

"evil eye": a behavioral technique, first described by Sally Blanchard, in which the bird is stopped from unwanted behavior by a stern, predator-like two-eyed gaze.

eye contact: the act of maintaining eye-to-eye gaze.

family: the order of parrots, *Psittaciformes.*

feather tracts: symmetrical lines of circulation along which feathers grow, molt out, and regrow. This incremental replacement of feathers gives balance to the bird in order to maintain flight ability during molting.

feral: previously captive animals living wild in habitats where they are non-native.

fight-or-flight response: instinctual, automatic reaction to real or perceived threats.

fledging: the process a young parrot goes through as it learns to fly for the first time.

flight: a cage or bird-proof space large enough to accommodate flight.

flock/flock members: as it applies to a companion bird, human companions sharing a home with a captive parrot.

forage: the search for and consumption of food.

free feeding: allowing access to food at all times.

genus (pl., genera): a group of related species sharing basic morphological and behavioral characteristics, such as the genus, *Amazona.* Also commonly called "group."

good hand/bad hand: a behavioral technique designed to distract a bird from biting (*see* p. 158).

grooming: the process of having the companion parrot's wing feathers trimmed, nails cut or filed, and beak shaped, if necessary.

group: a set of related species sharing basic morphological and behavioral characteristics, such as the group, *Amazona.* Also commonly called "genus."

habit: redundant behavior that has become a fixed part of the bird's behavior.

handfed: a parrot that as a neonate was fed by humans rather than birds.

handling techniques: methods used by humans to stimulate and maintain successful tactile interactions with companion parrots.

hide box: a place for a bird to have free access to hide any time it wants.

honeymoon period: a young parrot's first, impressionable weeks in the new home, an idyllic period before the baby bird's instincts for dominance and exploration develop. *See also:* baby days.

hookbill: a parrot.

human/mate: the human companion chosen by the bird to fill the role of mate. The bird will perform courtship displays for this person and protect this person as it would a mate of the same species.

imperfect: a bird with an obvious physical defect resulting from congenital anomaly or injury.

independence: improvising and enjoying self-rewarding behaviors.

juvenile: immature behaviors, especially in parrots, unrelated to nesting or breeding.

language: a method of verbal communication wherein multiple individuals use the same sounds or groups of sounds to convey the same meaning.

maladaptive: behaviors that decrease the bird's ability to function in its environment.

mandible: the lower beak; the horny protuberance with which the bird bites against the inside of the maxilla.

manzanita: commercially available hardwood branches, which, in small sizes, are suitable as perches for *Poicephalus.*

mate: The individual to whom the parrot is primarily bonded. *See also:* human/mate.

maxilla: the upper beak; the notched protuberance that gives the hookbill its name.

mimicking: to copy modeled behavior, especially vocalizations.

model: a learning process by which one individual copies behavior from another individual.

molt: the cyclical shedding and replacing of feathers.

nares: nostrils.

neonate: a baby parrot that cannot yet eat food on its own.

nest/nesting: the act of constructing a structure for the purpose of reproduction.

nest box: a human-constructed box for bird nesting.

night frights: unexplained thrashing in the night that is sometimes seen in cockatiels and other companion parrots.

nipping: an accidental, unintentional, or nonaggressive pinch not intended to cause damage.

nonpair bond species: nonmonogamous species such as *Eclectus* and ringnecks.

normal: the original animal that occurs wild; not a color mutation (pied, lutino, or albino).

overload: episodes of excitement resulting in displays of aggression. Probably part of sexual display common in Amazons and cockatoos.

parrot: a hookbill; a bird with a notched maxilla, a mallet shaped tongue, and four toes (two facing front and two facing back).

patterning: a learned habit. Establishing cooperative behavioral patterns with use of interactive drills performed by birds and humans together.

pecking order: the hierarchy of dominance within a group of birds or their companions.

pinch: a behavior designed to get a human's attention where the bird takes that person's skin in its beak and squeezes hard enough to cause pain, but not hard enough to break the skin.

preen: to groom the feathers, as with "combing" and "zipping" them with the beak.

prompt: a cue; the physical cue to used to stimulate a behavior.

Psittaciformes: the parrots.

quarantine: enforced isolation for the prevention of disease transmission.

race: subspecies.

reactive: to quickly revert to instinctual reactions such as aggression or fear.

recapture: to apprehend or recover possession of a parrot that has flown away.

recumbent: a cockatoo crest that tops off with a forward curve, such as that of a cockatiel.

recurve: a cockatoo crest that tops off with a backward curve, such as that of an umbrella cockatoo.

regurgitate: voluntary or involuntary production of partially digested food from the crop. *See also:* allofeeding.

reinforce: process of rewarding a behavior that humans wish to become habitual.

reprimand: punishment; action intended to discourage a behavior.

rescue: fortuitous removal from frightening circumstances.

rival: a competitor; one who competes for reinforcement or reward.

roaming: unsupervised explorations away from approved cage or play areas.

roost: the place where a bird usually sleeps.

scissor beak: condition where the mandible overgrows the edge of the maxilla on one side.

self-rewarding behavior: an activity that is enacted solely for the pleasure of doing it.

sexual behavior: self-rewarding breeding-related behavior.

sexual maturity: the period during which breeding-related behaviors become prominent in the bird's overall behavior.

species: subgenus; related groups of individuals that share common biological characteristics.

status: positioning related to dominance within the pecking order.

step-up: practice of giving the step-up command with the expectation that the bird will perform the behavior.

stress: any stimulus, especially fear or pain, that inhibits normal psychological, physical, or behavioral balance.

subspecies: a subdivision of species, especially by color or geographical characteristics.

substratum: material placed in the bottom of the bird's cage or play area to contain mess and droppings (pl., substrata).

terrible two's: a behavioral period wherein the bird's instincts for dominance, independence, and aggression are first manifest. *See also:* developmental period.

tool: an implement that is manipulated to accomplish a particular function.

toxin: any substance that causes illness or death through exposure to it.

toy: any tool for producing self-rewarding behavior.

treading: the style of mounted copulation used by most parrots.

vent: cloaca.

vocabulary: words or elements comprising a language.

weaned: when a baby parrot has learned to eat independently.

window of opportunity: a finite period during which something can be accomplished; a period of time during which behavior can be changed.

winking: a form of masturbation involving opening and closing the cloaca (exclusively Amazon behavior).

wobble correction: a behavioral correction performed during step-up practice (*see* p. 157).

Useful Addresses and Literature

Books

A Guide to Eclectus Parrots, Their Management, Care & Breeding, South Tweeds Head, Australia: Australian Birdkeeper, 1991.

Athan, Mattie Sue, *Guide to a Well-Behaved Parrot,* Hauppauge, NY: Barron's Educational Series, 1993.

Athan, Mattie Sue, *Guide to the Quaker Parrot,* Hauppauge, NY: Barron's Educational Series, 1997.

Athan, Mattie Sue and Deter, Dianalee, *Guide to the Senegal Parrot and Its Family,* Hauppauge, NY: Barron's Educational Series, 1998.

Bergman, Petra, *Feeding Your Pet Bird,* Hauppauge, NY: Barron's Educational Series, 1993.

Forshaw, Joseph M., *Parrots of the World,* Neptune, NJ: T.F.H. Publications, Inc., 1977.

Freud, Arthur, *The Complete Parrot,* New York, NY: MacMillan, 1995.

Gonzales, Fran, *African Greys,* Yorba Linda, CA: Neon Pet Publications, 1996.

Greeson, Linda, *Parrot Personalities,* Fruitland Park, FL: Greeson's Baby Parrots, 1993.

Harrison, Greg J., DVM and Harrison, Linda R., BS, *Clinical Avian Medicine and Surgery,* Philadelphia, PA: W. B. Saunders Company, 1986.

Jupiter, Tony and Parr, Mike, *Parrots: A Guide to Parrots of the World,* New Haven, CT: Yale University Press, 1998.

Lantermann, Werner and Susanne, *Amazon Parrots,* Hauppauge, NY: Barron's Educational Series, 1988.

Lantermann, Werner and Susanne, *Cockatoos,* Hauppauge, NY: Barron's Educational Series, 1989.

Low, Rosemary, *Encyclopedia of the Lories,* Blaine, WA: Hancock House, 1998.

Marquez, Garbriel Garcia, *Love in the Time of Cholera,* New York, NY: Viking Penguin, 1989.

McWatters, Alicia, *A Guide to a Naturally Healthy Bird,* East Canaan, CT: Safe Goods, 1997.

Murphy, James J., *Cockatoos Are Different Because They Have Crests,* Gilbert, PA: White Mountain Bird Farm, Inc., 1998.

Murphy, Kevin, *Training Your Parrot,* Neptune, NJ: T.F.H. Publications, Inc., 1983.

Ritchie, Harrison and Harrison, *Avian Medicine: Principles and Application,* Lake Worth, FL: Wingers Publishing, Inc., 1994.

Sweeney, Roger G., *The Eclectus,* Port Perry, ON: Silvio Mattacchione & Co., 1993.

Sweeney, Roger G., *Macaws,* Hauppauge, NY: Barron's Educational Series, 1992.

Vriends, Matthew, Ph.D., *Handfeeding and Raising Baby Birds,* Hauppauge, NY: Barron's Educational Series, 1993.

Vriends, Matthew, Ph.D., *Lories and Lorikeets,* Hauppauge, NY: Barron's Educational Series, 1993.

Vriends, Matthew, Ph.D., *The New Australian Parakeet Handbook,* Hauppauge, NY: Barron's Educational Series, 1992.

Vriends, Matthew, Ph.D., *Parrotlets,* Hauppauge, NY: Barron's Educational Series, 1998.

Wolter, Anette, *African Grey Parrots,* Hauppauge, NY: Barron's Educational Series, 1987.

Wolter, Anette, *The Long-Tailed Parakeets,* Hauppauge, NY: Barron's Educational Series, 1992.

Contributors

Sally Blanchard is the editor and publisher of *The Pet Bird Report.* She was first published in *Bird Talk* in 1988. She is the author of a book and a series of videos on the subject of companion parrot behavior. Interviews throughout 1998 and before.

Kashmir Csaky has studied behavior in companion parrots since 1965. She is a well-respected breeder specializing in hyacinth and scarlet macaws. She frequently lectures and writes, being a regular contributor to *The Pet Bird Report* and other avian publications. Correspondence, October 1998. Interview, November 1998.

Carol Darezzo became interested in parrots while owning Wild Birds Unlimited and began rescuing escaped birds at outdoor wild bird feeders. She taught high school biology for 20 years and is now committed to work in parrot rescue and education. Correspondence, 1998.

Dianalee Deter studied zoology and animal behavior at the University of Florida. She is the co-author of *Guide to the Senegal Parrot and Its Family* and *Guide to the African Grey Parrot* and consulting editor of this book. Consultations through 1998.

Layne Dicker is staff avian behaviorist at Wilshire Animal Hospital in Santa Monica, CA, and a behavior/care consultant to individuals, breeders, rescue organizations, and zoological parks. Layne is a very popular avian lecturer, author, and photographer. Article, *Bird Talk,* November 1998.

Ginger Elden is a long-time breeder of African greys, *Pionus*, Amazons, Goffin's cockatoos, and macaws.

Sybil Erden is founder and director of Oasis Sanctuary Foundation, established in 1994. Oasis is one of a very few nonprofit sanctuaries that neither breeds nor adopts birds but rather provides lifetime care for unwanted parrots and other exotic birds. Interview and correspondence, November 1998.

Heike Ewing is a well-known breeder of quakers and other parrots. She is list moderator on *quaker-parakeets@home. ease.lsoft.com,* a popular quaker-parakeet chat list. Correspondence, October 1998.

Dave Flom is a long-time breeder of companion, trick-trained, and free-flying macaws. He is the curator of the Rainforest Cafe. Interviews through 1998.

Linda Greeson is a breeder of quaker parrots and numerous other species. She has authored several well-known booklets and has been an important influence on avian publishing, including electronic publishing, for many years. Correspondence, October 1998.

Diane Grindol is the author of Howell's *The Complete Book of Cockatiels.*

She writes *Bird Talk's* "Small Talk," a column that features news and information about birds, research, conservation programs, and birds in the media. Interviews and correspondence, October 1998.

Diana Holloway is a long-time Amazon aficionado and current president of the Amazona Society.

Mary Karlquist is a well-respected breeder and lecturer specializing in macaws and cockatoos. Interviews, June 1998.

Betsy Lott works in parrot rescue and adoption in the south San Francisco Bay area. She is networked with other rescue programs and individuals all over the United States and Canada and serves on the Board of Directors for the Oasis Sanctuary Foundation. Interviews and correspondence, 1998.

Rosemary Low is the author of more than 20 books and hundreds of articles on parrots spanning more than 30 years. She is the former curator of two of the world's largest parrot collections, Loro Parque and Palmitos Park. Correspondence, October 1998.

Sandee Molenda has bred parrotlets for 15 years, producing six of the seven species, including color mutations. She founded the International Parrotlet Society.

James J. Murphy, MS, is a biologist specializing in the behavioral biology of birds and mammals. He breeds about 35 species of large psittacines. He is published in numerous professional and popular pet bird journals and is the editor of the *Amazona Quarterly.* Interviews, correspondence, and publications, 1998.

Julie Weiss Murad, also known as "The Birdbrain," is founder and president of the Gabriel Foundation, a nonprofit organization promoting education, rescue, rehabilitation, adoption, and sanctuary for companion parrots. Correspondence and interviews through 1998.

Nancy Newman is the owner of Sky-Dancers Aviary. She is a breeder of conures and cockatiels. Correspondence, September and October 1998.

Jean Pattison is president of the African Parrot Society, a frequent lecturer, writer, and a well-respected breeder of African parrots. She is sometimes called "The African Queen." Interviews and correspondence through 1998.

Tani Robar is a long-time professional animal trainer who turned her attention to birds and revolutionized the world of avian trick training with small birds never before used in shows including, astonishingly, a trick-trained, public performing African grey parrot. Interviews, October 1998, and videos, 1994.

Tom Roudybush, MS, is a nutritionist, writer, and founder and president of Roudybush, Inc. A pioneer in his field, Tom has studied the nutrient requirements of birds for more than 25 years. Interviews and correspondence, October and November 1998.

Rita Shimniok is a small breeder of primarily African parrots, operating Oakridge Feather Farm in Cross Plains, Wisconsin. Rita writes for several national avian magazines, and is most known for her research on the Jardine's parrots. Correspondence and interviews through 1997 and 1998.

Michele I. Traugutt has owned and bred various hookbills including lories, her favorites, for more than 15 years. Deter interview, October 1998.

Matthew Vriends, Ph.D., is a Dutch-born biologist/ornithologist who has several advanced degrees and has written more than 80 books in three languages. He has achieved many first-time breeding results in his extensive aviaries. Interviews, correspondence, and publications, 1998.

Ginger West is co-owner of one of the Pet Industry Joint Advisory Council's

"Ten Best Pet Stores in the United States." Correspondence and interviews through 1997 and 1998.

Liz Wilson, CVT, has 20 years experience as an avian technician, regularly writes for several magazines and veterinary textbooks, and consults with pet owners, aviculturists, and avian veterinarians. Correspondence and interviews, 1998.

Margaret Wissman, DVM, Diplomat, ABVP, is an extremely experienced and respected avian veterinarian practicing in Florida. She authors a regular *Bird Talk* column and has been published in other professional journals and textbooks. Correspondence and interviews, October and November 1998.

Organizations

The Amazona Society
P.O. Box 73547
Puyallup, WA 98373-4016

The African Parrot Society
P.O. Box 204
Clarinda, IA 51632-2731

American Federation of Aviculture
P.O. Box 56218
Phoenix, AZ 85079

Association of Avian Veterinarians
(556) 393-8901

British Columbia Avicultural Society
11784 - 9th Ave.
North Delta, B.C. V4C 3H6

Canadian Avicultural Society
32 Dronmore Ct.
Willlowdale, Ontario M2R 2H5

Canadian Parrot Association
Pine Oaks R.R. #3
Catherines, Ontario L2R 6P9

International Aviculturists Society
P.O. Box 2232
LaBelle, FL 33975

International Loriidae Society
17704 S. Tapps Drive East
Summer, WA 98390-9172

International Parrotlet Society
P.O. Box 2428
Santa Cruz, CA 95063

World Parrot Trust
P.O. Box 34114
Memphis, TN 38184

Rescue Organizations

The Gabriel Foundation
P.O. Box 11477
Aspen, CO 81612
(970) 923-1009

Oasis Parrot Sanctuary
P.O. Box 3104
Scottsdale, AZ 85271
(602) 265-6783

The Tropics Exotic Bird Refuge
Kannapolis, NC 28081
(704) 932-8041

Videos

"Fantastic Performing Parrots," Robar Productions, 1994.

"Parrots: Look Who's Talking," Thirteen/WNET and BBC-TV, 1995.

"Paulie," Dream Works Pictures, 1998.

"Pyrruhas: The Quiet Conures," The Feather Tree, 1997.

"Spirits of the Rainforest," Discovery Communications, Inc., 1993.

"Vanishing Birds of the Amazon," Audubon Productions and Turner Original Productions, 1996.

Index

BARRON'S BOOKS FOR BIRD OWNERS

Barron's offers a variety of specialized books on birds and bird care, all of them written by experienced breeders, veterinarians, or ornithologists. The books are filled with valuable general information, as well as detailed charts, tables, and more. Most books have beautiful full-color photos and instructive, high-quality line art.

 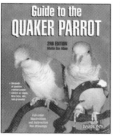 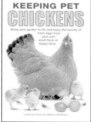

Feeding and Sheltering Backyard Birds	ISBN 0-8120-4252-2
Bateman's Backyard Birds	ISBN 0-7641-5882-1
Keeping Pet Chickens	ISBN 0-7641-3262-8
Hand-Feeding and Raising Baby Birds	ISBN 0-8120-9581-2
Guide to the Senegal Parrot and Its Family	ISBN 0-7641-0332-6
Guide to the Quaker Parrot	ISBN 0-7641-3668-2

All prices are in U.S. and Canadian dollars and subject to change without notice. Books may be purchased at your bookseller, or order direct adding 18% postage (minimum charge $5.95). New York, New Jersey, Michigan, Tennessee, and California residents add sales tax. All books are paperback editions. Prices subject to change without notice.

Barron's Educational Series, Inc.
250 Wireless Blvd., Hauppauge, NY 11788 • To order toll-free: 1-800-645-3476
In Canada: Georgetown Book Warehouse • 34 Armstrong Ave.,
Georgetown, Ont. L7G 4R9 • Order toll-free in Canada: 1-800-247-7160
Or order from your favorite bookstore or pet store
Visit our web site at: www.barronseduc.com

(62a) 7/07

A companion parrot is not a pet. It's an exotic animal that exhibits instinctual wild characteristics. It is precisely this fiery independence that makes parrots such irresistible companions.